Here's what au~~thors are~~ saying about ~~the~~ Romance Writer's Pink Pages:

". . . an incredibly impressive piece of work."
—Susan Wiggs, bestselling author of *Vows Made in Wine*

"Published and unpublished authors alike will benefit from this book, which is simply a gold mine of information."
—Rona Weisburg, *Affaire de Coeur*
book reviewer (★★★★★)

"[Agent] section alone is worth the price of the book. . . . Highly recommended."
—Kathryn Ptacek, publisher of
The Gila Queen's Guide to Markets

". . . highly recommend it to everyone . . ."
—Judy Di Canio, *Romantic Penns* book reviewer
and President of Futuristic, Fantasy and Paranormal
Chapter of Romance Writers of America

"Delivers the writer into the fascinating world of publishing . . . a must reference guide with the facts down cold."
—Laraine McDaniel, award-winning
Harlequin author of *Within the Law*

". . . one of the most helpful tools yet to come along for the aspiring romance novelist."
—Betty Webb, *Tribune* reviewer

". . . ideal for the novice writer since it answers many of the questions beginners don't know they should ask. It is also valuable for the experienced professional writer since it is an excellent source of information, all in one entertaining and well-written package."
—Sharon Wagner, author of more than
70 novels, including *Dark Cloister*

Romance Writer's Pink Pages

The Insider's Guide to Getting Your Romance Novel Published

Eve Paludan

PRIMA PUBLISHING

Follow your dreams,
for therein lies your talent.

PRIMA PUBLISHING and its colophon, which consists of the letter P over PRIMA, are trademarks of Prima Communications, Inc.

ISBN 1-7615-0168-1
ISSN 1076-0046

96 97 98 99 AA 10 9 8 7 6 5 4 3 2 1

Printed in the United States of America

How to Order
Single copies may be ordered from Prima Publishing, P.O. Box 1260, Rocklin, CA 95677; telephone (916) 632-4400. Quantity discounts are also available. On your letterhead, include information concerning the intended use of the books and the number of books you wish to purchase.

Contents

Acknowledgments

*N*o author can succeed alone. It takes the efforts of many to get a book from concept into the hands of readers. Thanks to all those professionals who shared their expertise about the romance publishing business.

A very special thank you to: Melissa Ann Singer at Tor Books, for exceeding my expectations for in-depth information; Tina Tsallas at Harlequin Enterprises, Ltd., for securing necessary international permissions to reprint copyrighted guidelines; Leslie Wainger at Silhouette, for being a wellspring of information; Beth Lieberman at Kensington (West Coast), for sharing innovative ideas and pioneer spirit; Ginjer Buchanan at Berkley, for providing detailed info for Quantam Leap books; Lynda Ryan, of Kelly and Kathryn Present, who wants to make romance a universal language; Jacqueline Young at *Midnite Interlude* for insight into ethnic romance publishing.

Thanks also to all the literary agents who helped with information for the book, especially my own hardworking agent, Evan Fogelman. Evan, thanks for believing in me, and for great career advice.

Thank you to the staff at Prima Publishing, especially Jennifer Sander in acquisitions, who believed I could do it again, and again; Ben Dominitz, my publisher, a man of vision; Andi Reese Brady, my dedicated editor; and Frank Ruiz in publicity.

Appreciation goes to all my friends whom I "met" on GeNie's Romance Exchange (RomEx) network. I am blessed with so many writer pals, that I cannot possibly name you all! Thanks for encouragement, friendship, and information.

Thanks to more than a hundred chapters of Romance Writers of America for your enthusiasm and encouragement.

Thanks to Romance Writers of Australia for insisting that local bookshops order this book.

Each person who contributed to this book has a special place in my heart. Especially my readers.

Last, but never least, thanks Ron, for being a real live romance hero, one who always says, "You can do it."

Introduction

*W*elcome to the third edition of *Romance Writer's Pink Pages.* This annually updated genre-specific reference was created to assist romance writers with their goals of publication by providing information about the industry.

This edition's agent section will introduce you to more than sixty agents who are new to this reference. Most of the agents listed do not charge reading fees or marketing fees.

Literary agents in Canada: there is a shortage of established Canadian literary agents who adhere to the Code of Ethics of the AAR and WGA (no reading fees, etc.). Canadian authors who want to sell to Harlequin in Toronto are in need of representation. If interested, write to the address below and request an agent's questionnaire. Preference may be given to agents who do not charge reading or marketing fees.

In the publisher's section, many editors have given *Romance Writer's Pink Pages* permission to reprint their guidelines. This saves writers the expense and time of mailing numerous SASEs for tip sheets. The ones here are the most current provided by the publishers.

Some book publishers who do not yet have their first titles released are not listed in this edition. The publishers who already have books in the marketplace are the ones listed here.

This directory is as complete and accurate as possible, but if there is an error in a listing, or a change of address, editors, etc., please contact the author, so it can be updated for the next edition.

Efforts have been made to make sure that everyone listed is reputable, but neither the author, nor Prima Publishing, necessarily endorses anyone, nor accepts liability for the results obtained from contacting anyone in this reference.

So, approach each agent or publisher in a professional manner. Ask questions. Read contracts carefully. Early on, consider career decisions, such as whether to use a pseudonym. Remember that writing under your real name gives you the flexibility to switch publishers but keep your readers. Reader recognition can be an important marketing tool to help your agent negotiate better book contracts for you.

Whether you are a writer, agent, or editor, I hope you will find this book to be a valuable reference. Many readers mark up their copies with post-its, handwritten notes, and highlighters. A reference book that gets used repeatedly is one of my goals.

Letters from readers (SASE appreciated) are welcome, especially suggestions and success stories.

Good luck with your romance writing!

Write to: Eve Paludan, P.O. Box 5234, Apache Junction, AZ 85278-5234. If you have access to an Internet Gateway or are on GEnie, the e-mail address is: R.Paludan1@GENIE.COM

1

How to Think About Literary Agency

Evan M. Fogelman

Once you've completed your first manuscript, you'll need to think about the business of publishing. A lot of writers feel intimidated by hard-core business details. The whole matter of the commercial exploitation of writing may be somewhat distasteful to you and you might want to leave those details to someone else. Whatever your own feelings on the subject may be, take responsibility for the development of your own career. Ask a lot of questions. Learn the basics of acquiring and distributing books. The quality of your decisions will rise in direct proportion to the amount of background understanding you've acquired about the topic at hand.

The right literary agent—someone who has a good knowledge of the publishing business and an understanding of the development of your career—can be of tremendous help. In some respects publishing is an agent-driven business. Nevertheless, one great author once referred to her agent as a "benevolent parasite," and there is some merit in her characterization. Still, the right agent can do much for your career, in terms of money and the other variables of the writer's professional life.

Before you begin assessing which agents or agencies are right for you, give some thought to what you want—besides that first sale—from the author-agent relationship. Much time at writers' conferences is devoted to agents, yet many authors seem to know little about the business of literary representation. Agents typically do much more than just send your manuscript to the right editors. Most good agents are true career managers and you'll need to know what that entails so you can make an informed choice about what may well prove to be one of your most important career decisions.

Begin with the premise that agents aren't really necessary. With the exception of situations where publishers require agented submissions, we're not. After all, few publishers will pay you royalties as high as 15%, so you need a very compelling set of reasons to give up that much of your income to someone else. If you're the type of person who prefers to do everything yourself, you may not want to associate with a literary representative. If, however, you want to delegate some of your responsibility to a qualified professional, you'll need to explore your requirements for the three areas in which agents work.

The first area is *editorial contact*. This may be the most overrated aspect of an agent's work—especially among the Romance Writers of America (RWA) where there are a manageable number of acquisitions editors and even the most novice of unpublished authors can meet editors at conferences. Also, some very savvy published authors know as many editors as some agents do. True, the martini or Perrier lunches do occur occasionally, but even the most delightful friendship between agent and editor can rarely be utilized to compel the acquisition of an unsalable manuscript. In category genre fiction there are a limited number of editors to begin with, and it certainly does not take great professional acumen to determine which editor acquires for a certain line. The mere acquaintance of editors appropriate for your manuscript does not in itself merit the compensation of an agent. You could probably hunt down the range of editors yourself and not be out the 15%.

However, the more complicated the area of editorial contacts becomes, the more you'll want to explore what an agent can do for you. For example, if you're writing for several lines or across genre boundaries, you may want someone to help manage your different obligations. Also, you'll need to consider the larger concerns of publishing programs. If you write more mainstream, single title books, you'll have to consider which publishers might really foster your talent and move you up the list. An agent might help you quite a bit in locating those editors whose sensibilities are in accord with your writing.

You might also consider the value of an agent's endeavors to your own relationship with an editor. Many editors like working with agents because it's clear who handles the business details and who handles the creative aspects. Thus, the author-editor relationship is freed from the encumbrances of commerce and can exist on a nurturing-of-talent level. It sounds pretty hopeful, yet it can actually happen that way and is something you should think about.

Once you're comfortable with evaluating the propriety of an agent's benefit in terms of editorial contacts, you'll want to explore a second area, *business management.* Business management is much more than advances and royalty rates; it's the area where agents can really earn their commissions. Yes, in some cases an agent can get you more money up front and a better royalty for a first book than you could get on your own—yet that alone might not be enough to justify the relationship. Particularly in the case of category works, the little extra money the agent might get for you could be more than eaten up by the agency commission you'll have to pay. Think of business management not only as a contract negotiation, but also as contract maintenance. Signing the contract is only the very beginning.

An increasingly important part of contract maintenance is subsidiary rights management. More and more publishers look toward subrights to help their profit margins. And there's a lot more to subrights than the glamorous TV and feature film options of which we're all happy to be a part. There are also foreign rights, reprints, audio, serializations, book club sales, and other sources of potential income that may be marketed throughout the life of the title. Depending upon the publishing contract, it is often the publisher who takes primary responsibility for garnering subrights income. In the case of author-retained rights, though, it is the author's agent who seeks the subrights deals.

There is also a business management side to the author-editor relationship. During the initial submission process, this involves handling revision suggestions and informing the author about the status of any negotiations. Once your book is acquired, your agent might be the liaison between you and your editor for any pre-press information the publisher requires. At times authors feel more comfortable having their agents make inquiries about the book. Though author and editor should be able to converse as needed without the unnecessary intervention of an agent, many authors feel uncomfortable asking questions about print runs and options.

When you understand the necessity of good business management, you're able to move on to the last area you'll need to evaluate in your decision about an agent, *career development.* This is the most underrated, yet perhaps the most important aspect of your decision. The right agent can help your career development by associating your talent with future deals. Here, your agent can act as a sounding board for your ideas and can provide specific input designed to keep you selling. There's a lot of value in being able to discuss your manuscripts with someone who has professional judgment. Though your first book may be a runaway bestseller, most publishers look at authors as incremental business successes. That is, your second book should be more successful than your first, your third more than your second, and so forth. Imagine how much more productive you might be along that route if someone were guiding you along the way.

This area of career development leads us naturally to perhaps the best criterion for measuring agents: *communication.* You should feel that your agent expresses an understanding of your work and your goals if she or he is to be a truly effective representative. Learn as much as you can about the agents you are considering. Make an effort to find out about their backgrounds, who they represent, and their recent sales. Don't blindly send your book to a list of agents who may or may not be receptive to your work. Look for the ones who accept unpublished authors, for those who have a good reputation in the romance genre, and for those about whom you feel generally confident.

Like most things in book publishing, finding the right agent is not nearly so easy as it sounds. Many agents do not accept unpublished authors. Since there are no particular qualifications needed to become an agent—and no certifications of any sort required—you should approach the matter cautiously. I think you'll find, though, that most agents don't run scam operations. All businesses have some dishonest individuals, yet there's no reason to assume that in book publishing there are any more than in other places.

Here it's appropriate to mention the controversial topic of reading fees. Some very successful agencies charge them. Thus, it would be a bit simplistic to say one should always avoid them. That's a decision you're going to have to make on your own. If you like what an agent has proposed to you, and you're comfortable that his or her reading fee will be worth it for you, perhaps there's no problem. However, you should inquire about the purposes of the fee. Is it designed to cover the agency's administrative costs? Is the fee used to compensate outside readers? If you're paying a fee for a critique, find out who's doing the job. If you must pay a fee, make sure the agency's record merits your involvement. Use common sense. Recently, some authors were amazed to learn of several colleagues who paid $250 each to a relatively unestablished agency. Their feeling was that the agent involved was not really in the business of literary representation, but instead was a fee collector disguised as an agent. Well, I'm sure by now you get the picture.

Fortunately the literary agent trade group, the Association of Author Representatives (AAR), mandates a policy against reading fees for new members and is in the process of phasing them out altogether for existing members who wish to maintain AAR membership. (Certain agencies that do charge reading fees were grandfathered in when the ILAA and SAR merged to form the AAR.) The AAR also prescribes ethical and accounting guidelines for its members. Thus, the AAR is a good place to start your search for an agent. Request their list of members and do some background checking on the ones that interest you. Cross-reference that list with the RWA's (Romance Writer's of America) list to determine which qualified agents are active in romance fiction.

Many fine agents are not AAR members. If you meet an agent at a conference and she or he impresses you, there's no reason to believe this person has to be an AAR member to successfully undertake representation on your behalf. Nevertheless, you've got to start somewhere, and unless you're spending a fortune attending conferences all over the country, you'll need a credible agency resource. Show respect for your career and do your homework on us. (Of course, there's no substitute for contacting your best friend's agent after he just got her a good contract.)

Agents have different policies about submission. Please follow them—they're designed to help us find the best writers and writing available. As a general rule, agents don't appreciate gimmicks. Some agents require a formal query letter before you send any manuscript. Others are perfectly amenable to seeing sample chapters right off the bat. Some like pre-submission phone calls; some frown on multiple submissions. The best thing you can do for yourself is to follow the procedures in a professional and courteous manner.

When you and an agent are ready to come to terms, I recommend you use a written agreement. It's good to require an articulation of your agent's responsibilities. Though writing is intensely personal, the elements of book publishing constitute business and all the relationships involved should be rooted in sound business practices.

Look for the following in writing:

1. A definition of the represented property. Are all genres or types included? What, if anything, is to be excluded?

2. An acknowledgment of the agent's commission. What about the rate for subsidiary rights and sales?

3. A clear statement of the accounting practices involved. Will the agent promptly forward to the writer all funds and statements? When? Will the agency provide accounting documentation separate from that of the publisher?

4. An unequivocal obligation to the author that the author will be informed about *all* offers relating to publication and licensing.

5. A clear statement of what expenses the agency will be responsible for, and which ones the author will pay. For example, what if five copies of the manuscript are needed to submit to various publishers?

6. An obligation for the agency to send to the writer copies of all correspondence related to the manuscript, and a similar requirement that the agent notify the author about all conversations concerning the book.

7. A provision of how the author-agent relationship can be terminated by either of the people involved.

Many other points may be perfectly acceptable. The main objective should be fairness to the author.

Finally, some thoughts about emerging technologies are appropriate. Publishing is going through some remarkable changes. Though retail book sales remain our taproot, computers and television possess a developmental impact we can't ignore. Category fiction may be the last to be affected by these changes, yet now is the time to become informed.

CD computer programs (CD-ROM) make books accessible in numbers and detail previously unthinkable. (For example, did you know that 900 books can fit on one CD-ROM disk?) We refer to these electronic rights as *new media* and believe the CD-I (interactive compact disk technology) may unite visual and print media for distribution to the mass-market. The entire publishing community is in the process of learning how to handle and profit from these rights.

You might also expect to see more books sold direct to buyers from television orders. What has happened to nonfiction books tied to infomercials may also be applied to direct sales of fiction. In-home shopping for all goods and services is a force to be considered.

Now you are ready. Supplied with creative property and business information, you can make good decisions about your career. It won't always be easy. A career as a published author involves a devotion that few people can really understand. You'll have to face rejection, deadlines, and all the encroachments life demands. Yet, if you're reading this, you probably suspect it'll all be worth it.

When all is said and done, there's one piece of advice that may be more important than anything else in these pages: Finish your book. The starters never succeed at anything—only those who finish their manuscripts get them published.

Good luck.

Evan M. Fogelman, member of the Association of Author's Representatives and the American Bar Association Forum on Entertainment Law, owns the literary agency that bears his name.

2

Directory of Agents

ANDREE ABERASSIS
Associate
Ann Elmo Agency, Inc.
60 E. 42nd Street
New York, NY 10165
(212) 661-2880   FAX: (212) 661-2883

Fees: No reading fee. Nominal $25 handling fee for unpublished authors.

Terms: 15% commission.

Recent Sales/Clients: Linda Turner, Vickie York, Kaitlin Girton, Charlotte Douglas, Ida Hills, Arlene Erlbach, Carol Culvar.

Submissions: Query first with SASE. OK to send synopsis and first three chapters. No unsolicited manuscripts.

Seeking: Contemporary (long), historical, mystery, paranormal, romantic suspense.

CHARLENE ADAMS
Client First Agency
P.O. Box 795
White House, TN 37188
(615) 325-4780

Professional Affiliations: Signatory to the Writers Guild.

Fees: No reading fees. No marketing fees.

Terms: 10% sale price.

Submissions: Query first by letter with SASE. No phone queries. No unsolicited manuscripts.

Seeking: Feature films in all genres.

RAJEEV AGARWAL
Literary Agent
Circle of Confusion, Ltd.
666 Fifth Avenue, Suite 303
New York, NY 10103

Professional Affiliations: Writers Guild of America.

Fees: No reading fees. No marketing fees.

Terms: 10% on sale.

Recent Sales/Clients: Available upon request.

Submissions: Query first with SASE. No phone queries. No unsolicited manuscripts.

Seeking: Contemporary (long), contemporary (short), ethnic, fantasy, futuristic, historical, mainstream, mystery, paranormal, romantic suspense, screenplays.

Comments: Screenplays are our primary focus.

PAMELA G. AHEARN
President
The Ahearn Agency
2021 Pine Street
New Orleans, LA 70118
(504) 861-8395   FAX: (504) 866-6434

Professional Affiliations: Romance Writers of America.

Fees: Charges small reading fee. No marketing fees.

Terms: 15% on domestic rights, 20–25% on dramatic/foreign.

Submissions: Query first with SASE. No phone queries. No unsolicited manuscripts. Only send synopsis and first three chapters if requested by agency.

Seeking: Contemporary (long) from published authors only, contemporary (short) from published authors only, ethnic, historical, mainstream, mystery, paranormal, romantic suspense.

JAMES ALLEN
President
James Allen Literary Agency
538 E. Harford Street/P.O. Box 278
Milford, PA 18337

Fees: No reading fees. No marketing fees.

Terms: 10% domestic print, 20% film and dramatic, 20% foreign.

Recent Sales/Clients: Judi Lind, Harlequin Intrigue; Jeanne Renick, HarperMonogram.

Submissions: Query by letter first. Prefers query letter with 2–3 page synopsis. No unsolicited manuscripts. Absolutely no first contacts by phone or fax accepted.

Seeking: Contemporary (long), fantasy, historical, mainstream, mystery, romantic suspense.

Comments: Prefers to consider established authors with at least a couple of book-length sales under their belts. Most (90%) of new clients are from referrals by established clients or editors.

ROBERT BRAD ALLRED
All-Star Talent Agency
7834 Alabama Avenue
Canoga Park, CA 91304-4905
(818) 346-4313

Professional Affiliations: Signatory to the Writers Guild, California license #TA2805.

Fees: No reading fees. No marketing fees.

Terms: 10%.

Recent Sales/Clients: Has eight clients.

Submissions: Query by letter first with SASE. No unsolicited manuscripts. No phone queries.

Seeking: Contemporary (short), ethnic, fantasy, futuristic, historical, mainstream, mystery, romantic suspense, other. Those that defy categorization also welcome. Also seeking screenplays of feature films, movies-of-the-week, romantic comedies, and woman-in-jeopardy.

Comments: Please keep queries and synopses short and to the point.

MARCIA AMSTERDAM
President
Marcia Amsterdam Agency
41 W. 82nd Street, Suite 9A
New York, NY 10024
(212) 873-4945

Professional Affiliations: Signatory to the Writers Guild of America.

Fees: No reading fees. No marketing fees.

Terms: Standard 15% domestic, 10% on film scripts.

Recent Sales: *Children of the Dawn* by Patricia Rowe, Warner.

Submissions: Query first by letter, or send synopsis and first three chapters. No unsolicited manuscripts. Enclose SASE or we don't return.

Seeking: Historical, mainstream, mystery, romantic suspense, screenplays (romantic comedies, woman-in-jeopardy).

Comments: We're always happy to find a voice with humor in it.

STEVEN AXELROD
President
The Axelrod Agency
54 Church Street
Lenox, MA 01240
(413) 637-2000   FAX: (413) 637-4725

Professional Affiliations: Association of Author's
Representatives.

Fees: No reading fees. No marketing fees.

Submissions: Query first with SASE.

Seeking: Contemporary (long), historical, mainstream, mystery,
romantic suspense.

AMY BERKOWER
Literary Agent
Writers House, Inc.
21 W. 26th Street
New York, NY 10010
(212) 685-2400   FAX: (212) 685-1871

Professional Affiliations: Association of Author's
Representatives.

Fees: No reading fees. No marketing fees.

Terms: 15% domestic, 20% foreign.

Recent Sales/Clients: Nora Roberts, Barbara Delinsky, Eileen
Goudge, Jane Feather, Betty Receveur, Barbara Veyle, Anne
Tolstoi Wallach, Modean Moon, Francine Pascal.

Submissions: Query first with SASE.

Seeking: Brilliant writing in any category.

Comments: Interested in experienced writers who feel they have the skills and energy to move from paperback into hardcover. We manage careers.

PAM BERNSTEIN
President
Pam Bernstein and Associates
790 Madison Avenue, Suite 310
New York, NY 10021
(212) 288-1700

Professional Affiliations: Association of Author's Representatives.

Fees: No reading fees. No marketing fees.

Terms: 15% commission.

Submissions: Query first by letter with SASE. No phone queries. No unsolicited manuscripts.

Seeking: Contemporary (long), ethnic, historical, mainstream, mystery, romantic suspense.

CAROLE D. BODEY
Senior Editor
Aabaal Literary Associates
P.O. Box 482
Hoquiam, WA 98550
(360) 538-1251

Professional Affiliations: Signatory to the Writers Guild, National Press Women, Washington Press Association, League of American Pen Women.

Fees: No reading fees. No marketing fees.

Terms: A straight 10% commission.

Recent Sales/Clients: Paul Gromosiak, Stephanie Mita. More names of clients upon request.

Submissions: Queries by phone are acceptable. We do prefer the complete manuscript, plus synopsis. Unsolicited manuscripts are OK. Please enclose SASE plus self-addressed container and return postage for your manuscript. Also have the postal clerk attach a certified card, so you will learn the date the manuscript is received by Aabaal.

Seeking: Contemporary (long), contemporary (short), ethnic, historical, mainstream, mystery, romantic suspense, screenplays.

Comments: We are a Signatory of the Writers Guild of America. (Besides book manuscripts) we handle feature films and movies-of-the-week that do not contain violence. Romantic comedies have been requested by many (film) producers.

BARBARA BOVA

President
Barbara Bova Literary Agency
3951 Gulf Shore Boulevard, PH-1B
Naples, FL 33940
(813) 649-7237   FAX: (813) 649-0757

Fees: No reading fees. No marketing fees.

Terms: 15%.

Recent Sales/Clients: Confidential.

Submissions: Please query first by letter, or send synopsis and first three chapters. No unsolicited manuscripts. No phone queries.

Seeking: Contemporary (long), contemporary (short), ethnic, fantasy, futuristic, historical, mainstream, mystery, paranormal, romantic suspense.

HELEN BREITWIESER
Associate
William Morris Agency
1325 Avenue of the Americas, 16th Floor
New York, NY 10019
(212) 903-1159   FAX: (212) 262-7747

Fees: No reading fees. No marketing fees.

Terms: 10%.

Submissions: Query first by letter with SASE. No phone queries. OK to send synopsis and first three chapters, but no unsolicited manuscripts.

Seeking: Contemporary (long), contemporary (short), historical, mainstream, mystery, romantic suspense.

DEBORAH T. BROWN
Associate Agent
Peter Lampack Agency, Inc.
551 Fifth Avenue, Suite 1613
New York, NY 10176
(212) 687-9106   FAX: (212) 687-9109

Professional Affiliations: We attend the American Booksellers' Association convention only!

Fees: No reading fees. No marketing fees.

Terms: Flat 15% commission.

Recent Sales/Clients: No straight romance clients yet, but other clients include Doris Mortman, Johanna Kingsley, Clive Cussler, Judith Kelman, Jessica March, Fred Mustard Stuart.

Submissions: Query first by letter with SASE. No phone queries. No unsolicited manuscripts. Brown is the only applicable agent at this agency for high quality romance.

Seeking: Historical (prefers from Medieval-Renaissance to 16th century), mystery, romantic suspense.

Comments: My preference for 12th–16th century background reflects my own affinity for the period. I also think Regency is glutted. Suspense and mystery are always a plus and a way to stand out in this genre. I do demand excellent writing skills—only the best! No screenplays. Only handle scripts and screenplays if book properties are sold to motion picture or TV industry.

PEMA BROWNE AND PERRY BROWNE
Pema Browne Ltd.
Pine Road HCR, Box 104B
Neversink, NY 12765
(914) 985-2936   FAX: (914) 985-7635

Professional Affiliations: Signatory to the Writers Guild.

Fees: No reading fees for romance.

Recent Sales/Clients: Romances to Avon, Zebra, Silhouette, Thomas Nelson, Bradford Exchange.

Submissions: Query first with SASE. OK to send synopsis and first three chapters with SASE. No FAX queries!

Seeking: Contemporary (long), mainstream, mystery, screenplays (only for screenwriters with credits).

Comments: Write according to guidelines. We also look for nonfiction proposals, too, including offerings for the Christian market.

LEWIS CHAMBERS
Co-Owner
The Norma-Lewis Agency
360 W. 53rd Street, Suite BA
New York, NY 10019
(212) 664-0807   FAX: (212) 664-0462

Fees: No reading fees. No marketing fees.

Terms: 15% domestic and Canada, 20% to all other.

Recent Sales/Clients: *Viper Quarry* by Dean Feldmeyer; *Pitchfork Hollow* by Dean Feldmeyer.

Submissions: Please query first with SASE. OK to send synopsis and first three chapters. No phone queries. No unsolicited scripts.

Seeking: Contemporary (long), contemporary (short), ethnic, historical, mainstream, mystery, romantic suspense. Also seeking screenplays for dramatic series and cable series.

TED CHICHAK

Scovil, Chichak, Galen Literary Agency, Inc.
381 Park Avenue South, Suite 1020
New York, NY 10016
(212) 679-8686   FAX: (212) 679-6710

Fees: No reading fees. No marketing fees.

Terms: 15% domestic, 20% foreign.

Recent Sales/Clients: *Preternatural* by Margaret Wander Bonanno, Pocket Books; *Murder She Wrote* novel series by Donald Bain, Signet; *First Ladies* by Margaret Truman, Random House; *Harvest of Fire* by Poul Anderson, Tor Books; *Colombo* by William Harrington, Tor Books.

Submissions: Please query first by letter with SASE, or send synopsis and first three chapters with cover letter. No phone queries. Only send manuscript if OK'd after query. Ted Chichak will read material from newer writers after requesting it subsequent to query.

Seeking: All kinds of books.

Comments: Ted Chichak is interested in every kind of book and is particularly interested in working with writers for whom he can build careers. Not interested in having a great number of clients and will devote himself to selected list.

FRANCINE CISKE

Ciske & Dietz Literary Agency
P.O. Box 555
Neenah, WI 54957
(414) 722-5944

Professional Affiliations: Romance Writers of America.

Fees: No reading fees. No marketing fees.

Terms: 15% commission on domestic sales.

Submissions: No phone queries, please. Instead of a query letter, send synopsis and first three chapters. Unsolicited partial manuscripts are OK.

Seeking: Contemporary (long), contemporary (short), ethnic, historical, mainstream, mystery, romantic suspense.

Comments: Francine Ciske handles romance. For mystery and suspense (not necessarily romance), see Patricia Dietz.

NANCY COFFEY
Literary Agent
Jay Garon-Brooke Associates, Inc.
101 W. 55th Street., Suite 5K
New York, NY 10019
(212) 581-8300   FAX: (212) 581-8397

Professional Affiliations: Association of Author's Representatives, Writers Guild of America.

Fees: No reading fees. No marketing fees.

Terms: 15% domestic, 30% foreign.

Submissions: Query by mail only. Query should include synopsis of story, author bio, and SASE! No phone queries. No unsolicited manuscripts.

Seeking: Mainstream book manuscripts. Also handles theatrical and feature film scripts. Query first.

SUSAN COHEN
Writers House, Inc.
21 W. 26th Street
New York, NY 10010
(212) 685-2400   FAX: (212) 685-1871

Professional Affiliations: Association of Author's Representatives.

Fees: No reading fees. No marketing fees.

Terms: 15% domestic, 20% foreign.

Recent Sales/Clients: Nora Roberts, Barbara Delinsky, Eileen Goudge, Jane Feather,Betty Receveur, Barbara Veyle, Anne Tolstoi Wallach, Modean Moon, Francine Pascal.

Submissions: Query first with SASE.

Seeking: Brilliant writing in any category.

Comments: Interested in experienced writers who feel they have the skills and energy to move from paperback into hardcover. We manage careers.

FRANCES COLLIN, AGENT/OWNER
Frances Collin, Literary Agent
P.O. Box 33
Wayne, PA 19087-0033
(610) 254-0555

Professional Affiliations: Association of Author's Representatives.

Fees: No reading fees. No marketing fees.

Terms: 15% domestic sales, 20% foreign and film rights.

Recent Sales/Clients: Diane Austell, Barbara Hambly, Lee Wallingford.

Submissions: Query by mail. OK to send synopsis and first three chapters. All queries must be accompanied by reply envelope and sufficient return postage. No phone queries. No unsolicited manuscripts.

Seeking: Contemporary (long), contemporary (short), ethnic, fantasy, historical, mainstream, mystery, romantic suspense.

Comments: I look for unusually strong writing and unusually graceful use of language as well as strong characterizations and obviously good research. Mine is an especially broad general trade list with fantasy and science fiction specialities as well as historical romances and romantic suspense. No original screenplays. I do handle film rights for the books I place.

NYANI COLOM
President
Genesis Press
611 Broadway, Suite 428
New York, NY 10012
(212) 780-9800   FAX: (212) 780-0308

Fees: No reading fees. No marketing fees.

Recent Sales/Clients: Rochelle Alers, Elsie B. Washington, and more.

Submissions: No phone queries. Send cover letter with SASE, author bio, synopsis, and first three chapters. Unsolicited manuscripts are acceptable.

Seeking: Contemporary (long), contemporary (short), ethnic, fantasy, historical, mainstream, romantic suspense.

Comments: We specialize in (representation of) African-American romance. We are also publishers of African-American romances.

MARI CRONIN
Associate
Ann Elmo Agency, Inc.
60 E. 42nd Street
New York, NY 10165
(212) 661-2880   FAX: (212) 661-2883

Fees: No reading fee. Nominal $25 handling fee for unpublished writers.

Terms: 15% commission.

Recent Sales/Clients: Linda Turner, Vickie York, Kaitlin Girton, Charlotte Douglas, Ida Hills, Arlene Erlbach, Carol Culvar.

Submissions: Query first with SASE. OK to send synopsis and first three chapters. No unsolicited manuscripts.

Seeking: Contemporary (long), historical, mystery, paranormal, romantic suspense.

RICHARD CURTIS
Richard Curtis Associates
171 E. 74th Street, Suite 2
New York, NY 10021
(212) 772-7363   FAX: (212) 772-7393

Professional Affiliations: Member Romance Writers of America, Science Fiction Writers of America, Western Writers of America, Mystery Writers of America, and Agent for Science Fiction Writers of America.

Fees: No reading fees. No marketing fees.

Terms: 15% commission. We absorb cost of postage, photocopying, and other expenses.

Recent Sales/Clients: Janet Dailey, Jennifer Blake, Alexandra Thorne, Laura Kinsale, Kristin Hannah.

Submissions: Please query first by letter, or send synopsis and first three chapters. No unsolicited manuscripts.

Seeking: Contemporary (long), contemporary (short), ethnic, fantasy, futuristic, historical, mainstream, mystery, romantic suspense.

ANITA DIAMANT
President
Anita Diamant Agency
310 Madison Avenue, #1508
New York, NY 10017
(212) 687-1122   FAX: (212) 972-1756

Professional Affiliations: Association of Author's Representatives.

Fees: No reading fees. No marketing fees.

Terms: 15% commission.

Recent Sales/Clients: V. C. Andrews, Linda Howard, Ann Major, Lisa Jackson.

Submissions: Query first with SASE. OK to send synopsis and first three chapters after querying.

Seeking: Contemporary (long), contemporary (short), ethnic, historical, mainstream, mystery, nonfiction, romantic suspense.

PATRICIA DIETZ
Ciske & Dietz Literary Agency
P.O. Box 555
Neenah, WI 54957
(414) 864-7702

Professional Affiliations: Romance Writers of America.

Fees: No reading fees. No marketing fees.

Terms: 15% commission on domestic sales.

Submissions: Instead of query letter, send synopsis and first three chapters. Unsolicited partial manuscripts are OK.

Seeking: Contemporary (long), contemporary (short), fantasy, futuristic, ethnic, historical, mainstream, mystery, romantic suspense.

Comments: Patricia handles mystery, suspense (not necessarily romance). See also Francine Ciske. No phone queries please.

B. J. DOYEN
President
Doyen Literary Services, Inc.
1931 660th Street
Newell, IA 50568
(712) 272-3300

Professional Affiliations: Romance Writers of America, and many more.

Fees: No reading fees. No marketing fees.

Recent Sales/Clients: Confidential.

Submissions: Query letter first with SASE. No phone queries. Only send synopsis and first three chapters when requested. No unsolicited manuscripts.

Seeking: Historical, mainstream, mystery, romantic suspense.

ETHAN ELLENBERG
President
The Ethan Ellenberg Literary Agency
548 Broadway, #5-E
New York, NY 10012
(212) 431-4554   FAX: (212) 941-4652

Professional Affiliations: Romance Writers of America, Science Fiction Writers of America, Mystery Writers of America, Western Writers of America, Novelist's Inc.

Fees: Never a reading fee. No marketing fees.

Recent Sales/Clients: Christine Michels, Andrea Parnell, Angela Benson, Laura Hayden, Dallas Schulze, Curtiss Ann Matlock, Sonya Birmingham, Susan Sizemore, Debbie Cowan, Peggy Morse (a.k.a. Peggy Moreland), Diane Stuckart.

Submissions: Accepts query letters, but prefers sample chapters with synopsis. No phone queries, please. Unsolicited manuscripts are OK.

Seeking: Contemporary (long), contemporary (short), ethnic, fantasy, futuristic, historical, mainstream, mystery, paranormal, romantic suspense.

Comments: We are very committed to the romance genre and taking new clients at all stages of their careers. We only take clients we have a personal enthusiasm for. If we love your work, we'll work hard and effectively for you. We've been in business ten years and handle most commercial fiction. Previous work includes jobs at Bantam and Berkley/Jove.

MICHELLE FIELDEN
Client First Agency
P.O. Box 795
White House, TN 37188
(615) 325-4780

Professional Affiliations: Signatory to the Writers Guild.

Fees: No reading fees. No marketing fees.

Terms: 10% sale price.

Submissions: Query first by letter with SASE. No phone queries. No unsolicited manuscripts.

Seeking: Feature films in all genres.

JOYCE A. FLAHERTY
Literary Agent
816 Lynda Court
St. Louis, MO 63122
(314) 966-3057

Professional Affiliations: Association of Author's Representatives, Romance Writers of America, Mystery Writers of America, Western Writers of America, Authors Guild.

Fees: No reading fee. $50 marketing fee for unpublished book authors.

Terms: 15% U.S., plus co-agent when foreign rights are retained.

Recent Sales/Clients: 4 book contract for Elizabeth August to Silhouette, 3 book historical contract for Charlene Cross to Pocket.

Submissions: Query first with SASE. OK to send synopsis and first three chapters. No unsolicited manuscripts.

Seeking: Contemporary (long), contemporary (short), historical, mainstream, paranormal, romantic suspense. No screenplays unless book has been sold for movies. Has co-agent in Hollywood.

Comments: We are mainly taking on published authors, but will consider current Romance Writers of America finalists and winners in their Golden Heart contest.

EVAN M. FOGELMAN
President
The Fogelman Literary Agency
7515 Greenville Avenue, Suite 712
Dallas, TX 75231
(214) 361-9956   FAX: (214) 361-9553

Professional Affiliations: Association of Author's Representatives, Romance Writers of America, American Bar Association Forum on Entertainment Law, board advisor for Published Authors Network.

Fees: No reading fees. No marketing fees.

Terms: 15% domestic, including all agency-negotiated subsidiary-rights deals; 10% foreign.

Recent Sales/Clients: Katherine Sutcliffe, Julie Beard, Helen R. Myers, Teresa Warfield, Jo Anne Cassity, S. K. Epperson, Judith Hill, Elizabeth Leigh, Lauryn Chandler, among others.

Submissions: Query letter with SASE. Phone queries are OK. Do not send unsolicited manuscripts or partials.

Seeking: Contemporary (long), contemporary (short), historical, mystery, romantic suspense. Occasionally handles screenplays, according to Guild and generally accepted packaging standards—please call first.

SHARRON FORREST
President
SF Literary Agency
P.O. Box 546
Larkspur, CA 94977
(415) 924-0222

Professional Affiliations: Romance Writers of America, Authors Guild.

Fees: No reading fees. No marketing fees.

Terms: A percentage on all money earned on projects placed by the agency.

Submissions: Query first with synopsis and first three chapters and SASE. No phone queries. No unsolicited manuscripts.

Seeking: Contemporary (long), contemporary (short), mainstream, mystery.

JEAN FREE
Literary Agent
Jay Garon-Brooke Associates, Inc.
101 W. 55th Street, Suite 5K
New York, NY 10019
(212) 581-8300   FAX: (212) 581-8397

Professional Affiliations: Association of Author's Representatives, Writers Guild of America.

Fees: No reading fees. No marketing fees.

Terms: 15% domestic; 30% foreign.

Submissions: Query by mail only. Query should include synopsis of story, author bio, and SASE! No phone queries. No unsolicited manuscripts.

Seeking: Mainstream book manuscripts. Also handles theatrical and feature film scripts—query first.

RUSS GALEN
Scovil, Chichak, Galen Agency, Inc.
381 Park Avenue South, Suite 1020
New York, NY 10016
(212) 679-8686   FAX: (212) 679-6710

Fees: No reading fees. No marketing fees.

Terms: 15% domestic, 20% foreign.

Submissions: Query first by letter with SASE. No phone queries. OK to send synopsis and first three chapters. Manuscript may be requested after query letter.

Seeking: Query first.

JAY GARON
President
Jay Garon-Brooke Associates, Inc.
101 W. 55th Street, Suite 5K
New York, NY 10019
(212) 581-8300   FAX: (212) 581-8397

Professional Affiliations: Association of Author's Representatives, Writers Guild of America.

Fees: No reading fees. No marketing fees.

Terms: 15% domestic, 30% foreign.

Recent Sales/Clients: *The Rainmaker* by John Grisham, Doubleday.

Submissions: Query by mail only. Query should include synopsis of story, author bio, and SASE! No phone queries. No unsolicited manuscripts.

Seeking: Mainstream book manuscripts. Also handles theatrical and feature film scripts—query first.

CHUCK GEBUHR
Literary Agent
International Leonards Corporation
3612 N. Washington Boulevard
Indianapolis, IN 46205-3534
(317) 926-7566

Professional Affiliations: Writers Guild of America East and West.

Fees: No reading fees. No marketing fees.

Terms: Writers Guild of America terms (10%).

Submissions: Query first by letter. Do not phone, please. Be a writer and write! No unsolicited materials. We represent only movies and TV scripts. No book manuscripts. Always enclose SASE with query.

Seeking: Screenplays/teleplays only. Contemporary, ethnic, fantasy, futuristic, historical, mainstream, mystery, paranormal, and romantic suspense are all OK. We are not looking for anything in particular—just good writing!

SUSAN GINSBURG
Writers House, Inc.
21 W. 26th Street
New York, NY 10010
(212) 685-2400   FAX: (212) 685-1871

Professional Affiliations: Association of Author's Representatives.

Fees: No reading fees. No marketing fees.

Terms: 15% domestic.

Recent Sales/Clients: *Vanity* by Jane Feather.

Submissions: Query first with SASE.

Seeking: Well-written, commercially oriented fiction. Any genre acceptable, as long as the work is accessible and affecting.

BARBARA J. GISLASON

Attorney
The Gislason Agency
219 S.E. Main Street, Suite 506
Minneapolis, MN 55415
(612) 331-8033   FAX: (612) 331-8115

Fees: No reading fees. No marketing fees.

Terms: 15% of first North American hardcover and softcover rights; 20% of other rights.

Recent Sales/Clients: Jeri Smith-Youness, Nancy Parra, Wendelin Parsons, Hazel White.

Submissions: Query first with SASE. No phone queries. OK to send synopsis and first three chapters. All correspondence, especially manuscripts, should have SASE enclosed.

Seeking: Contemporary (long), contemporary (short), ethnic, fantasy, futuristic, historical, mainstream, mystery, paranormal, romantic suspense, science fiction, true crime.

Comments: Regarding screenplays, this agency prefers to handle book manuscripts. Most film rights handled are attached to books.

AMY S. GOLDBERGER

President
Publishing Services
525 E. 86th Street, Suite PHA
New York, NY 10028
(212) 535-6248   FAX (212) 988-1073

Fees: No reading fees. No marketing fees.

Recent Sales/Clients: Barbara Anne Pauley, Vida George.

Submissions: Query first with SASE. OK to include synopsis and first three chapters. No unsolicited manuscripts.

Seeking: Historical.

IRENE GOODMAN
Irene Goodman Literary Agency
521 Fifth Avenue, Suite 1700
New York, NY 10175
(212) 682-1978   FAX: (212) 490-6502

Professional Affiliations: Association of Author's Representatives.

Fees: No reading fees. No marketing fees.

Terms: 10–15%.

Recent Sales/Clients: Linda Lael Miller, Debbie Macomber, Pamela Morsi.

Submissions: Query first with SASE. No phone queries. No unsolicited partials or manuscripts.

Seeking: Contemporary (long), contemporary (short), historical, mainstream, mystery, paranormal.

BILL GRAHAM
Aabaal Literary Associates
P.O. Box 482
Hoquiam, WA 98550
(360) 538-1251

Professional Affiliations: Signatory to the Writers Guild of America, National Press Women, Washington Press Association, League of American Pen Women.

Fees: No reading fees. No marketing fees.

Terms: A straight 10% commission.

Recent Sales/Clients: Paul Gromosiak and Stephanie Mita. Many more names available upon request.

Submissions: Queries by phone are acceptable, or send synopsis and first three chapters. We do prefer the complete manuscript plus synopsis. Please enclose SASE, plus self-addressed container and return postage for your manuscript. Also have the postal clerk attach a certified card, so you will learn the date the manuscript is received by Aabaal.

Seeking: Contemporary (long), contemporary (short), ethnic, historical, mainstream, mystery, romantic suspense. Also seeking screenplays.

Comments: We are a Signatory of the Writers Guild of America. (Besides book manuscripts) we handle feature films and movies-of-the-week that do not contain violence. Romantic comedies have been requested by many producers.

NANCY GUMMERY
Literary Agent
Montgomery-West
7450 Butter Hills Drive
Salt Lake City, Utah 84121

Professional Affiliations: Signatory to the Writers Guild of America West.

Fees: No reading fees. Charges marketing fees for phone calls and postage.

Recent Sales/Clients: *Sporeless* to Fox, *Long Hello* to Tongue River Productions.

Submissions: Query first by letter with SASE. No unsolicited scripts.

Seeking: No novels. Handles only screenplays for feature films and movies-of-the-week in the areas of romantic comedy, romantic suspense, ethnic, futuristic, mystery, woman-in-jeopardy, and mainstream.

Comments: No longer handles novelists. Screenwriters only.

LEO P. HAFFEY, JR.
Attorney at Law
Client First Agency
P.O. Box 795
White House, TN 37188
(615) 325-4780

Professional Affiliations: Signatory to the Writers Guild of America, licensed attorney.

Fees: No reading fees. No marketing fees.

Terms: 10% sale price.

Recent Sales/Clients: *Days of the Dead* by Agnes Bushell.

Submissions: Query first with SASE. No phone queries. No unsolicited manuscripts or partials.

Seeking: Handles feature films in all genres.

MERRILEE HEIFETZ
Writers House, Inc.
21 W. 26th Street
New York, NY 10010
(212) 685-2400   FAX: (212) 685-1781

Professional Affiliations: Association of Author's Representatives.

Fees: No reading fees. No marketing fees.

Terms: 15% domestic, 20% foreign.

Recent Sales/Clients: Nora Roberts, Barbara Delinsky, Eileen Goudge, Jane Feather, Betty Receveur, Barbara Veyle, Anne Tolstoi Wallach, Modean Moon, Francine Pascal.

Submissions: Query first with SASE.

Seeking: Brilliant writing in any category.

Comments: Interested in experienced writers who feel they have the skills and energy to move from paperback into hardcover. We manage careers.

DR. MYRL D. HERMANN
Aabaal Literary Associates
P.O. Box 482
Hoquiam, WA 98550
(360) 538-1251

Professional Affiliations: Signatory to the Writers Guild of America, National Press Women, Washington Press Association, League of American Pen Women.

Fees: No reading fees. No marketing fees.

Terms: A straight 10% commission.

Recent Sales/Clients: Paul Gromosiak and Stephanie Mita. Many more names available upon request.

Submissions: Queries by phone are acceptable, or send synopsis and first three chapters. We do prefer the complete manuscript plus synopsis. Please enclose SASE, plus self-addressed container and return postage for your manuscript. Also have the postal clerk attach a certified card, so you will learn the date the manuscript is received by Aabaal.

Seeking: Contemporary (long), contemporary (short), ethnic, historical, mainstream, mystery, romantic suspense. Also seeking screenplays.

Comments: We are a Signatory of the Writers Guild of America. (Besides book manuscripts) we handle feature films and movies-of-the-week that do not contain violence. Romantic comedies have been requested by many producers.

SUSAN HERNER
President
Susan Herner Rights Agency, Inc.
P.O. Box 303
Scarsdale, NY 10583
(914) 725-8967   FAX: (914) 725-8969

Fees: No reading fees. No marketing fees.

Terms: 15% domestic, 20% foreign and performance.

Recent Sales/Clients: Libby Sykes, Joanne Pence, Linda Anderson, Gayle Feyrer.

Submissions: Query first with SASE. No phone queries. OK to send synopsis and first three chapters. No unsolicited manuscripts.

Seeking: Contemporary (long), fantasy, historical, mainstream, mystery, romantic suspense.

CAROLYN HODGES

Carolyn Hodges Agency
1980 Glenwood Drive
Boulder, CO 80304
(303) 443-4636   FAX: same

Professional Affiliations: Writers Guild of America, Rocky Mountain Writer's Guild.

Fees: No reading fees. No marketing fees.

Terms: 10% of gross.

Submissions: Query by letter first. No unsolicited materials. This agency represents screenplays only, no manuscripts.

Seeking: Screenplays only, no book manuscripts, in the areas of feature films in any genre except westerns. No TV scripts except movie-of-the-week scripts, especially true crime/true life stories.

PAM HOPKINS

Elaine Davie Literary Agency
620 Park Avenue
Rochester, NY 14607
(716) 442-0830   FAX: (716) 461-1641

Fees: No reading fees. No marketing fees.

Terms: No contracts. 15% commission when book sells, 20% on foreign and film rights.

Recent Sales/Clients: Kit Garland, Merline Lovelace, Jane Kidder, Sue Krinard, Tina Wainscott.

Submissions: Prefers query letter with synopsis and first three chapters, and SASE, of course. Speedy replies are given to queries, partials are responded to in one month. No phone queries, please. No FAX queries. (Does not represent short stories, poetry, novellas, or children's books.)

Seeking: Contemporary (long), contemporary (short), historical. All genre romances, especially category, mystery, fantasy, westerns (a few), women's fiction. Also handle well-written nonfiction.

YVONNE TRUDEAU HUBBS
President
Yvonne Trudeau Hubbs Literary Agency
32371 Alipaz, Suite 101
San Juan Capistrano, CA 92675
(714) 496-1970

Professional Affiliations: Romance Writers of America.

Fees: Charges reading fee of $50 to unpublished authors, which includes light editing and critique. If agent sells manuscript within 1 year, $50 is refunded to author. $25 office expense fee.

Recent Sales/Clients: Privileged information. I have many published writers as clients.

Submissions: Prefers a query letter first with SASE. No phone queries. No unsolicited manuscripts.

Seeking: Contemporary (long), contemporary (short), ethnic, fantasy, historical, mainstream, mystery, paranormal, romantic suspense, time travel. Handles screenplays only if connected to published book.

Comments: Works with unpublished writers with goals of publication and career-building.

JENNIFER JACKSON
Assistant Agent
Donald Maass Literary Agency
157 W. 57th Street, Suite 1003
New York, NY 10019
(212) 757-7755

Professional Affiliations: Agency membership in Association of Author's Representatives.

Fees: No reading fees. No marketing fees.

Terms: 15% domestic, 20% overseas.

Submissions: Please query first with SASE. No phone queries. No unsolicited manuscripts or partials.

Seeking: Contemporary (long), contemporary (short), fantasy, futuristic, historical, paranormal, romantic suspense.

ELAINE JACOBS
Literary Agent
Westchester Literary Agency
4278 D'Este Court, #203
Lake Worth, FL 33467
(407) 642-2908   FAX: (407) 965-4258

Fees: No reading fees. No marketing fees.

Terms: 15% domestic, 20% foreign.

Recent Sales/Clients: *Please Don't Let Him Hurt Me Anymore* by Alexis Asker, Burning Gate; *Clearwater Summer* by John Keegan, Carol & Graf; *Blackfeet* by Teresa Lacey, Chelsea House.

Submissions: Query first with SASE. OK to send synopsis and first three chapters.

Seeking: Contemporary (long), mainstream, mystery, romantic suspense.

ELEANORE JEFFER AND MEDWIN JEFFER
Literary Agents
Westchester Literary Agency
4278 D'Este Court, #203
Lake Worth, FL 33467
(407) 642-2908   FAX: (407) 965-4258

Fees: No reading fees. No marketing fees.

Terms: 15% domestic, 20% foreign.

Recent Sales/Clients: *Please Don't Let Him Hurt Me Anymore* by Alexis Asker, Burning Gate; *Clearwater Summer* by John Keegan, Carol & Graf; *Blackfeet* by Teresa Lacey, Chelsea House.

Submissions: Query first with SASE. OK to send synopsis and first three chapters.

Seeking: Contemporary (long), mainstream, mystery, romantic suspense.

MARTHA JEWETT
Associate
The Evan Marshall Agency
6 Tristam Place
Pine Brook, NJ 07058-9445
(201) 882-1122   FAX: (201) 882-3099

Professional Affiliations: Association of Author's Representatives, Romance Writers of America.

Fees: No reading fees. No marketing fees. Handling fee of $38 for unpublished writers.

Terms: 15% commission on domestic, 20% on foreign.

Recent Sales/Clients: Confidential.

Submissions: Query first with SASE. No phone queries. No unsolicited manuscripts or partials.

Seeking: Contemporary (long), contemporary (short), ethnic, fantasy, futuristic, historical, mainstream, mystery, paranormal, romantic suspense. Also seeking screenplays for feature films and movies-of-the-week.

CHARLÈNE KAY
President
Charlène Kay Agency
901 Beaudry, Suite 6
St-Jean/Richelieu, Quebec J3A 1C6
CANADA

Professional Affiliations: Writers Guild of America, Broadcast Music, Inc.

Fees: No reading fees. No marketing fees.

Terms: 10% on domestic and foreign sales.

Submissions: Phone queries or letter queries are acceptable. OK to send synopsis or unsolicited scripts.

Seeking: Screenplays and teleplays of fantasy, futuristic, mainstream, family drama, or true stories.

Comments: This agency handles only screenplays and teleplays. No books, novels, or short stories, unless those can be written in script form. We handle feature films and movies-of-the-week, sometimes episodic sitcoms, dramas, and cable films. No daytime serial or prime-time serial teleplays.

KAY KIDDE
Chief Associate
Kidde, Hoyt & Picard
335 E. 51st Street
New York, NY 10022
(212) 755-9461

Professional Affiliations: Association of Author's Representatives.

Fees: No reading fees. No marketing fees.

Recent Sales/Clients: Diana Haviland, Zebra; Nancy Christiansen, Zebra; Chloe Gardner Diamond, Harper; Barry King, Ballantine.

Submissions: Query by letter with SASE. No unsolicited manuscripts.

Seeking: Contemporary (long), contemporary (short), historical, mainstream, mystery, romantic suspense.

Comments: We only want to take on authors of romance if we feel they have the potential for hardcover, or lead titles.

SAM KLEIN
C.E.O.
Kick Entertainment
1934 E. 123rd Street
Cleveland, OH 44106
(216) 791-2515   FAX: same

Professional Affiliations: Writers Guild of America.

Fees: No reading fees. No marketing fees.

Terms: 10% of sale price.

Submissions: Query first with SASE.

Seeking: Feature film screenplays only, in the areas of mystery, futuristic, or romantic suspense.

ROBERT KNIGHT
Aabaal Literary Associates
P.O. Box 482
Hoquiam, WA 98550
(360) 538-1251

Professional Affiliations: National Press Women, Washington Press Association, League of American Pen Women, Signatory of the Writers Guild of America.

Fees: No reading fees. No marketing fees.

Terms: A straight 10% commission.

Recent Sales/Clients: Paul Gromosiak and Stephanie Mita. Many more names available upon request.

Submissions: Queries by phone are acceptable, or send synopsis and first three chapters. We do prefer the complete manuscript plus synopsis. Please enclose SASE, plus self-addressed container and return postage for your manuscript. Also have the postal clerk attach a certified card, so you will learn the date the manuscript is received by Aabaal.

Seeking: Contemporary (long), contemporary (short), ethnic, historical, mainstream, mystery, romantic suspense. Also seeking screenplays.

Comments: We are a Signatory of the Writers Guild of America. (Besides book manuscripts) we handle feature films and movies-of-the-week that do not contain violence. Romantic comedies have been requested by many producers.

LINDA DIEHL KRUGER
Vice President
The Fogelman Literary Agency
7515 Greenville Avenue, Suite 712
Dallas, TX 75231
(214) 361-9956   FAX: (214) 361-9553

Professional Affiliations: Association of Author's Representatives and Romance Writers of America.

Fees: No reading fees. No marketing fees.

Recent Sales/Clients: Karen Leabo; Two untitled books by Susan Macias, Harper; *Cowboy Homecoming* by Pamela

Ingrahm, Silhouette; *Dark Hunter* by Leeann Harris, Denise Little Presents; *Forever and a Day* by Victoria Chancellor, Leisure; *Kelly and the Coach* by Teresa Southwick, Silhouette; *Lady Vengeance* by Sarah Eagle, Harper; Three titles by April Kihlstrom to NAL/Signet; *Texas Lonesome* by Alice Duncan, Harper.

Submissions: Query by letter with SASE or query by phone. No unsolicited manuscripts or partials.

Seeking: Contemporary (long), contemporary (short), ethnic, historicals of any time period, paranormal, Regency, select non-fiction.

JASMINE LAM
Literary Agent
Circle of Confusion, Ltd.
666 Fifth Avenue, Suite 303
New York, NY 10103

Professional Affiliations: Writers Guild of America.

Fees: No reading fees. No marketing fees.

Terms: 10% on sale.

Recent Sales/Clients: Available upon request.

Submissions: Query first with SASE. No phone queries. No unsolicited manuscripts.

Seeking: Contemporary (long), contemporary (short), ethnic, fantasy, futuristic, historical, mainstream, mystery, paranormal, romantic suspense, screenplays.

Comments: Screenplays are our primary focus.

DICK LANDERMAN
Affiliate
Montgomery-West
7450 Butter Hills Drive
Salt Lake City, Utah 84121

Professional Affiliations: Signatory to the Writers Guild of America West.

Fees: No reading fees. Charges marketing fees for phone calls and postage.

Recent Sales/Clients: *Sporeless* to Fox; *Long Hello* to Tongue River Productions.

Submissions: Query first by letter with SASE. No unsolicited scripts.

Seeking: Only screenplays for feature films and movies-of-the-week in the areas of romantic comedy, romantic suspense, ethnic, futuristic, mystery, woman-in-jeopardy, and mainstream.

Comments: No longer handles novelists. Screenwriters only.

JAMES L'ANGELLE
Cyberstorm!
P.O. Box 6330
Reno, NV 89513

Fees: No reading fees. No marketing fees.

Terms: 20%.

Submissions: No phone calls please! Send synopsis of 1–2 pages with cover letter and SASE.

Seeking: Mystery, paranormal, and other unusual, bizarre. Will assist in placement of screenplays with agents and producers.

Comments: Would like to see some extremely imaginative stories centered around romance, strictly intelligent and novel material.

LAURA LANGLIE

Associate
Kidde, Hoyt & Picard
335 E. 51st Street
New York, NY 10022
(212) 755-9461

Professional Affiliations: Association of Author's Representatives.

Fees: No reading fees. No marketing fees.

Recent Sales/Clients: Diana Haviland, Zebra; Nancy Christiansen, Zebra; Chloe Gardner Diamond, Harper; Barry King, Ballantine.

Submissions: Query by letter with SASE. No unsolicited manuscripts.

Seeking: Contemporary (long), contemporary (short), historical, mainstream, mystery, romantic suspense.

Comments: We only want to take on authors of romance if we feel they have the potential for hardcover, or lead titles.

MICHAEL LARSEN

Partner
Michael Larsen/Elizabeth Pomada Literary Agents
1029 Jones Street
San Francisco, CA 94109
(415) 673-0939

Professional Affiliations: Association of Author's Representatives, American Society of Journalists and Authors, Women's National Book Association, Authors Guild, National Writer's Union, National Writer's Club.

Fees: No reading fees. No marketing fees.

Recent Sales/Clients: *A Crack in Forever* by Jeannie Brewer, Simon and Schuster; *Palace* by Katharine Kerr, Bantam; *Drums of Chaos* by Jo Clayton, Tor.

Submissions: Don't query. For fiction, send the first 30 pages with synopsis, SASE, and phone number. For nonfiction only, call first.

Seeking: Contemporary (long), contemporary (short), fantasy, historical, mainstream, mystery, romantic suspense. No screenplays, "although we do sell our novels to Hollywood."

Comments: Looking for romance novels that will stand on their own as good books first—good romance second. Fresh voices and new ideas are vital.

FRAN LEBOWITZ

Literary Agent
Writers House, Inc.
21 W. 26th Street
New York, NY 10010
(212) 685-2400   FAX: (212) 685-1871

Professional Affiliations: Association of Author's Representatives.

Fees: No reading fees. No marketing fees.

Terms: 15% domestic, 20% foreign.

Recent Sales/Clients: Nora Roberts, Barbara Delinsky, Eileen Goudge, Jane Feather, Betty Receveur, Barbara Veyle, Anne Tolstoi Wallach, Modean Moon, Francine Pascal.

Submissions: Query first with SASE.

Seeking: Brilliant writing in any category.

Comments: Interested in experienced writers who feel they have the skills and energy to move from paperback into hard-cover. We manage careers.

LETTIE LEE
Associate
Ann Elmo Agency, Inc.
60 E. 42nd Street
New York, NY 10165
(212) 661-2880   FAX: (212) 661-2883

Professional Affiliations: Association of Author's Representatives.

Fees: No reading fee. $25 nominal handling fee for unpublished writers.

Terms: 15% commission.

Recent Sales/Clients: Linda Turner, Vickie York, Kaitlin Girton, Charlotte Douglas, Ida Hills, Arlene Erlbach, Carol Culvar.

Submissions: Query first with SASE. OK to send synopsis and first three chapters. No unsolicited manuscripts.

Seeking: Contemporary (long), historical, mystery, paranormal, romantic suspense.

DAVID LEONARDS
President
International Leonards Corporation
3612 N. Washington Boulevard
Indianapolis, IN 46205-3534
(317) 926-7566

Professional Affiliations: Writers Guild of America East and West.

Fees: No reading fees. No marketing fees.

Terms: Writers Guild of America terms (10%).

Submissions: Query first by letter. Do not telephone, please. Be a writer and write! No unsolicited materials. We represent only movies and TV scripts. No book manuscripts. Always enclose SASE with query.

Seeking: Screenplays/teleplays only. Contemporary, ethnic, fantasy, futuristic, historical, mainstream, mystery, paranormal, and romantic suspense are all OK. We are not looking for anything in particular—just good writing!

NORMA LIEBERT
Co-Owner
The Norma-Lewis Agency
360 W. 53rd Street, Suite BA
New York, NY 10019
(212) 664-0807   FAX: (212) 664-0462

Fees: No reading fees. No marketing fees.

Terms: 15% domestic and Canada, 20% to all other.

Recent Sales/Clients: *Viper Quarry* by Dean Feldmeyer; *Pitchfork Hollow* by Dean Feldmeyer.

Submissions: Please query first with SASE. OK to send synopsis and first three chapters. No phone queries. No unsolicited scripts.

Seeking: Contemporary (long), contemporary (short), ethnic, historical, mainstream, mystery, romantic suspense. Also seeking screenplays for dramatic series and cable series.

ROBERT MADSEN
President
The Robert Madsen Literary Agency
1331 E. 34th Street, #1
Oakland, CA 94602
(510) 223-2090

Fees: No reading fees. No marketing fees.

Terms: 10% + 10% to foreign agents for overseas sales.

Recent Sales/Clients: So far, our sales have been nonfiction and New Age. We're hopeful about finding a good romance to sell.

Submissions: No phone queries. Query by letter or send synopsis and first three chapters. No unsolicited manuscripts.

Seeking: Contemporary (short), ethnic, fantasy, futuristic, historical, mainstream, mystery, paranormal, romantic suspense. Also handles screenplays for feature films, movies-of-the-week, sitcoms, dramatic series, romantic comedies, cable series, almost everything, except soaps.

DENISE MARCIL
President
Denise Marcil Literary Agency
685 West End Avenue, #9C
New York, NY 10025
(212) 932-3110   FAX: (212) 932-3113

Professional Affiliations: Association of Author's Representatives, past board member, past vice president.

Fees: Charges small reading fee. No marketing fees.

Terms: Domestic, 15% commission; foreign, 20% commission.

Recent Sales/Clients: Arnette Lamb, Anita Mills, Roseanne Bittner, Carla Neggers.

Submissions: Always query with a one page letter and SASE, only. No phone queries. No unsolicited manuscripts or partials.

Seeking: Contemporary (long), mainstream.

Comments: I will consider previously published authors only.

EVAN MARSHALL
President
The Evan Marshall Agency
6 Tristam Place
Pine Brook, NJ 07058-9445
(201) 882-1122   FAX: (201) 882-3099

Professional Affiliations: Association of Author's Representatives, Romance Writers of America.

Fees: No reading fees. No marketing fees. Handling fee of $38 for unpublished writers.

Terms: 15% commission on domestic, 20% on foreign.

Recent Sales/Clients: Confidential.

Submissions: Query first with SASE. No phone queries. No unsolicited manuscripts or partials.

Seeking: Contemporary (long), contemporary (short), ethnic, fantasy, futuristic, historical, mainstream, mystery, paranormal, romantic suspense. Also seeking screenplays for feature films and movies-of-the-week.

LAWRENCE MATTIS
Literary Agent
Circle of Confusion, Ltd.
666 Fifth Avenue, Suite 303
New York, NY 10103

Professional Affiliations: Writers Guild of America.

Fees: No reading fees. No marketing fees.

Terms: 10% on sale.

Recent Sales/Clients: Available upon request.

Submissions: Query first with SASE. No phone queries. No unsolicited manuscripts.

Seeking: Contemporary (long), contemporary (short), ethnic, fantasy, futuristic, historical, mainstream, mystery, paranormal, romantic suspense, screenplays.

Comments: Screenplays are our primary focus.

LOUISE MEYERS
Director of Development
Charlène Kay Agency
901 Beaudry, Suite 6
St-Jean/Richelieu, Quebec J3A 1C6
CANADA

Professional Affiliations: Writers Guild of America, Broadcast Music, Inc.

Fees: No reading fees. No marketing fees.

Terms: 10% on domestic and foreign sales.

Submissions: Query by letter or phone, or send synopsis with cover letter. Unsolicited scripts are OK.

Seeking: Screenplays and teleplays *only.* No books, novels, or short stories, unless these can be written in script form. Looking for fantasy, futuristic, mainstream, family drama, or true stories.

Comments: Handles feature films and movies-of-the week, sometimes episodic sitcoms, dramas, and cable films. No daytime serial or prime-time serial teleplays.

MAUREEN MORAN
Senior Editor
Donald MacCampbell, Inc.
P.O. Box 20191, Park West Station
New York, NY 10025
(212) 683-5580

Fees: No reading fees. No marketing fees.

Terms: 10% U.S., 15% Canada, 20% elsewhere; 15% first book sale.

Submissions: Query first by letter with SASE.

Seeking: Contemporary romance and mainstream novels. Does not represent fantasy, futuristic, horror, paranormal, or young adult.

Comments: Donald MacCampbell died in late 1994. Maureen Moran is continuing the agency, which has been in business for many years.

HOWARD MORHAIM
President
Howard Morhaim Literary Agency
175 Fifth Avenue, Suite 709
New York, NY 10010
(212) 529-4433   FAX: (212) 995-1112

Professional Affiliations: Association of Author's Representatives, Romance Writers of America, Mystery Writers of America.

Fees: No reading fees. No marketing fees.

Terms: 15% domestic, 20% foreign.

Submissions: Query first with SASE. OK to send synopsis and first three chapters. No phone queries. No unsolicited manuscripts.

Seeking: Contemporary (long), historical, mainstream, mystery, romantic suspense.

DARA MOSKOWITZ
Associate Agent
The Gislason Agency
219 S.E. Main Street, Suite 506
Minneapolis, MN 55415
(612) 331-8033   FAX: (612) 331-8115

Fees: No reading fees. No marketing fees.

Terms: 15% of first North American hardcover and softcover rights, 20% of other rights.

Recent Sales/Clients: Jeri Smith-Youness, Nancy Parra, Wendelin Parsons, Hazel White.

Submissions: Query first with SASE. No phone queries. OK to send synopsis and first three chapters. All correspondence, especially manuscripts, should have SASE enclosed.

Seeking: Contemporary (long), contemporary (short), ethnic, fantasy, futuristic, historical, mainstream, mystery, paranormal, romantic suspense.

Comments: Regarding screenplays, this agency prefers to represent book manuscripts; most film rights handled are attached to books.

ALLISON MULLEN
Literary Agent
Howard Morhaim Literary Agency
175 Fifth Avenue, Suite 709
New York, NY 10010
(212) 529-4433   FAX: (212) 995-1112

Professional Affiliations: Association of Author's Representatives, Romance Writers of America, Mystery Writers of America.

Fees: No reading fees. No marketing fees.

Terms: 15% domestic, 20% foreign.

Submissions: Query first with SASE. OK to send synopsis and first three chapters. No phone queries. No unsolicited manuscripts.

Seeking: Contemporary (long), historical, mainstream, mystery, romantic suspense.

ANN MARIE NEGRETTI
Literary Agent
Circle of Confusion, Ltd.
666 Fifth Avenue, Suite 303
New York, NY 10103

Professional Affiliations: Writers Guild of America.

Fees: No reading fees. No marketing fees.

Terms: 10% on sale.

Recent Sales/Clients: Available upon request.

Submissions: Query first with SASE. No phone queries. No unsolicited manuscripts.

Seeking: Contemporary (long), contemporary (short), ethnic, fantasy, futuristic, historical, mainstream, mystery, paranormal, romantic suspense, screenplays.

Comments: Screenplays are our primary focus.

KIM VAN NGUYEN
Senior Editor
The Robert Madsen Literary Agency
1331 E. 34th Street, #1
Oakland, CA 94602
(510) 223-2090

Fees: No reading fees. No marketing fees.

Terms: 10% + 10% to foreign agents for overseas sales.

Recent Sales/Clients: So far, our sales have been nonfiction and New Age. We're hopeful about finding a good romance to sell.

Submissions: No phone queries. Query by letter or send synopsis and first three chapters. No unsolicited manuscripts.

Seeking: Contemporary (short), ethnic, fantasy, futuristic, historical, mainstream, mystery, paranormal, romantic suspense. Also handles screenplays for feature films, movies-of-the-week, sitcoms, dramatic series, romantic comedies, cable series, almost everything, except soaps.

M. NICHOLAS PIRO
Client First Agency
P.O. Box 795
White House, TN 37188

Professional Affiliations: Signatory to the Writers Guild of America.

Fees: No reading fees. No marketing fees.

Terms: 10% of sale price.

Submissions: Query first by letter with SASE. No phone queries. No unsolicited manuscripts.

Seeking: Feature films in all genres.

ELIZABETH POMADA

Partner
Michael Larsen/Elizabeth Pomada Literary Agents
1029 Jones Street
San Francisco, CA 94109
(415) 673-0939

Professional Affiliations: Association of Author's Representatives, American Society of Journalists and Authors, Women's National Book Association, Authors Guild, National Writer's Union, National Writer's Club.

Fees: No reading fees. No marketing fees.

Recent Sales/Clients: *A Crack in Forever* by Jeannie Brewer, Simon and Schuster; *Palace* by Katharine Kerr, Bantam; *Drums of Chaos* by Jo Clayton, Tor.

Submissions: Don't query. For fiction, send the first 30 pages with synopsis, SASE, and phone number. For nonfiction only, call first.

Seeking: Contemporary (long), contemporary (short), fantasy, historical, mainstream, mystery, romantic suspense. No screenplays, "although we do sell our novels to Hollywood."

Comments: Looking for romance novels that will stand on their own as good books first—good romance second. Fresh voices and new ideas are vital.

HARRY PRESTON
Consultant/Agent
Stanton & Associates Literary Agency
4413 Clemson Drive
Garland, TX 75042
(214) 276-5427   FAX: (214) 276-5426

Professional Affiliations: Signatory to the Writers Guild of America West.

Fees: No reading fees. No marketing fees.

Submissions: Handles only screenplays, no book manuscripts. Query first by letter with SASE or call. Do not send unsolicited scripts.

Seeking: Screenplays only for feature films and movies-of-the-week, especially woman-in-jeopardy and romantic comedies. No spec scripts for existing TV series.

Comments: Reading fees are not allowed by the WGA. We do, however, (sometimes) refer screenwriters to professional editors and rewrite persons.

JULIA A. RHYNE
Attorney at Law
Rhyne & Stevens, Attorneys at Law
Authors' Representatives
8325 N. Meridian Street
Indianpolis, IN 46260
(317) 255-0331   FAX: same

Professional Affiliations: Romance Writers of America, Published Authors Network, Novelists, Inc., American Bookseller's Association, International Bookseller's Association, Indianapolis Bar Association.

Fees: A processing charge of $50 per project is repaid out of the first sale, for authors not previously published in the genre in which they are submitting.

Terms: 15% on North American sales, 20% on sale of extended rights.

Recent Sales/Clients: *Knight of a Billion Stars* by Donna Lanier, Leisure.

Submissions: Send one page query letter with SASE. Phone queries are also acceptable. OK to send synopsis and first three chapters, but please no unsolicited manuscripts. We don't have room.

Seeking: Contemporary (long), contemporary (short), ethnic, fantasy, futuristic, historical, mainstream, mystery, nonfiction, paranormal, romantic suspense. Does not handle screenplays, but can refer to contacts in LA.

Comments: Because we are lawyers and writers, we have wide expertise. We are actively seeking clients for our young business. (Julia Rhyne has a BA and MLS from Indiana University and a Law Degree from the Indiana University School of Law at Indianapolis. She specializes in copyright law, intellectual property law, and publishing.)

MICHAEL ROBINSON
Client First Agency
P.O. Box 795
White House, TN 37188
(615) 325-4780

Professional Affiliations: Signatory to the Writers Guild of America.

Fees: No reading fees. No marketing fees.

Terms: 10% of sale price.

Submissions: Query first by letter with SASE. No phone queries. No unsolicited manuscripts.

Seeking: Feature films in all genres.

DAMARIS ROWLAND
President
The Damaris Rowland Agency
R.R. #1, Box 513A
Wallingford, VT 05773
(802) 446-3146   FAX: (802) 446-3224

Professional Affiliations: Association of Author's Representatives, Romance Writers of America.

Fees: No reading fee. No marketing fee.

Terms: 15% commission.

Recent Sales/Clients: Haywood Smith, Connie Brockway, Connie Rinehold, Tracey Tillis.

Submissions: Send query letter or synopsis and first three chapters. Unsolicited manuscripts are OK. Enclose SASE. No phone queries, please.

Seeking: Contemporary (long), contemporary (short), ethnic, historical, mainstream, mystery, paranormal, romantic suspense.

Comments: Affiliated with Steven Axelrod Agency.

DAVID ROYCE

Storr, Royce & Associates
Box 10, 9944 33rd Avenue
Edmonton, Alberta T6N 1E8
CANADA

Fees: No reading fees. No marketing fees.

Submissions: Preferred submission is outline with complete manuscript. Do not send queries or sample chapters. No phone queries please. Canadian stamps must be on the SASE, or authors must provide International Reply Coupons and response envelope, otherwise material will be recycled. Submit to Jason Storr/David Royce. Response is usually in 4 to 6 weeks.

Seeking: This new Canadian literary agency is currently seeking nonfiction and fiction in all categories and genres.

Note: This literary agency is enthusiastically endorsed by Shaun Donnelly, the publisher of *Writer's Block Magazine*, who knows the agents at this agency and vouches for their professional reputation.

PESHA RUBINSTEIN

Pesha Rubinstein Literary Agency, Inc.
37 Overlook Terrace, #1D
New York, NY 10033
(212) 781-7845

Professional Affiliations: Association of Author's Representatives, Romance Writers of America, Mystery Writers of America, Society of Children's Book Writers and Illustrators.

Fees: No reading fees. No marketing fees.

Terms: 15% commission domestic, 20% foreign.

Recent Sales/Clients: Tanya Crosby to Avon, Penelope Neri to Zebra, Karyn Monk to Bantam.

Submissions: No phone queries. Query letter first with SASE, or send synopsis and first fifteen pages. No unsolicited manuscripts. SASE is essential.

Seeking: Contemporary (long), contemporary (short), ethnic, historical, mainstream, mystery, paranormal, other. Invent something new and wonderful!

Comments: No sci-fi or poetry. Submissions must be double-spaced. Without SASE, material won't be returned. I am looking for marvelous stories. Editors want to find the story that breaks the rules or creates new frontiers in romance in ways that are entirely convincing. "Boy meets girl, they have a conflict, they resolve it and live happily ever after" still works, but the ways in which the formula works must be refreshing. I look forward to reading irresistible stories. By the way, I am a believer in correct spelling and grammar, so please proofread!

ROBIN RUE
Literary Agent
Anita Diamant Agency
310 Madison Avenue, #1508
New York, NY 10017
(212) 687-1122   FAX: (212) 972-1756

Professional Affiliations: Association of Author's Representatives.

Fees: No reading fees. No marketing fees.

Terms: 15% commission.

Recent Sales/Clients: V. C. Andrews, Linda Howard, Ann Major, Lisa Jackson.

Submissions: Query first with SASE. OK to send synopsis and first three chapters after querying.

Seeking: Contemporary (long), contemporary (short), ethnic, historical, mainstream, mystery, nonfiction, romantic suspense.

KELLY ST. CLAIR
St. Clair Literary Agency
4501 Colonial Avenue
Norfolk, VA 23508
(804) 623-0288   FAX: same, but call first

Professional Affiliations: Romance Writers of America.

Fees: No reading fee. No marketing fee.

Terms: 15% commission. Agency pays for postage, copies, etc.

Recent Sales/Clients: Prefers not to disclose without clients' permission.

Submissions: Prefers synopsis and first three chapters at initial contact. No query letters or phone queries.

Seeking: Contemporary (long), contemporary (short), ethnic, fantasy, futuristic, historical, mainstream, mystery, paranormal, romantic suspense.

LAURENS R. SCHWARTZ, ESQ.

Literary, Film and Art Representative
5 E. 22nd Street, Suite 15D
New York, NY 10010-5315
(212) 228-2614   FAX: (212) 228-6093

Professional Affiliations: Signatory to the Writers Guild of America.

Fees: No reading fees. No marketing fees.

Terms: 15% domestic, 25% foreign, 10% screenplay/teleplay.

Submissions: Query first by letter with SASE. No phone queries. OK to send synopsis and first three chapters. No unsolicited manuscripts.

Seeking: Contemporary (long), mainstream, mystery, paranormal, romantic suspense. Also handles screenplays of all types, including feature films, movies-of-the-week, sitcoms, dramatic series, daytime or prime-time soap scripts, romantic comedies, woman-in-jeopardy, cable series.

JACK SCOVIL

Scovil, Chichak, Galen Literary Agency, Inc.
381 Park Avenue South, Suite 1020
New York, NY 10016
(212) 679-8686   FAX: (212) 679-6710

Fees: No reading fees. No marketing fees.

Terms: 15% domestic, 20% foreign.

Submissions: Query first by letter with SASE. No phone queries. OK to send synopsis and first three chapters. No unsolicited manuscripts, unless OK'd after query.

Seeking: Query first.

MICHAEL SHORTT

Agency Director
Talent Source
P.O. Box 14120
Savannah, GA 31416
(912) 232-9390   FAX: (912) 232-8213

Professional Affiliations: Writers Guild of America.

Fees: No reading fee. No marketing fee.

Terms: 10%.

Submissions: Send query letter first with SASE. Phone queries are OK. OK to send synopsis with query letter. No unsolicited manuscripts. Always enclose SASE.

Seeking: Screenplays only!

Comments: We work primarily in film and television. Adaptations and original screenplays are of interest.

BOBBE SIEGEL

President
Bobbe Siegel Agency
41 W. 83rd Street
New York, NY 10024
(212) 877-4985   FAX: same

Fees: No reading fee. No marketing fee.

Terms: 15% commission on domestic sales. 10% foreign sales.

Recent Sales/Clients: *Travelling* to Macmillan; *The Storytellers* to Macmillan; *The Feel of Silence* to Temple University Press.

Submissions: Send query letter first. No unsolicited manuscripts. Only send synopsis and first three chapters if requested. Enclose SASE. No phone queries, please.

Seeking: Fantasy, historical, mainstream, mystery, paranormal.

HENRY STANTON
President
Stanton and Associates Literary Agency
4413 Clemson Drive
Garland, TX 75042
(214) 276-5427   FAX: (214) 276-5426

Professional Affiliations: Signatory to the Writers Guild of America West.

Fees: No reading fees. No marketing fees.

Submissions: Handles only screenplays, no book manuscripts. Query first by letter with SASE or call. Do not send unsolicited scripts.

Seeking: Screenplays only for feature films and movies-of-the-week, especially woman-in-jeopardy and romantic comedies. No spec scripts for existing TV series.

Comments: Reading fees are not allowed by the WGA. We do, however, (sometimes) refer screenwriters to professional editors and rewrite persons.

PATTIE STEELE-PERKINS

Elaine Davie Literary Agency
620 Park Avenue
Rochester, NY 14607
(716) 442-0830   FAX: (716) 461-1641

Professional Affiliations: Association of Author's Representatives, Mystery Writers of America, Sisters in Crime.

Fees: No reading fees. No marketing fees.

Terms: No contracts. 15% commission when book sells; 20% on foreign and film rights.

Recent Sales/Clients: Kit Garland, Merline Lovelace, Jane Kidder, Sue Krinard, Tina Wainscott.

Submissions: Prefers query letter with synopsis and first three chapters, and SASE, of course. Speedy replies are given to queries, partials are responded to in a month. No telephone queries, please. No FAX queries. (Does not represent short stories, poetry, novellas, or children's books.)

Seeking: Contemporary (long), contemporary (short), historical, all genre romances, especially category, mystery, fantasy, westerns (a few), women's fiction. Also handle well-written nonfiction.

THERESA A. STEVENS

Attorney at Law
Rhyne & Stevens, Attorneys at Law
Authors' Representatives
8325 N. Meridian Street
Indianpolis, IN 46260
(317) 255-0331   FAX: same

Professional Affiliations: Romance Writers of America, Published Authors Network, Novelists, Inc., American Bookseller's Association, International Bookseller's Association, Indianapolis Bar Association.

Fees: A processing charge of $50 per project is repaid out of the first sale, for authors not previously published in the genre in which they are submitting.

Terms: 15% on North American sales; 20% on sale of extended rights.

Recent Sales/Clients: *Knight of a Trillion Stars* by Dara Joy, Leisure.

Submissions: Send one page query letter with SASE. Phone queries are also acceptable. OK to send synopsis and first three chapters, but please no unsolicited manuscripts. We don't have room.

Seeking: Contemporary (long), contemporary (short), ethnic, fantasy, futuristic, historical, mainstream, mystery, paranormal, romantic suspense, nonfiction. Does not handle screenplays, but can refer to contacts in LA.

Comments: Because we are lawyers and writers, we have wide expertise. We are actively seeking clients for our young business. (Theresa A. Stevens has a BA in creative writing from Purdue University and a Law Degree from the Indiana University School of Law at Indianapolis. She specializes in trademark law and entertainment law, including talent contracts.)

DENISE STINSON
President
Stinson Literary Agency, Inc.
8120 E. Jefferson, Suite 6H
Detroit, MI 48214

Fees: No reading fees. No marketing fees.

Recent Sales/Clients: A two book deal for Jane Archer to Pocket Books, plus a movie deal for one of the books.

Submissions: Query first by phone. OK to send synopsis and first three chapters. Unsolicited manuscripts are OK.

Seeking: Contemporary (long), ethnic. Does not handle screenplays, but sells movie-of-the-week and feature films from book manuscripts.

JASON STORR
Storr, Royce & Associates
Box 10, 9944 33rd Avenue
Edmonton, Alberta T6N 1E8
CANADA

Fees: No reading fees. No marketing fees.

Submissions: Preferred submission is outline with complete manuscript. Do not send queries, or sample chapters. No phone queries please. Canadian stamps must be on the SASE, or authors must provide International Reply Coupons and response envelope, otherwise material will be recycled. Submit to Jason Storr/David Royce. Response is usually in 4 to 6 weeks.

Seeking: This new Canadian literary agency is currently seeking nonfiction and fiction in all categories and genres.

Note: This literary agency is enthusiastically endorsed by Shaun Donnelly, the publisher of *Writer's Block Magazine*, who knows the agents at this agency and vouches for their professional reputation.

GENO TRUNZO
Executive Vice President—Creative Affairs
Kick Entertainment
1934 E. 123rd Street
Cleveland, OH 44106
(216) 791-2515   FAX: same

Professional Affiliations: Writers Guild of America.

Fees: No reading fees. No marketing fees.

Terms: 10% of sale price.

Submissions: Query first with SASE.

Seeking: Feature film screenplays only, in the areas of mystery, futuristic, or romantic suspense.

DEE DEE UNDERWOOD
Client First Agency
P.O. Box 795
White House, TN 37188
(615) 325-4780

Professional Affiliations: Signatory to the Writers Guild of America.

Fees: No reading fees. No marketing fees.

Terms: 10% of sale price.

Submissions: Query first by letter with SASE. No phone queries. No unsolicited manuscripts.

Seeking: Feature films in all genres.

WENDY VALENTINE
Administrative Assistant
The Gislason Agency
219 S.E. Main Street, Suite 506
Minneapolis, MN 55415
(612) 331-8033   FAX: (612) 331-8115

Fees: No reading fees. No marketing fees.

Terms: 15% of first North American hardcover and softcover rights; 20% of other rights.

Submissions: Query first by letter with SASE. No phone queries. OK to send synopsis and first three chapters. All correspondence, especially manuscripts, should have SASE enclosed.

Seeking: Contemporary (long), contemporary (short), ethnic, fantasy, futuristic, historical, mainstream, mystery, paranormal, romantic suspense, science fiction, true crime.

Comments: Regarding screenplays, this agency prefers book manuscripts. Most film rights are attached to books.

JESSICA WAINWRIGHT
Literary Agent/Foreign Rights Director
The Literary Group International
270 Lafayette Street, Suite 1505
New York, NY 10012

Fees: No reading fees. No marketing fees.

Terms: 15% domestic, 20% foreign.

Submissions: Query by letter with SASE. OK to include synopsis and first three chapters. No unsolicited manuscripts.

Seeking: Historical.

SCOTT WAXMAN
Literary Agent
The Literary Group International
270 Lafayette Street, Suite 1505
New York, NY 10012

Fees: No reading fees. No marketing fees.

Terms: 15% domestic, 20% foreign.

Submissions: Query by letter with SASE. OK to include synopsis and first three chapters. No unsolicited manuscripts.

Seeking: Historical.

FRANK WEIMANN
President
The Literary Group International
270 Lafayette Street, Suite 1505
New York, NY 10012

Fees: No reading fees. No marketing fees.

Terms: 15% domestic, 20% foreign.

Submissions: Query by letter with SASE. OK to include synopsis and first three chapters. No unsolicited manuscripts.

Seeking: Historical.

CAROLE WESTERN
Montgomery-West
7450 Butter Hills Drive
Salt Lake City, Utah 84121

Professional Affiliations: Signatory to the Writers Guild of America West.

Fees: No reading fees. Charges marketing fees for phone calls and postage.

Recent Sales/Clients: *Sporeless* to Fox; *Long Hello* to Tongue River Productions.

Submissions: Query first by letter with SASE. No unsolicited scripts.

Seeking: Screenplays *only* for feature films and movies-of-the-week in the areas of romantic comedy, romantic suspense, ethnic, futuristic, mystery, woman-in-jeopardy, and mainstream.

Comments: No longer handles novelists. Screenwriters only.

SUE YUEN
Associate
Susan Herner Rights Agency, Inc.
P.O. Box 303
Scarsdale, NY 10583
(914) 725-8967   FAX: (914) 725-8969

Fees: No reading fees. No marketing fees.

Terms: 15% domestic, 20% foreign and performance.

Recent Sales/Clients: Libby Sykes, Joanne Pence, Linda Anderson, Gayle Feyrer.

Submissions: Query first with SASE. No phone queries. OK to send synopsis and first three chapters. No unsolicited manuscripts.

Seeking: Contemporary (long), fantasy, historical, mainstream, mystery, romantic suspense.

Agents Who Do Not Charge Reading Fees

Compiled from the previous listings, here are the names of 90 agents, whom, to the best of our knowledge do NOT charge reading fees, marketing fees, or handling fees:

Charlene Adams, Rajeev Agarwal, James Allen, Robert Brad Allred, Marcia Amsterdam, Steven Axelrod, Amy Berkower, Pam Bernstein, Carole D. Bodey, Barbara Bova, Helen Breitwieser, Deborah T. Brown, Pema Browne, Perry Browne, Lewis Chambers, Ted Chichak, Francine Ciske, Nancy Coffey, Susan Cohen, Frances Collin, Nyani Colom, Richard Curtis, Anita Diamant, Patricia Dietz, B. J. Doyen, Ethan Ellenberg, Michelle Fielden, Evan M. Fogelman, Sharron Forrest, Jean Free, Russ Galen, Jay Garon, Chuck Gebuhr, Susan Ginsburg, Barbara J. Gislason, Amy S. Goldberger, Irene Goodman, Bill Graham, Leo P. Haffey, Merrilee Heifetz, Dr. Myrl D. Hermann, Susan Herner, Carolyn Hodges, Pam Hopkins, Jennifer Jackson, Elaine Jacobs, Eleanore Jeffer, Medwin Jeffer, Martha Jewett, Charléne Kay, Kay Kidde, Sam Klein, Robert Knight, Linda Diehl Kruger, Jasmine Lam, James L'Angelle, Laura Langlie, Michael Larsen, Fran Lebowitz, David Leonards, Norma Liebert, Robert Madsen, Lawrence Mattis, Louise Meyers, Maureen Moran, Howard Morhaim, Dara Moskowitz, Allison Mullen, Ann Marie Negretti, Kim Van Nguyen, M. Nicholas Piro, Elizabeth Pomada, Harry Preston, Michael Robinson, Damaris Rowland, David Royce, Pesha

Rubinstein, Robin Rue, Kelly St. Clair, Laurens R. Schwartz, Jack Scovil, Michael Shortt, Bobbe Siegel, Henry Stanton, Pattie Steele-Perkins, Denise Stinson, Jason Storr, Geno Trunzo, Dee Dee Underwood, Wendy Valentine, Jessica Wainwright, Scott Waxman, Frank Weimann, Sue Yuen.

Agents Listed by Subject Interests

Compiled from all the agent listings, here are the names of agents, categorized by their subject interests:

Christian
Pema Browne, Perry Browne.

Contemporary, Long
Andree Aberassis, Rajeev Agarwal, Pamela G. Ahearn, James Allen, Steven Axelrod, Amy Berkower, Pam Bernstein, Carole D. Bodey, Barbara Bova, Helen Breitwieser, Pema Browne, Perry Browne, Lewis Chambers, Ted Chichak, Francine Ciske, Susan Cohen, Frances Collin, Nyani Colom, Mari Cronin, Richard Curtis, Anita Diamant, Patricia Dietz, Ethan Ellenberg, Joyce Flaherty, Evan M. Fogelman, Sharron Forrest, Russ Galen, Susan Ginsburg, Barbara J. Gislason, Irene Goodman, Bill Graham, Merrilee Heifetz, Dr. Myrl D. Hermann, Susan Herner, Pam Hopkins, Yvonne Trudeau Hubbs, Jennifer Jackson, Elaine Jacobs, Eleanore Jeffer, Medwin Jeffer, Martha Jewett, Kay Kidde, Robert Knight, Linda Diehl Kruger, Jasmine Lam, Laura Langlie, Michael Larsen, Fran Lebowitz, Lettie Lee, Norma Liebert, Denise Marcil, Evan Marshall, Lawrence Mattis, Maureen Moran, Howard Morhaim, Dara Moskowitz, Allison Mullen, Ann Marie Negretti, Elizabeth Pomada, Julia A. Rhyne, Michael Robinson, Damaris Rowland, David Royce, Pesha Rubinstein, Robin Rue, Kelly St. Clair, Laurens R. Schwartz, Jack Scovil, Pattie Steele-Perkins, Theresa Stevens, Denise Stinson, Jason Storr, Wendy Valentine, Sue Yuen.

Contemporary, Short

Rajeev Agarwal, Pamela G. Ahearn, Robert Brad Allred, Amy
Berkower, Carole D. Bodey, Barbara Bova, Helen Breitwieser,
Lewis Chambers, Ted Chichak, Francine Ciske, Susan Cohen,
Frances Collin, Nyani Colom, Richard Curtis, Anita Diamant,
Patricia Dietz, Ethan Ellenberg, Joyce Flaherty, Evan M.
Fogelman, Sharron Forrest, Susan Ginsburg, Barbara Gislason,
Irene Goodman, Bill Graham, Merrilee Heifetz, Dr. Myrl D.
Hermann, Pam Hopkins, Yvonne Trudeau Hubbs, Jennifer
Jackson, Martha Jewett, Kay Kidde, Robert Knight, Linda Diehl
Kruger, Jasmine Lam, Laura Langlie, Michael Larsen, Fran
Lebowitz, Norma Liebert, Robert Madsen, Evan Marshall,
Lawrence Mattis, Dara Moskowitz, Ann Marie Negretti, Kim
Van Nguyen, Elizabeth Pomada, Julia A. Rhyne, Damaris
Rowland, David Royce, Pesha Rubinstein, Robin Rue, Kelly St.
Clair, Pattie Steele-Perkins, Theresa A. Stevens, Jason Storr,
Wendy Valentine.

Ethnic

Rajeev Agarwal, Pamela G. Ahearn, Robert Brad Allred, Amy
Berkower, Pam Bernstein, Carole D. Bodey, Barbara Bova,
Lewis Chambers, Ted Chichak, Francine Ciske, Susan Cohen,
Frances Collin, Nyani Colom, Richard Curtis, Anita Diamant,
Patricia Dietz, Ethan Ellenberg, Susan Ginsburg, Barbara
Gislason, Bill Graham, Merrilee Heifetz, Dr. Myrl D. Hermann,
Yvonne Trudeau Hubbs, Martha Jewett, Robert Knight, Linda
Diehl Kruger, Jasmine Lam, Fran Lebowitz, Norma Liebert,
Robert Madsen, Evan Marshall, Lawrence Mattis, Dara
Moskowitz, Ann Marie Negretti, Kim Van Nguyen, Julia A.
Rhyne, Damaris Rowland, David Royce, Pesha Rubinstein,
Robin Rue, Kelly St. Clair, Theresa A. Stevens, Denise Stinson,
Jason Storr, Wendy Valentine.

Fantasy

Rajeev Agarwal, James Allen, Robert Brad Allred, Amy
Berkower, Barbara Bova, Ted Chichak, Susan Cohen, Frances
Collin, Nyani Colom, Richard Curtis, Patricia Dietz, Ethan

Ellenberg, Susan Ginsburg, Barbara Gislason, Merrilee Heifetz,
Susan Herner, Pam Hopkins, Yvonne Trudeau Hubbs, Jennifer
Jackson, Martha Jewett, Jasmine Lam, Michael Larsen, Fran
Lebowitz, Robert Madsen, Evan Marshall, Lawrence Mattis,
Dara Moskowitz, Ann Marie Negretti, Kim Van Nguyen,
Elizabeth Pomada, Julia A. Rhyne, David Royce, Kelly St. Clair,
Bobbe Siegel, Pattie Steele-Perkins, Theresa A. Stevens, Jason
Storr, Wendy Valentine, Sue Yuen.

Futuristic
Rajeev Agarwal, Robert Brad Allred, Amy Berkower, Barbara
Bova, Ted Chichak, Susan Cohen, Richard Curtis, Patricia Dietz,
Ethan Ellenberg, Susan Ginsburg, Barbara Gislason, Merrilee
Heifetz, Jennifer Jackson, Martha Jewett, Jasmine Lam, Fran
Lebowitz, Robert Madsen, Evan Marshall, Lawrence Mattis,
Dara Moskowitz, Ann Marie Negretti, Kim Van Nguyen, Julia A.
Rhyne, David Royce, Kelly St. Clair, Theresa A. Stevens, Jason
Storr, Wendy Valentine.

Historical
Andree Aberassis, Rajeev Agarwal, Pamela G. Ahearn, James
Allen, Robert Brad Allred, Marcia Amsterdam, Steven Axelrod,
Amy Berkower, Pam Bernstein, Carole D. Bodey, Barbara Bova,
Helen Breitwieser, Deborah T. Brown, Lewis Chambers, Ted
Chichak, Francine Ciske, Susan Cohen, Frances Collin, Nyani
Colom, Mari Cronin, Richard Curtis, Anita Diamant, Patricia
Dietz, B. J. Doyen, Ethan Ellenberg, Joyce Flaherty, Evan M.
Fogelman, Susan Ginsburg, Barbara Gislason, Amy S.
Goldberger, Irene Goodman, Bill Graham, Merrilee Heifetz, Dr.
Myrl D. Hermann, Susan Herner, Pam Hopkins, Yvonne
Trudeau Hubbs, Jennifer Jackson, Martha Jewett, Kay Kidde,
Robert Knight, Linda Diehl Kruger, Jasmine Lam, Laura
Langlie, Michael Larsen, Fran Lebowitz, Lettie Lee, Norma
Liebert, Robert Madsen, Evan Marshall, Lawrence Mattis,
Howard Morhaim, Dara Moskowitz, Allison Mullen, Ann Marie
Negretti, Kim Van Nguyen, Elizabeth Pomada, Julia A. Rhyne,
Damaris Rowland, David Royce, Pesha Rubinstein, Robin Rue,

Kelly St. Clair, Bobbe Siegel, Pattie Steele-Perkins, Theresa A. Stevens, Jason Storr, Wendy Valentine, Jessica Wainwright, Scott Waxman, Frank Weimann, Sue Yuen.

Mainstream
Rajeev Agarwal, Pamela G. Ahearn, James Allen, Robert Brad Allred, Marcia Amsterdam, Steven Axelrod, Amy Berkower, Pam Bernstein, Carole D. Bodey, Barbara Bova, Helen Breitwieser, Pema Browne, Perry Browne, Lewis Chambers, Ted Chichak, Francine Ciske, Nancy Coffey, Susan Cohen, Frances Collin, Nyani Colom, Richard Curtis, Anita Diamant, Patricia Dietz, B. J. Doyen, Ethan Ellenberg, Joyce Flaherty, Sharron Forrest, Jean Free, Jay Garon, Susan Ginsburg, Barbara Gislason, Irene Goodman, Bill Graham, Merrilee Heifetz, Dr. Myrl D. Hermann, Susan Herner, Yvonne Trudeau Hubbs, Elaine Jacobs, Eleanore Jeffer, Medwin Jeffer, Martha Jewett, Kay Kidde, Robert Knight, Jasmine Lam, Laura Langlie, Michael Larsen, Fran Lebowitz, Norma Liebert, Robert Madsen, Denise Marcil, Evan Marshall, Lawrence Mattis, Maureen Moran, Howard Morhaim, Dara Moskowitz, Allison Mullen, Ann Marie Negretti, Kim Van Nguyen, Elizabeth Pomada, Julia A. Rhyne, Damaris Rowland, David Royce, Pesha Rubinstein, Robin Rue, Kelly St. Clair, Laurens R. Schwartz, Bobbe Siegel, Theresa A. Stevens, Jason Storr, Wendy Valentine, Sue Yuen.

Mystery
Andree Aberassis, Rajeev Agarwal, Pamela G. Ahearn, James Allen, Robert Brad Allred, Marcia Amsterdam, Steven Axelrod, Amy Berkower, Pam Bernstein, Carole D. Bodey, Barbara Bova, Helen Breitwieser, Deborah T. Brown, Pema Browne, Perry Browne, Lewis Chambers, Ted Chichak, Francine Ciske, Susan Cohen, Frances Collin, Mari Cronin, Richard Curtis, Anita Diamant, Patricia Dietz, B. J. Doyen, Ethan Ellenberg, Evan M. Fogelman, Sharron Forrest, Susan Ginsburg, Barbara Gislason, Irene Goodman, Bill Graham, Merrilee Heifetz, Dr. Myrl D. Hermann, Susan Herner, Pam Hopkins, Yvonne Trudeau Hubbs, Elaine Jacobs, Eleanore Jeffer, Medwin Jeffer, Martha

Jewett, Kay Kidde, Robert Knight, Jasmine Lam, James
L'Angelle, Laura Langlie, Michael Larsen, Fran Lebowitz, Lettie
Lee, Norma Liebert, Robert Madsen, Evan Marshall, Lawrence
Mattis, Howard Morhaim, Dara Moskowitz, Allison Mullen, Ann
Marie Negretti, Kim Van Nguyen, Elizabeth Pomada, Julia A.
Rhyne, Damaris Rowland, David Royce, Pesha Rubinstein,
Robin Rue, Kelly St. Clair, Laurens R. Schwartz, Bobbe Siegel,
Pattie Steele-Perkins, Theresa A. Stevens, Jason Storr, Wendy
Valentine, Sue Yuen.

New Age
Robert Madsen, Kim Van Nguyen.

Nonfiction
Pema Browne, Perry Browne, Anita Diamant, Pam Hopkins,
Linda Diehl Kruger, Robert Madsen, Kim Van Nguyen, Julia A.
Rhyne, David Royce, Robin Rue, Theresa A. Stevens, Jason
Storr.

Paranormal
Andree Aberassis, Rajeev Agarwal, Pamela G. Ahearn, Robert
Brad Allred, Amy Berkower, Barbara Bova, Ted Chichak, Susan
Cohen, Mari Cronin, Ethan Ellenberg, Joyce Flaherty, Susan
Ginsburg, Barbara Gislason, Irene Goodman, Merrilee Heifetz,
Yvonne Trudeau Hubbs, Jennifer Jackson, Martha Jewett, Linda
Diehl Kruger, Jasmine Lam, James L'Angelle, Fran Lebowitz,
Lettie Lee, Robert Madsen, Evan Marshall, Lawrence Mattis,
Maureen Moran, Dara Moskowitz, Ann Marie Negretti, Kim
Van Nguyen, Julia A. Rhyne, Damaris Rowland, David Royce,
Pesha Rubenstein, Kelly St. Clair, Laurens R. Schwartz, Bobbe
Siegel, Theresa A. Stevens, Jason Storr, Wendy Valentine.

Regency (see also Historical)
Linda Diehl Kruger.

Romantic Suspense
Andree Aberassis, Rajeev Agarwal, Pamela G. Ahearn, James
Allen, Robert Brad Allred, Marcia Amsterdam, Steven Axelrod,

Amy Berkower, Pam Bernstein, Carole D. Bodey, Barbara Bova, Helen Breitwieser, Deborah T. Brown, Lewis Chambers, Ted Chichak, Francine Ciske, Susan Cohen, Frances Collin, Nyani Colom, Mari Cronin, Richard Curtis, Anita Diamant, Patricia Dietz, B. J. Doyen, Ethan Ellenberg, Joyce Flaherty, Evan M. Fogelman, Susan Ginsburg, Barbara Gislason, Bill Graham, Merrilee Heifetz, Dr. Myrl D. Hermann, Susan Herner, Yvonne Trudeau Hubbs, Jennifer Jackson, Elaine Jacobs, Eleanore Jeffer, Medwin Jeffer, Martha Jewett, Kay Kidde, Robert Knight, Jasmine Lam, Laura Langlie, Michael Larsen, Fran Lebowitz, Lettie Lee, Norma Liebert, Robert Madsen, Evan Marshall, Lawrence Mattis, Howard Morhaim, Dara Moskowitz, Allison Mullen, Ann Marie Negretti, Kim Van Nguyen, Elizabeth Pomada, Julia A. Rhyne, Damaris Rowland, David Royce, Robin Rue, Kelly St. Clair, Laurens R. Schwartz, Pattie Steele-Perkins, Theresa A. Stevens, Jason Storr, Wendy Valentine, Sue Yuen.

Science Fiction
Barbara Gislason, Dara Moskowitz, Wendy Valentine.

Screenplays
Charlene Adams, Rajeev Agarwal, Robert Brad Allred, Marcia Amsterdam, Carole D. Bodey, Pema Browne, Perry Browne, Lewis Chambers, Nancy Coffey, Michelle Fielden, Evan M. Fogelman, Jean Free, Jay Garon, Chuck Gebuhr, Bill Graham, Nancy Gummery, Leo P. Haffey, Dr. Myrl D. Hermann, Carolyn Hodges, Yvonne Trudeau Hubbs, Martha Jewett, Charlène Kay, Sam Klein, Robert Knight, Jasmine Lam, Dick Landerman, James L'Angelle, David Leonards, Norma Liebert, Robert Madsen, Evan Marshall, Lawrence Mattis, Louise Meyers, Ann Marie Negretti, Kim Van Nguyen, M. Nicholas Piro, Harry Preston, Michael Robinson, Laurens R. Schwartz, Michael Shortt, Henry Stanton, Gene Trunzo, Dee Dee Underwood, Carole Western.

Time Travel (See also Paranormal)
Yvonne Trudeau Hubbs.

True Crime
Barbara Gislason, Dara Moskowitz, Wendy Valentine.

Westerns (see also Historical)
Pam Hopkins, Pattie Steele-Perkins.

Women's Fiction (see also Mainstream)
Pam Hopkins, Pattie Steele-Perkins.

3

Melissa Ann Singer Gives Writers a Tour, of Tor Books!

Romance readers in the mood for "something different" can always find a Tor/Forge title to whet their book-hungry appetites. If you aren't familiar with Tor/Forge offerings, you're missing out on some good reading, and also the opportunity to sell to a competitive publishing company that annually releases about 200+ mass-market paperback titles and 150–200 hardcover and trade titles. The number of books in each imprint varies each month, as does the breakdown of genres.

Melissa Ann Singer, Senior Editor at Tor, gives writers some background information about Tom Doherty Associates, Inc. (TDA) the parent company of Tor:

"TDA has several imprints, including Forge, Tor Books, Tor Science Fiction, Tor Fantasy, and Orb. Orb is not open to submissions, as it is a line of trade paperback reprints of science fiction and fantasy titles of literary merit. Tor Science Fiction and Tor Fantasy are mass market imprints; in hardcover the science fiction and fantasy titles carry the Tor Books logo.

"For your audience (romance writers), publishing opportunities lie within the Forge and Tor Books lists. These imprints are published in both hardcover and mass market."

What kinds of books does this company publish? Melissa Ann Singer responds:

"We do not publish anything that might be considered traditional romance, or anything that would fit into a category romance line. We require that each book have a plot other than the boy-meets-girl plot, and that this other plot be at least equal in strength to the romance plot, if not stronger."

Keeping that information in mind, let's take an analytical look at some recent, representative Tor/Forge titles:

Romance readers worldwide are familiar with Aimee Thurlo's memorable Native American-themed Harlequin Intrigues. Now Aimee and her husband David have teamed up to co-author *Blackening Song,* the first in a series of hardcover romantic mysteries from Tor/Forge. The novels feature the investigation adventures of Ella Clah, a Navajo FBI agent. Murder, and more, will keep readers enthralled. Tony Hillerman, make way for the Thurlos!

Romantic suspense dons a politically-correct fur coat in the popular series of Midnight Louie murder mysteries, which are set in Las Vegas. The series stars a feline detective whose wicked wit and romantic im-purr-tinence are the cat's pajamas in *Cat in a Crimson Haze* (and others) by Carole Nelson Douglas.

Suspense dives into the big blue of an undersea sci-fi world when a woman banker hires a bodyguard to protect her from terrorists in Maureen F. McHugh's *Half the Day Is Night.*

In David Alexander Smith's *In the Cube,* a futuristic Boston is the setting for a woman private investigator who finds missing persons in a labyrinth teeming with danger after a loathsome human holocaust.

Romance readers with a taste for fantasy fare will get hooked on L. E. Modesitt's Recluce series, which pits the island kingdom of Recluce against the White Wizards of the East. In *The Order War,* hero Justen risks all when he envisions a new technology that can harness Chaos forces and protect the Black Order.

As you can see, the diversity of Tor/Forge titles offers opportunities for reading pleasure to a wide audience with varied tastes, as well as opportunities for writers with wildly creative imaginations and writing talent. Descriptions of these Tor Books should light a fire under romance writers whose book manuscripts may be too offbeat or unusual for category houses because of science fiction or fantasy elements.

But books are not the only unique aspect of Tor. Melissa Ann Singer is one of the few editors in the industry who thinks it's perfectly acceptable for writers to make phone queries. She writes:

"In the last couple of years we have almost completely stopped looking at query letters; most writers seem to have a great deal of difficulty boiling their work down to a single page. We would prefer to see approximately fifty pages (wherever there's a convenient chapter break near fifty pages) plus a complete synopsis of a novel. Character breakdowns are not necessary.

"If a writer has previously published at novel length, the writer may submit a complete manuscript. All submissions, except those from literary agents, and including queries, must be accompanied by return postage. We do not accept FAX submissions of any kind.

"Any writer may call any editor here, to determine if his or her work is right for the company or the particular editor in question, or to determine to which editor to submit. If a submitting writer is familiar with our line and wishes to submit to the editor of a particular writer, call and ask. We're always willing to spend five minutes on the phone with an aspiring writer."

The editors at Tor with an interest in some types of romantic fiction are: Melissa Ann Singer, Senior Editor; Claire Eddy, Editor; Natalia Aponte, Associate Editor.

What kinds of manuscripts are these editors looking to acquire? Melissa Ann Singer has specific interests at this time:

"We are interested in historical fiction primarily in two areas: books set in North or South America at any point in time (but less interested in urban fiction of the Victorian/Edwardian era), with special emphasis on the period of western expansion of the United States; and what we call Ancient Civilization historicals (Greece, Roman Empire, Egypt, dynastic China, etc.).

"We are interested in both science fiction and fantasy romances, but our requirements here are very strict. Since many of our editors have edited science fiction and fantasy during their careers, they tend to be rigorous in their review of time travel, futuristic, and other of these type of romances. We are not looking for rehashed *Star Trek* episodes, but for books in which the science or fantasy elements have internal logic, are properly extrapolated, and are not merely window dressing. If the novel would be no different if everyone in it were human or wearing contemporary clothes, it's not for us.

"The same strictures apply to paranormal—we have a strong background in horror/occult/vampire/paranormal fiction, and apply the standards of these genres to romance novels."

About romantic suspense, Melissa Ann Singer writes:

"We are publishing less romantic suspense than we were a couple of years ago, because there seems to be less and less new and interesting material in this genre. But someone with a fresh approach is always welcome."

All right, romance writers. Melissa Ann Singer has been very detailed about what she wants to acquire—now, it's up to you to wow her! If you do choose to call an editor at Tor/Forge with a book pitch, be professional. You want to be able to articulate the basics of your story. Before you even pick up that phone, make some note cards with a few sentences about your book, so you don't get flustered when the editor asks questions. You want to be able to clearly and briefly describe your story, so that the editor will be able to visualize the characters, settings, conflicts, and events that help to shape it.

When pitching to this publisher, remember that while romance is an important element of the story, it is probably secondary to the main adventures and goals of the hero and heroine. Current titles released by this publisher have some common elements that should be heeded by the writer who wants to be a Tor/Forge author.

Many of Tor's books are fast-paced page-turners with chapter endings that reveal intriguing questions, surprising situations, or even cliff-hangers. The pacing increases as the plot and characters hurtle toward the climax of the story, where the main conflict will be solved. The "epilogue" chapters are short and leave the reader wanting more, which is imperative in a continuing series.

Danger is also a common thread in Tor Books, as are the protagonist's personal sacrifices for the greater good. There is usually more at stake than a romance, often it is the lives of the main characters.

Dialogue is the primary vehicle for unfurling the plot and revealing character. In Piers Anthony's *Harpy Thyme,* Metria, a demoness, exclaims, "Oh, stink horns!" and other colorful euphemisms. By the way, the heroine of *Harpy Thyme* is a beautiful half-goblin/half-harpy on an adventurous quest for true love. How's that for original?

Long passages of narrative are rarely seen in Tor Books, except in historicals such as *Irene's Last Waltz* by Carole Nelson Douglas, which is written in the first-person point of view. Be aware that it takes great skill and aplomb to pull off this point of view as well as accomplished author Douglas.

Most of Tor's books are written in third person and present different characters' viewpoints in the stories that require it. Preferred point of view is only one of the issues you might discuss with a prospective editor.

Become familiar with Tor's books (this goes for any publisher you want to pitch to). Analyzing editorial styles and common themes will help you to break into the market. Go to the bookstore or library and do thorough research before pitching a story. You only get one chance to make a first impression.

A point to consider before picking up that phone: Can you tell the editor which of their recent releases you really liked, and why? Or how your book manuscript might fit in with Tor's other titles? Or, perhaps, how your story is new and different, but still in keeping with the type of fiction that is unique to Tor?

When you call a Tor/Forge editor, remember to listen to her comments and answers. Take brief notes of any suggestions or comments that could help you polish your manuscript before submitting it. Here are some sample questions that are likely to come up in conversation between writer and editor:

- Is your romance a historical, a fantasy, a science fiction, a paranormal (etc.)?

- If it is a historical, in what year and setting does the story take place?

- If it is a science fiction, fantasy, or futuristic novel, have you invented a believable world? (*The Writer's Guide to Creating a Science Fiction Universe* is a helpful resource book.) Are the situations in this unique world a part of the conflict that the protagonists face?

- Describe the main conflict of your book.

- Describe the main characters. How does the outcome of the main conflict impact the love relationship? What are some of the inner conflicts to be overcome? What do the characters have to sacrifice to be together?

- Are the characters strong enough for a possible series?

- How long is the manuscript? Is it finished?

These can be difficult questions to answer in a five minute phone call if you're not ready. But don't be scared, be prepared!

Now that Melissa Ann Singer's method for scouting new writing talent has been revealed, I just want to say that I hope Melissa has one of those phone holder gadgets for her shoulder. She's going to need it!

Many thanks to Melissa Ann Singer, Senior Editor, for taking the time to provide a letter with detailed information about Tor/Forge.

4

Murder, Magic, and Men in Kilts

Women in hot water and the men who love them. No, it isn't a topic on a late afternoon talk show. It's a peaking trend in the romance novel industry that has agents adding "romantic suspense" to their list of desired manuscripts, publishers adding the same request to their tip sheets, and romance readers asking for more. In fact more than 60% of the agents listed in this reference want romantic suspense manuscripts and the majority of the book publishers do, too.

Authors like Sandra Brown, Eileen Dreyer, Nora Roberts, and Meryl Sawyer have known for a long time that danger and romance make excellent bedfellows in a novel.

There is often much more in a romance novel than a boy-meets-girl relationship. Danger is a savvy spice that seasons the story with suspense and suspects. What was recently called woman-in-jeopardy, and earlier, contemporary Gothic, is now usually called romantic suspense, and almost anything goes, as long as the setting is contemporary, the pace is fast, the romance heats up as danger threatens, and the plot is as compelling as the characters.

HarperMonogram isn't shy about putting "romantic suspense" on the spine of books like *Mantrap* by Louise Titchener, in which the heroine teams up with a rugged police detective to check out the demise of her ex-fiancé. Did he take a voluntary swan dive off a bridge, or was it murder? As she and the cop hero get closer to the truth, they get closer to each other.

Zebra has labeled the spines "suspense" or "mystery" on Pat Warren's character-linked single titles, such as *Shattered Vows,* in which the heroine dons her murdered cousin's religious habit to bait a serial killer with an obsession for nuns. On hand is a handsome police detective who steals her heart.

Pocket also is in on the single-title romantic suspense scene too, with offerings such as Linda Howard's *Dream Man,* another compelling cop story. This one falls in love with a woman psychic who witnesses murders through the eyes of a slasher serial killer.

Leisure's Love Spell line is a great place to sell those offbeat, dark romantic suspense tales, though they publish other types of romance, too. In Lori Handeland's *Shadow Lover,* the heroine plots to avenge her brother's death, and the hero is her intended target. She never expects to fall in love with the disfigured actor.

Also on the series front, Silhouette Intimate Moments and Harlequin Intrigue specialize in romantic suspense novels that feature everything from pregnant kidnapped teenagers and black market babies in Karen Leabo's *Into Thin Air,* to Patricia Rosemoor's *Drop Dead Gorgeous,* which features the best friend of a missing bride, who suspects the sexy son of a notorious crime boss. Another romantic suspense, Merline Lovelace's page-turner *Night of the Jaguar,* stars a mercenary/secret agent who infiltrates rebels in Central America to rescue an enigmatic woman and a group of captive children.

Danger and suspense are no less prevalent in historical romances, and popular settings are the American West that Margaret Brownley favors, Tudor England tales from Susan Wiggs, and especially Scotland, in all periods of history, from many authors. Scotland?

The truth is real men *do* wear kilts. Well, they did anyway! Sorry, Prince Charles, but Mel Gibson, Liam Neeson, and those "Highlander" guys really know how to fill out a kilt, and dangerously, too. The rumor is, there's nothing underneath!

Notwithstanding Hollywood's broad influence, the handsome-legged heroes from Scotland are hotly holding their own in historical romance novels at nearly all the romance publishing houses. *Highland Fling* by Amanda Scott, is from Pinnacle/Denise Little Presents. The heroine is a Scottish lass with important messages for Bonnie Prince Charlie. The hero is an English Earl who takes over her father's lands. HarperMonogram offers *Fool of Hearts* by Teri Lynn Wilhelm and features a heroine who hides her father's body from a reckless Scottish laird who might take over her lands if he finds out he's been appointed her guardian. Leisure keeps the danger alive with Scottish warring clans in *White Heather* by Helene Lehr, in which the heroine falls in love with her kidnapper from a rival clan. Harlequin Historical's Suzanne Barclay makes medieval Scotland come alive with betrayal and treachery in *Lion of the North*. Zebra presents medieval Scotland too, in Hannah Howell's feisty and sweet tale *Only for You*, in which the hero and heroine must save their homeland and themselves from danger. Pocket pays its respect to the plaid, as Arnette Lamb's *Maiden of Inverness* must be rescued from the English in order to save Scotland and unite the clans.

Can't anyone save Scotland from the English? Maybe they need some magic to pull it off . . . Yes, those unexplained things that go bump in the night are steadily gathering a hungry romance-reading audience who want their own spooky, spine-tingling tales.

Senior Editor Denise Little at Kensington has a good eye for magical romances. One of her star authors, Deb Stover, penned a first novel, *Shades of Rose,* which had shades of everything paranormal in it: time travel, ghosts, and more. Sounds offbeat, but rave reviews and books disappearing by the hundreds at book signings are the readers' response!

With a little magic from St. Martin's Press, and from above, Tina Wainscott's heroine in *On the Way to Heaven* came back to life after she died, except that she was reincarnated in someone else's body. Unfortunately, the sexy new body is a skin-deep covering for a troubled woman who was a thief, a philanderer, and about to get a divorce from her rich, gorgeous, faithful husband. (Don't miss this one!)

More magic (aka paranormal) romances are planned by these publishers: Ace, Avon, Ballantine, Bantam, Berkley, Tor, Dutton, Goodfellow, Harper, Kelly and Kathryn Present, Kensington, Leisure, Penguin (UK), St. Martin's, and more. Check the publisher's directory in the next chapter for details of what editors want and how to submit.

The next time a hunk in a kilt shows up for hero duty, or a heroine leaps into a murder investigation, or a little bit of magic throws together an unlikely couple, listen to your fictional characters, get their story on paper, and then go for the happy ending. Yours—when you sell it!

Directory of
Book Publishers

ACE BOOKS
200 Madison Avenue
New York, NY 10016

Acquisitions: Laura Ann Gilman, Editor of Ace Science Fiction

Media Type: Paperback and hardcover, 6–10 titles per month.

Submissions: Don't query. Send a synopsis and first three chapters with SASE. Unsolicited manuscripts are OK. Unagented manuscripts are OK, but please, no simultaneous submissions. Agents may call. Response time is from 3–6 months and can vary widely.

Pay Rate: Standard for industry.

Seeking: Fantasy and vampire of 70,000–80,000 words.

Tips: Write with SASE for current guidelines.

ALADDIN BOOKS
A Division of Macmillan
866 Third Avenue, 24th Floor
New York, NY 10022
(212) 702-3880

Acquisitions: Julia Sibert, Executive Editor

Media Type: Paperback.

Submissions: Slots are limited. Recommend authors query first with SASE and request current guidelines.

Pay Rate: Competitive advance plus royalties. Editor says Aladdin is not a "book packager."

Seeking: Young adult series, including novels based on characters from TV series *Saved by the Bell,* and middle grade series novels.

ARCHWAY PAPERBACKS/MINSTREL BOOKS
(See Pocket Books)

AVALON BOOKS (THOMAS BOUREGY & CO.)
401 Lafayette Street, 2nd Floor
New York, NY 10003
(212) 598-0222

Acquisitions: Marcia Markland, Vice President/Publisher

Media Type: Hardcover, 60 per year.

Submissions: Send first three chapters and 2–3 page synopsis, double-spaced. Unagented manuscripts are OK. Simultaneous submissions are OK, if indicated in cover letter that it is a multiple submission. Because of large number of submissions, material cannot be returned. If publisher thinks novel might be suitable for their list, author will be contacted.

Seeking: Under its Avalon Books imprint, Thomas Bouregy & Co., Inc. publishes hardcover mysteries, romances, and westerns. Our books are wholesome adult fiction, suitable for family reading. There is no graphic sex or profanity in our novels. Books range in length from 40,000–50,000 words.

Tips: Many libraries subscribe to Avalon Books. See current titles to determine what editor is buying.

Note: Avalon did not return completed questionnaire by press time. Information for this listing is from their writers' guidelines. Write for current tip sheet. Enclose SASE.

AVON
1350 Avenue of the Americas
New York, NY 10019
(212) 261-6833

Acquisitions: Ellen Edwards, Executive Editor, Romance; Micki Nuding, Editorial Assistant

Media Type: Paperback, 4–6 titles per month.

Submissions: Query by letter with SASE. OK to send synopsis and first three chapters. Unsolicited manuscripts are OK. No phone queries. No dot matrix. Manuscripts must be double-spaced. Usual response time is 3–4 months.

Pay Rate: Individually negotiated.

Seeking: Contemporary of 90,000–100,000 words; ethnic; historical of 100,000–125,000 words (preferred time periods are Viking and Middle Ages to end of 19th century); paranormal; romantic suspense; time travel.

Turn-offs/Taboos: No violence against women (including rape), childhood abuse, wimpy heroines, sex without emotional intimacy and commitment.

Editor's Wish List: Larger-than-life heroes and heroines in big, sweeping stories.

Avon Books Writer's Guidelines

At the heart of Avon's romance program are some of the most talented, well-respected, and creative individuals in the world of romance publishing today. We are proud of our authors and the fact that we publish the best in the romance genre. We are committed to helping our authors write better books and reach an ever-larger audience. And we are always on the lookout for the fresh, exciting, new voices of tomorrow! Each month, Avon publishes several romance titles.

Lead Women's Fiction is reserved for well-established authors whose substantial sales allow them to compete against non-romance titles on national bestseller lists. Avon publishes at least one lead historical romance or contemporary women's novel every month.

The Avon Romantic Treasure is a program designed for authors whose previous historical romances have shown exceptional promise, and whose sales have earned them a degree of recognition within the romance buying community. Treasure authors are carefully selected by Avon's editorial staff to join this prestigious program. Some Treasure writers are Avon authors who have "moved up" and others come to this program with already-established track records at other houses. We publish one Romantic Treasure a month.

The Avon Romance program, now over ten years old, was created for new or almost-new writers of historical romance. Avon Romances are 100,000–125,000 words long (400–500 manuscript pages) and take place in any time period from the Middle Ages to the end of the 19th century. We publish two Avon Romances each month.

Regency Romance: Avon publishes one Regency romance every month. However, we are not looking for Regency submissions at this time.

Contemporary Women's Fiction: Avon publishes contemporary women's fiction by both new and established writers. This is an important growth area for Avon and has fewer guidelines or restrictions. We will consider novels that include romance, "mainstream" elements, and supernatural or magical elements, in a variety of tones and styles. We are not interested in futuristic romances or in science fiction and fantasy elements as found in the fantasy genre (for example, no talking animals, please). However, we do welcome time travel romances. Ghosts, angels, and other unusual elements are also acceptable if they are handled skillfully.

Manuscripts should be 90,000–100,000 words (360–400 manuscript pages); more elaborate secondary characters and subplots are possible and desired. Avon does not publish short contemporary romances (like Harlequins, Silhouettes, and Loveswepts).

If you love romances and have an active imagination, enjoy writing, and are willing to work hard to become a published writer, we encourage you to try your hand at writing a romance for Avon. Here are some helpful hints to get you started.

Hook the reader with a strong opening that makes her want to keep reading.

The hero and heroine should meet early in the book, and once they've met, they should not be separated for lengthy periods.

Start by creating an appealing and memorable hero and heroine who interact in exciting, original, sexy, and romantic ways. Know your characters thoroughly. Know why, besides sexual attraction, they're drawn to each other and fall in love.

The hero and heroine should make love in sensual, tastefully described love scenes—but not before you've established a degree of emotional intimacy between them.

The heroine shouldn't make love with anyone but the hero. (I'm afraid the double standard still applies; it's OK for the hero to make love with other women, but preferably not after he makes love with the heroine.)

Make sure the focus of your book is the romantic relationship between the hero and heroine. Everything you include should contribute to the development of that relationship in some way.

Avon historicals take place in any time period from the Middle Ages to the end of the 19th century. We will consider Viking romances that are set earlier than the Middle Ages. Do careful research. Historical accuracy is a must. Try to capture the special flavor of the particular time and place you're writing about. Be original. Read other romances to know what story ideas have been overused. Do something different; find variations on the tried and true themes.

Master the technique of writing well. A good story will come alive for the reader only if you tell it skillfully and energetically.

Be critical of your work. Make sure it's your very best work. Keep asking yourself: Will a "jaded" romance reader who's read dozens of romances find my manuscript entertaining? Make sure your book ends "happily ever after."

AVON FLARE BOOKS
1350 Avenue of the Americas
New York, NY 10019
(212) 261-6800   FAX: (212) 261-6895

Acquisitions: Ellen Kreiger, Young Adult Romance

Submissions: Query first with SASE. Write for guidelines.

Seeking: Young adult novels.

BALLANTINE/DEL REY
201 E. 50th Street
New York, NY 10022
(212) 572-2149

Acquisitions: Barbara Dicks, Senior Editor

Media Type: Paperback.

Submissions: Unagented manuscripts are OK. Submit complete manuscripts or partials (synopsis and first three chapters) with SASE. Manuscripts should be double-spaced with no blank lines between paragraphs, except scene breaks. Paragraphs are indented five spaces. Don't bind manuscript. Response time is several months. Reads all manuscripts. Printed form rejections are usual, due to volume of submissions.

Pay Rate: "Competitive" advances and royalties. Contracts are individually negotiated.

Seeking: Editor Barbara Dicks is actively seeking 100,000–125,000 word historicals and 70,000–75,000 word Regencies for Fawcett/Ballantine. Send synopsis and first three chapters or the entire manuscript (preferred).

Barbara Dicks also seeks adult fantasy (and science fiction) for Del Rey between 60,000 and 100,000+ words. Fantasy plots and characters are propelled by magic and the supernatural.

Tips: No UFO or occult works. No coincidence solutions. Read McCaffrey, Foster, and Chalker to see what kind of fantasy is published. Romance is usually light and sweet when it is a plot element.

BANTAM BOOKS

Bantam Fanfare/Bantam Loveswept
1540 Broadway
New York, NY 10036
(212) 354-6500   FAX: (212) 782-9523

Acquisitions: Beth de Guzman, Senior Editor; Wendy McCurdy, Senior Editor; Shauna Summers, Associate Editor; Susan Brailey, Editor

Media Type: Paperback, hardcover, audio; 1–2 Fanfare per month, 4 Loveswepts, 2–4 general list.

Submissions: Beth de Guzman and Shauna Summers prefer authors to query first by letter with SASE. No phone queries. No unsolicited manuscripts or partials. Enclose return postage on all submissions. Wendy McCurdy prefers to be sent the synopsis and first three chapters with cover letter and SASE.

Pay Rate: Confidential advances and royalties.

Seeking: Contemporary, ethnic, fantasy, futuristic, historical, mainstream, mystery, paranormal, prairie romance, romantic suspense, time travel. Loveswept (category) romances are 60,000 words. (Editor Susan Brailey informed us that pseudonyms have been eliminated for Loveswept authors. She also wants to add more paranormal and mystery/suspense to the romance.) Loveswepts are shaped by events; hero and heroine meet early in the book and don't stay apart for many pages. Internal conflicts are based on hopes, dreams, and fears of characters. Keep dialogue witty. Novel length for manuscripts other than Loveswepts are 90,000–150,000 words.

Tips: Read what we publish (Shauna Summers).

Editor's Wish List: Wonderful and interesting stories that are well-written (Shauna Summers). Send me something wonderful. Quality women's novels (Wendy McCurdy).

Bantam News for Authors

At Bantam Books there are no guidelines for Women's Fiction—the stories and styles of our books cover the entire spectrum of the genre. If you wish to submit your work for consideration by Bantam and are unagented, send us a query letter. The query letter should be no more than three pages covering the basics of who your characters are, what the conflict is that they face, and how your plot develops. It usually takes eight weeks to receive a response from us. Please don't submit sample chapters or a complete manuscript until we request them. Unfortunately, we cannot give comments on many submissions. Be sure to include SASE; we cannot respond to queries that are not accompanied by return postage.

We advise you to review the titles we have published during the last several years by such bestselling authors as Sandra Brown, Amanda Quick, Iris Johansen, Debra Dixon, Tami Hoag, Teresa Medeiros, Rosanne Bittner, Susan Johnson, Kay Hooper, Suzanne Robinson, Pat Potter, Betina Krahn, Jane Feather, and Jessica Bryan.

We're constantly searching for the stars of tomorrow, the new authors who are the genre's lifeblood. If you write a great book, we'll buy it!

Bantam Loveswept Guidelines for Writers

Thanks for your interest in our Loveswept line. Here are some pertinent facts about our romances: Loveswepts run about 60,000 words and are set in the present. The books are wonderfully written and feature sparkling dialogue rather than long narrative. Quickly paced, our Loveswepts are page-turners!

The characters are deftly crafted, well-rounded people whom readers care about and root for. They should meet as close to page one as possible and never be apart for more than 8 to 10 manuscript pages. The sexual tension and attraction between the hero and heroine should be apparent from their first encounter on, but their love for each other should be based on emotions and feelings, not simply on sexual attraction.

We expect mystery/intrigue/adventure/paranormal, and other elements to be kept to a minimum and that the romance remain the focus of the story at all times. Secondary characters should also be limited in number and in importance. More valuable than any "tip sheet" or "guideline," the books themselves are your best tools for learning what we're looking for in a Loveswept. Read as many as possible before you submit to us. Send us a query letter if you don't have an agent. The query should be no more than two or three pages, but it should cover the basics of who your characters are, what the conflict is that they face, and how your plot develops. It usually takes eight weeks to receive a response from us. Please don't submit sample chapters or a complete manuscript until we request them. Unfortunately, we cannot give comments on any submissions. Be sure to include an SASE; we cannot respond to queries that are not accompanied by return postage.

We're constantly searching for the stars of tomorrow, the new authors who are the genre's lifeblood. Write a great book, and we'll buy it!

BARBOUR AND COMPANY, INC.

Heartsong Presents
P.O. Box 719, 1810 Barbour Drive
Uhrichsville, OH 44683
(614) 922-6045   FAX: (614) 922-5948

Acquisitions: Stephen Reginald, Vice President Editorial; Rebecca Germany, Senior Editor

Media Type: Paperback, 4 per month.

Submissions: Send cover letter with synopsis and three chapters. Unsolicited manuscripts are OK. Please enclose SASE for response. See Guidelines below for additional information.

Pay Rate: Outright purchase of all rights for $1,500–$2,500.

Seeking: Contemporary and historical romances of 50,000–55,000 words. All of our romances are Christian/Inspirational.

Tips: Romance between the hero and heroine is the main focus.

Turn-offs/Taboos: Anything that is crude or offensive to our evangelical audience.

Heartsong Presents Guidelines for Writers and Editors

The Basics: All manuscripts in the Heartsong Presents inspirational line should present a conservative, evangelical Christian world view. Manuscripts that do not reflect this position will be returned to the author(s).

Specifics: Heartsong Presents will consider contemporary and historical manuscripts between 50,000–55,000 words. A historical manuscript, for our purposes, is any time period covering the years prior to and during World War II. A contemporary manuscript would be any time period after World War II, although strictly speaking, we would probably not consider a manuscript set in the 1950s as contemporary. Since all of the contemporaries we have published thus far have been set in the 1990s, your best bet for acceptance is the present time period.

Things to Consider: The underlying theme in all of our romances is the belief that a true and honest faith in God is the foundation for any romantic relationship. Although we are not looking for "sermons in novel form," the importance and need for a personal relationship with Jesus Christ should be apparent. Our readers are primarily women who consider themselves born again Christians. One of the reasons they choose Heartsong Presents books over other reading material is because our books confirm their values and beliefs. As a writer/editor, you must take this into consideration.

Things to Avoid: Avoid the truly controversial. Although conflict is important for any storyline, certain matters should be avoided at all costs. Stay away from language that could be considered foul. Avoid euphemisms like heck or darn. To many of our readers these words are substitutes for curses, and in their minds as bad, or worse. Main characters should be Christians (or Christians by the end of the book) and should act accordingly. They need not be "saints," but their actions should be consistent with Christian teaching.

The hero and the heroine should not be divorced. This is acceptable for secondary and non-Christian characters. The idea of divorce and remarriage is a problem for most of our readers. Most of our readers also find a woman as pastor, or even assistant pastor, unbiblical. If your heroine is a woman who is a pastor or youth pastor, etc., we will not consider your manuscript.

The use of alcohol is offensive and incompatible with Christian teaching, according to many of our readers. While drinking is unacceptable for Christian characters, for non-Christian characters, this conflict can be explored.

Avoid controversial doctrinal issues. We will not list these (there are too many); however, if you keep in mind that we are appealing to a broad range of Christian evangelical readers, we believe you will be on the right track.

Physical tension between characters should not be overdone. Do not be overly descriptive when describing how characters feel when kissing, embracing, and so on. Characters, especially women characters, should be modestly dressed.

Summary: One particular biblical message should be threaded throughout if possible. This can be presented from many different characters, through symbols and so on. The main element of the books is the romance and to that end characters must be perceived as appealing and capable of finding each other attractive. Conflict within the relationship will draw hero and heroine closer and involve readers more personally.

Few would doubt the breathless appeal of a love story. But a Christian love story combines the elements of enchantment and inspiration to produce a tale that is unforgettable.

To Submit: If you believe that you have an inspirational romance that would fit Heartsong Presents guidelines, please send a summary of the story along with three to four randomly selected chapters.

COMPUTER PREPARATION OF MANUSCRIPTS:
If you will be typing your manuscript on a computer, it would save us a great deal of time if you send us the manuscript on disks along with a printout. This simplifies production and prevents errors in typesetting. This can only be done if you have an IBM or IBM-compatible computer using an MS-DOS operating system (no Apples). The word processing program you use generally doesn't matter. If your manuscript has already been typed into your computer, do the following: 1) Print out the manuscript (double-spaced). 2) Label disks with your name and the correct order of the disks. 3) Enclose in your cover letter the brand of computer you used and the name and version of your word processing program. 4) Package everything carefully, by using disk mailers or protecting disks with heavy cardboard. Mail the disks together with the manuscript to avoid mixups.

If you haven't typed in the manuscript yet, do the following: 1) As you type, only hit RETURN at the end of a paragraph, never at the end of a line. Let the computer wrap the text itself until you reach the end of a paragraph, then use one RETURN to indicate a new paragraph. 2) Use no centering, no flush right, no boldface, no italics. Instead, indicate these with a note within parenthesis. 3) Use uniform tabs or indents. 4) You may use underlines to indicate italics. 5) Double space the manuscript. 6) Use Arabic numbers instead of Roman numerals. 7) Be sure to include dedications and/or acknowledgements on disk. 8) Print out the manuscript, then follow the directions above for mailing. If you want, you can indicate on the manuscript such things as subheads, extracts, etc. To avoid loss of disks, please wait to send disks until the publisher requests them. Thanks for your help. (Note: This publisher's request for flush left printout format is unique to Heartsong Presents. So, in case your manuscript is rejected here, always save a backup copy of the manuscript's files with complete formatting. Read The Road Before Me by Susannah Hayden.)

THE BERKLEY PUBLISHING GROUP

Putnam Berkley Publishing Group—Quantam Leap
200 Madison Avenue, 12th floor
New York, NY 10016
(212) 951-8830   FAX: (212) 545-8917

Acquisitions: Ginjer Buchanan, Executive Editor, Sci-Fi and Fantasy (she also acquires for Boulevard Books and Quantam Leap novels).

Media Type: Paperback, 2–4 titles per month (and 4 Quantam Leap titles per year).

Submissions: Send synopsis and first three chapters with cover letter and SASE. Unsolicited manuscripts are OK, but only for Quantam Leap novels.

Pay Rate: Competitive. The Quantam Leap books are writer-for-hire. They do not necessarily include a royalty.

Seeking: Science fiction and fantasy.

Tips: Note that we do *not* do the Star Trek novels. They are published by Pocket Books.

General Guide

(6/9/95 letter from Ginjer Buchanan, Executive Editor, Sci-Fi and Fantasy)

Dear Author,

I receive a lot of requests for guidelines for the Quantam Leap novels. The fact is that there aren't any "official" ones, either from Universal or Bellasarius Productions. So I have developed some general guides, based on conversations with people who are responsible for the approval process, and a review of what has been approved so far.

    1) All of the novels are to be set before the "Mirror Image" episode. I think that we have to leave it up to Don Bellasario to let us know how the fourth season would have worked out.

    2) As with the Star Trek novels, no major permanent changes can be made in the lives of the primary characters. If someone is to be killed off, if heretofore unsuspected children are to be written in for Al or Sam, they must disappear at the end of the book, one way or another. Sammy Jo stories, however, are acceptable, as are stories involving Sam or Al's families, insofar as information about them was given in the (TV) show. The Evil Leapers, Angela, and Edward St. John are fair game, too. I would caution anyone attempting a "personal" story to try to keep it in balance. Most often in the series, when we learned background information about Sam or Al, it was given as a part of a subplot, a sidebar to the Leap. A concentration on the personal usually works better as fan fiction. (Written for fun, not profit, fan fiction uses existing fictional characters and is published in noncommercial magazines called fanzines.)

    3) If you are a published author, please send along samples of your work, in addition to a proposal and 50–60 pages of text. Fan fiction is acceptable, but make certain that you choose your best.

    4) If you are not a published author, you need to send, initially, a proposal and the standard 50–60 pages. If I think that your idea has promise, I will let you know, so that you can continue to work on the manuscript. It is highly unlikely that MCA would approve "on spec" from an author who has never been

published before. Both of the first-time writers that have done
Quantam Leap novels to date were contracted from finished
manuscripts.

    5) For purposes of the Leap program, a novel is a minimum of 75,000 words.

    6) Follow standard manuscript form, and be sure to attach
a self-addressed stamped envelope large enough to return your
material, if you want it back.

    Please be aware of two things: I am only filling four slots a
year (for QL), and, as I mentioned above, only two authors have
been approved who did not have prior professional publishing
credits. I wish you luck!

THE BERKLEY PUBLISHING GROUP
Putnam Berkley Publishing Group—Romance
200 Madison Avenue
New York, NY 10016
(212) 951-8830   FAX: (212) 545-8917

Acquisitions: Judith Stern, Senior Editor; Hillary Cige, Senior
Editor; Gail Fortune, Editor

Media Type: Paperback, hardcover.

Submissions: Query first with SASE. Only send synopsis and
sample chapters after querying. The complete manuscript
should not be sent unless requested. New authors are encouraged to send submissions. Query first rather than sending unsolicited or unagented manuscripts. Simultaneous submissions are
OK, but please tell us in your letter. Usual response time is six
weeks. Of course, agents may call.

Pay Rate: Books are normally published about nine to twelve months after acceptance. Average advance varies. Average royalty not disclosed.

Seeking: Historical of 90,000–100,000 words; contemporary of 90,000–100,000 words; ethnic of 90,000–100,000 words; mainstream; mystery/suspense of 60,000–90,000 words; time travel of 90,000–100,000 words; paranormal of 90,000–100,000 words. Our romances are sweet, spicy, sensual, or sexy.

NEWS FROM BERKLEY (excerpted)

At Putnam Berkley Group we pride ourselves on the diversity of our woman's fiction program. With our three imprints (Berkley, Jove, Diamond) we publish a minimum of four romances a month. Our novels range from historical romance, contemporary, mainstream, and romantic suspense, to woman-in-jeopardy, prehistory novels, and Regencies.

We are open to publishing historical romances in any setting and time period. In addition we have a line called Homespun. Homespun Romances are sweeter historical romances set in 19th century American small towns and countrysides. The focus of these books is the love story but they also feature family relationships. All Homespuns have a child worked into the storyline. Presently we are also looking for strong sensual romances, taking place between the years of 1300 to 1900 in any setting. All of our historical romances range from 85,000–100,000 words.

We prefer agented submissions, but if you are unagented, please send a query letter to a specific editor, including a brief description of the plot, previously published works, if applicable, as well as any other pertinent information. Please allow eight weeks for replies to manuscripts requested by an editor.

BETHANY HOUSE
11300 Hampshire Avenue South
Minneapolis, MN 55438
(612) 829-2500   FAX: (612) 829-2768

Acquisitions: Carol A. Johnson, Editorial Director

Bethany House Writer's Guidelines (excerpted)

We are happy to share these guidelines with you, but they come
with this note of caution: We have discovered that the publishing
commitments we already have made to Bethany House
Publishers' authors and to other writers whom we have commis-
sioned make it very unlikely that there will be room in our publishing program in the foreseeable future for additional projects.

Bethany House is an evangelical publisher of books in a
broad range of categories, and the leading publisher of religious
fiction. (Besides Bible Study References, Personal Growth
Books, Devotionals, Contemporary Issues, and Marriage and
Family Principles Books) . . . We are seeking a series of historical
novels for adults and children offering a strong and clear spiritual
truth.

The following are some of the fiction categories in our list.

Prairie Romance: Our bestsellers in this category are of course
the Janette Oke novels. Attempting to actually copy her style is
not likely to work, but we will consider other manuscripts in the
general category (e.g. series such as The Starlight Trilogy by
Marian Wells).

Historical Fiction: This category includes stories in a historical
setting, such as *The Stonewycke* by Michael Phillips and Judith
Pella, the *Zion Chronicles* by Bodie Thoene, and the House of
Winslow Series by Gilbert Morris.

Young Adult Fiction: See Cedar River Daydreams series by Judy Baer for examples of style, etc.

Juvenile Fiction: See Mandie series, An American Adventure series.

We do not publish formula romance, but are instead looking for:

1. An intriguing, well-written story with strong characterization and complex and colorful description.

2. One main scriptural teaching, skillfully incorporated into the story without being preachy or too obscure.

3. Historical/geographical/social accuracy without sacrificing plot or characterization.

4. A romantic relationship, which usually is not essential to the resolution of the plot. Instead of "love scenes," you should portray the true meaning of love—commitment and responsibility, rather than only the emotional and physical attraction.

5. Series possibilities with the same characters or historical setting. Adult manuscripts should be 60,000 words or longer.

How to Submit to Bethany House Publishers

1. Send a synopsis and three sample chapters. (Keep your original.)

2. Manuscript must be typed, double-spaced. Photocopies and quality dot matrix are acceptable.

3. Include a brief description of your qualifications.

4. Compare your book with other Christian novels (e.g. "my book is like title/author/brief description, but is different because . . . ")

5. SASE is required for return of your material.

6. Address submissions to the Editorial Dept. Response in two to nine weeks. Sorry, we do not provide critiques.

Once a contracted manuscript satisfies our editorial requirements, we assume all costs of production and distribution. . . . The author receives a royalty for each book sold, the rate being comparable to that paid by other publishers.

Our books are promoted through our trade catalog, dealer mailings, and ads in bookseller's journals and leading Christian magazines. Bookstore sales are by a nationwide network of sales representatives, by major American and Canadian distributors, and by distributors in over 20 foreign countries.

BROWNDEER PRESS

A Division of Harcourt, Brace and Company
9 Monroe Parkway, Suite 240
Lake Oswego, OR 97035

Acquisitions: Linda Zuckerman, Editorial Director

Submissions: Query first with cover letter, synopsis and first three chapters. No unsolicited materials.

Seeking: Contemporary middle-grade and young adult novels.

Tips: SASE for current guidelines.

DAW BOOKS

375 Hudson Street
New York, NY 10014

Acquisitions: Peter Stampfel

Submissions: Correspondence goes to Peter Stampfel.

Seeking: No romance novels, per se. Only publishing science fiction and fantasy. (Romance may be a subplot.)

DELL BOOKS

1540 Broadway, 19th Floor
New York, NY 10036
(212) 354-6500

Acquisitions: Marjorie Brannon, Executive Editor; Mary Ellen O'Neill, Senior Editor; Laura Cifelli, Associate Editor

Media Type: Paperback, 2 romance titles per month.

Submissions: Send synopsis and first three chapters with cover letter and SASE. For annual contest, usually held in September–November, send SASE for complete rules/entry form.

Pay Rate: Competitive contracts. Unpublished author who wins annual Dell Diamond Debut Award is awarded $5,000 advance plus 8% royalty contract.

Seeking: Historical preferred to contemporary. Historical or long contemporary novels for contest. No romantic suspense or short contemporary novels for contest. Length is 90,000–125,000 words.

Tips: The annual contest is a great opportunity for unpublished authors to become published. Mary Ellen O'Neill also edits Dell nonfiction (women's topics). (We obtained this information from a writer's conference.)

DEL REY BOOKS

(See Ballantine)

DORCHESTER PUBLISHING CO., INC.

Leisure Books and Love Spell
276 Fifth Avenue, Room 1008
New York, NY 10001
(212) 725-8811   FAX: (212) 532-1054

Acquisitions: Joanna Cagan, Editor; Edith Wilson, Editorial Assistant; Alicia Condon, Executive Editor; Kimberly Waltemyer, Editorial Assistant

Media Type: Paperback; 10 titles per month for Leisure, 4 per month for Love Spell.

Submissions: Query first or send synopsis and sample chapters. SASE a must. New authors are encouraged. No simultaneous submissions. Agents may call. Usual response time is 2 months. (See Guidelines below.)

Pay Rate: Average advance is negotiable. Average royalty not given. Books are normally published about 12 months after acceptance.

Seeking: Historicals, futuristic, time travel, and paranormal of 120,000 words. (Send these to Joanna Cagan or Edith Wilson.) Alicia Condon is launching a romantic suspense line and also a limited series of romance novels that are based on fairy tales. Send these types of manuscripts to her attention.

Tips: Read a romance before you try to write one. Do your research. Read Guidelines (below) and keep writing and rewriting (practice makes perfect).

Editor's Wish List: A plot that is interesting and well thought through; strong conflict between the hero and heroine; something new and interesting.

Editorial Guidelines for Leisure and Love Spell

The following are the *only* categories of original fiction we are currently acquiring.

Historical Romance: Sensual romances with strong plots and carefully thought-out characterizations. Spunky heroine whose love for the hero never wavers; he's the only one she makes love with and she's as passionate as he, although he may have to instruct her in the ways of love, since she's almost invariably untouched before she falls in love with the hero. Hero is often arrogant, overbearing; heroine often can't stand him at first, but discovers that beneath the surface lies a tender, virile, and experienced lover. It helps if both the heroine and hero have a sense of humor—a certain amount of wit leavens the heavy-breathing passion. Hero and heroine are constantly separated by emotional conflict or the twists and turns of the plot, but in the end they overcome the barriers between them and live happily ever after.

We don't want a heroine who sleeps around, or a hero who's sadistic, although if there's a villain or villainess, he or she can be as nasty as possible.

Historical background, details of costume, etc., should be accurate; however, we don't want endless descriptions of battles, the political climate of the period, or a treatise on contemporary social history. Our readers are more interested in the trials, tribulations, and love life of the heroine than in how many men Napoleon lost at the battle of Waterloo.

Futuristic Romance: Futuristic romances contain all the elements of historical romances—beautiful herione, dashing hero, some conflict that separates them, a happy ending, etc.—but they are set in lavish lands on distant worlds. (Avoid sci-fi type hardware, technology, etc.)

Time Travel Romance: A modern-day hero or heroine goes back in time and falls in love. Traditional guidelines for historical romances apply. The challenge here is to maintain credibility during the transition between the present and the past. The fun is seeing history and another way of life through the eyes of someone from our own time. The conflict and resolution of the romance arises from the fact that the hero and heroine are from different eras. Beware of a lot of philosophizing about fate, the meaning of time, and how the past affects the present. No time machines, please.

Paranormal Romance: Either historical or contemporary romance with magic, witches, ghosts, vampires, etc., as a subsidiary element. Must have a happy ending.

Angel Romance: Historical, time travel, or contemporary romance in which a guardian angel lends a hand in bringing the lovers together.

Guidelines for Submission to Leisure and Love Spell

Please query or submit synopsis and first three chapters only— no complete manuscripts unless specifically requested. Include SASE (of sufficient size) for possible return of proposal or manuscript. No material will be returned without SASE. Synopsis, sample chapters, and manuscript, if requested must be typed, double-spaced. Word processors are OK, but letter quality only. Please retain a copy of all material sent in case the original gets lost in the mail. For a free catalogue of Leisure Books, please send SASE (#10) to the above address.

DOUBLEDAY

(No response from Doubleday editors. See also Bantam.)

DUTTON/SIGNET

Dutton, Signet, Onyx, Topaz
375 Hudson Street
New York, NY 10014-3757
(212) 366-2000   FAX: (212) 366-2888

Acquisitions: Audrey LaFehr, Executive Editor; Hilary Ross, Associate Executive Editor; Constance Martin, Senior Editor

Media Type: Paperback, hardcover, audio.

Submissions: Please query first by letter with SASE. No unsolicited manuscripts or partials. Response time is approximately 8–10 weeks. Please let editor know if this is a multiple submission.

Seeking: Audrey LaFehr is looking for contemporary romance, ethnic, historical, mainstream, vampire, romantic suspense. Word count depends on story.

Constance Martin is looking for contemporary romance, historicals from the time periods 1500–1900, paranormal, Regency, romantic suspense, and time travel. Word counts are 75,000 for Regency and 100,000–120,000 for others.

Hilary Ross likes single-title commercial novels, romantic suspense, and time travel/paranormal books with contemporary or historical settings.

Tips: Study the market and read as much as you can of the successful authors in the genre. Humor is welcome, especially of the Patricia Gaffney, *A Crooked Heart*, type (Audrey LaFehr).

Unagented manuscripts are handled on a monthly basis by editorial assistants (Jeanmarie LeMense, former editor).

Turn-offs/Taboos: A clear ignorance of the market or our particular needs. Poor presentation of any kind. Ancient history doesn't sell well and isn't recommended (Audrey LaFehr).

Ghosts, angels, and vampires are fine, but werewolves are too hairy for my taste (Hilary Ross).

Editor's Wish List: Big mainstream "female suspense" as opposed to romantic suspense. The bestseller list is filled with "male suspense"—where are the authors of mainstream books? Women love to read Grisham, le Carre. I'd love to find talented female authors writing big thrillers (Audrey LaFehr).

FAWCETT BOOKS
201 E. 50th Street
New York, NY 10022

Acquisitions: Barbara Dicks, Executive Editor of romance.

Media Type: Paperback.

Submissions: Mostly acquires through established literary agents. Send cover letter with synopsis and first three chapters. SASE for new writer's guidelines.

Seeking: Contemporary, historical, including Regency. Young adult novels are under the Fawcett Juniper imprint.

GENESIS PRESS
611 Broadway, Suite 428
New York, NY 10012
(212) 780-9800

Acquisitions: Nyani Colom, Publisher

Media Type: Paperback, 2 titles per month.

Submissions: Send cover letter with synopsis and first three chapters, along with your author bio and SASE. Unsolicited manuscripts are OK.

Pay Rate: Not disclosed.

Seeking: Contemporary romance, ethnic, historical, romantic suspense. Genesis Press specializes in African-American romances.

Note: No writer's guidelines were provided by the publisher. Recommend writers who want to submit manuscripts to this publisher read *Breeze* by Robin Lynette Hampton.

GOODFELLOW PRESS, INC.
16625 Redmond Way, #M20
Redmond, WA 98053-4499
(206) 868-7323   FAX: (206) 867-0737

Acquisitions: Pamela R. Goodfellow, President/Editorial Director

Media Type: Quality trade paperback, 10 titles per year; audio.

Submissions: Query first by letter with SASE. Unsolicited manuscripts are OK, but must follow our guidelines exactly. (See detailed Guidelines below.) To enter Goodfellow Press's twice-a-year writers' contest, send an SASE and request contest information.

Pay Rate: Pays advance plus 6–10% payback for first time authors; advance plus 10–15% payback for experienced authors.

Seeking: Contemporary romance, ethnic, fantasy, historical (all time periods), inspirational/sweet, mainstream, mystery, paranormal, prairie romance, romantic suspense, time travel, other (all types of character-based fiction). Length is 100,000–150,000 words.

Tips: Goodfellow Press publishes all kinds of character-based fiction—that is the main criterion. Other rules do not apply at this company.

Turn-offs/Taboos: Criminals who eat their victims.

Editor's Wish List: To find new authors, or established authors, willing to work extra hard to develop their voice into all it can be.

Note: Goodfellow Press publishes their books as quality trade paperbacks, using recycled paper and soy inks. No cover stripping by bookstores is permitted, and GP backlists their titles.

What kind of books does GP publish? Read *Glass Ceiling* by C. J. Wycoff or *White Powder* by Mary Sharon Plowman.

Goodfellow Press Editorial Guidelines

The intention of Goodfellow Press is to publish fiction that is smooth and seamless, peopled with characters who will live beyond the confines of the book covers. Diversity in interests and backgrounds is appreciated, but emphasis is placed on the importance of respecting the humanity of both character and reader. You must not paint your "bad guys" all black or allow your "good guys" to wear halos.

For a character to be memorable, he or she must always be believable. An author must know how each character would uniquely think, feel, and react in any given circumstance. What makes your character laugh? What makes him cry? Who took care of her when she was young and how does she feel about that person now? Has he or she ever been in love? When and where, and if not, why not? You must know and be able to demonstrate more details of your character's personality than you will ever be able to use within the confines of a single novel.

Conflict is integral to every book that hopes to sustain a reader's interest. This conflict may be physical or emotional, in-

ternal or external, but it will always arise from the unique interaction of the characters you, the author, have created.

A well-crafted book is founded in five major scenes. The
first meeting can be the first time the reader meets the main
character or the first time your two main characters meet one
another. An emotional scene will be comprised of sensual, sexual,
or physical action. A fight or confrontation scene exemplifies aspects of a character's personality only visible in times of undue
stress. A tender moment is when we see characters show true respect for one another. The resolution ties up loose ends, and if
characters are strong, the reader will want more.

The target length of a manuscript should be 85,000 to
120,000 words. However, your work need not be completed to
send a proposal. Please submit detailed character profiles of the
protagonists, one polished major scene and synopses of the other
four scenes. We ask that you double-space all submission material and please enclose SASE. Proposals for nonfiction projects
will be reviewed for consideration based on merit and compati-
bility with the goals of Goodfellow Press.

Five Scene Scaffold for Goodfellow Press

First Meeting: The first meeting is the first time your reader
meets your main characters. If you have more than one character
who is integral to your story, you may have more than one first
meeting scene. First meeting scene should foreshadow the conflict. It does not have to be at the beginning of your book.

Fight/Conflict Scene: We all react to anger differently and we
all say and do things when angry that we would not normally do.
In the conflict scene, the major obstacles to resolving your story
must come to a head. The main characters must reveal to the
reader an important detail. Characters will also react uniquely to
the aftereffects of anger and these can be equally revealing. This
scene exemplifies the conflict or fight. It does not have to resolve
it. It can open new wounds, new areas of difficulty to be overcome. It can help or heal, hurt or hinder.

Physical/Action/Sensual Scene: The purpose of this scene is to practice and perfect the orchestration of moving your characters through space. In a sex or fight scene, the author must make certain the characters have the correct number of fingers, toes, arms, and legs and that they use them in ways that are possible for human beings. The scene can be as simple as two people walking across a room or as complex as children playing tag, but it must be perfectly orchestrated.

Tender Moment: I am an advocate for the human spirit and I insist upon respectful treatment of characters. I do not like "bad guys" who are all bad, nor do I like "good guys" who are saints. The tender moment is the foundation for respect. At some point in your story there must come an opportunity for your characters to realize that they do respect one another. The conflict does not need to be resolved, but when characters realize that underneath everything else that is burdening them, they can respect the integrity and human spirit of the other character, it is a powerful moment.

Resolution: The resolution is exactly what it sounds like. All the loose ends must be tied up, while leaving enough white space that the reader would like to see more. It does not have to be the final scene of your book. It does have to resolve the main conflict.

HARCOURT BRACE TRADE DIVISION

Odyssey Paperbacks, Voyager, Jane Yolen Books, Gulliver
525 B Street, Suite 1900
San Diego, CA 92101-4495
(619) 699-6810   FAX: (619) 699-6777

Media Type: Paperback, 75+ new titles per year, plus reprints.

Submissions: Agented only! No phone calls, please.

Seeking: Young adult and children's novels.

HARLEQUIN AMERICAN ROMANCE

300 E. 42nd Street, 6th Floor
New York, NY 10017
(212) 682-6080

Acquisitions: Debra Matteucci, Senior Editor and Editorial Coordinator; Julianne Moore, Editor; Denise O'Sullivan, Associate Editor; Bonnie Crisalli, Assistant Editor

Media Type: Paperback, 48 titles per year. Also see General Information on Harlequin below.

Submissions: Please query first. Send the complete manuscript if we request it. Published authors may send synopsis and sample chapters at initial contact. New authors are encouraged. Unagented manuscripts are OK. Asbolutely no simultaneous submissions. Agents may call. Usual response time is about 12 weeks.

Seeking: Contemporary romance of 70,000–75,000 words. Also seeking "some" paranormal and time travel.

Tips: Show, don't tell. We want lively, upbeat, action-packed material. Above all, we look for a strong hook, with the focus on hero and heroine.

Turn-offs/Taboos: Plots dealing with environmental problems, archaeology, treasure hunts, or featuring the movie, theater, or sports world.

Editor's Wish List: Bad boys, Cinderella stories, new twists on babies and weddings.

Harlequin American Romance Writer's Guidelines

In this fun, fast-paced, well-plotted page-turner, a dynamic premise hooks the reader instantly, sweeping her into a 70,000–75,000 word contemporary fairy tale where anything is

possible and all dreams come true. Whether themes are innovative or romantic staples—such as marriage-of-convenience and
brides-on-the-run—or suddenly take daring, imaginative new
twists, our adventurous heroes always meet their greatest challenge in a sassy, headstrong heroine. Sizzling repartee and spirited one-upmanship barely mask the attraction that underlies
their every moment together. They're bound to encounter the
unexpected in their situation, in each other, and in a world where
anything is possible!

Plot: Show, don't tell! We want lively, upbeat, action-packed material that is not problem-based or introspective. Aim for fictional
credibility, not realism, looking to your imagination and dreams
for inspiration, rather than to everyday life. Above all, we look for
a strong hook or premise: the conflicts that grow out of this initial situation lead to a big "payoff"—where everything comes out
right in the end. The focus is tightly on the relationship between
the hero and heroine, so subplotting is kept to a minimum.

Hero: He's not the boy next door! This 90s man is a man no
woman can resist. Whether he's rough around the edges, or earthy,
or slick and sophisticated, every reader will fall in love with him.
He is so dynamic, he may even be the focus in a hero-led story.

Heroine: She is sassy, strong, and full of spunk and never wimps
out to her hero. In fact, this highly contemporary woman occasionally bests him, which fuels his desire, as so few women have.

Setting: Anywhere.

Sensuality: These stories are intense, passionate, and filled with
all the emotions of falling in love.

General Information from
Harlequin Enterprises Limited

Submission Format: Query letter—state the length of your
manuscript and enclose a brief synopsis as well as any pertinent

information about yourself, including publishing credits and professional affiliations. Partial—three chapters and a synopsis (preferably one page and not more than three pages). Agents: We give equal consideration to manuscripts sent by authors and agents. We do not give recommendations.

Return Postage: Please include sufficient return postage, preferably a money order or international reply coupons.

Customs Value: The declared value of a manuscript copy should be a maximum of $10.00 to expedite processing through Canadian customs. This does not apply to manuscripts mailed in the United States to our New York office.

Simultaneous Submissions: We will not consider any submission that has been sent simultaneously to another publisher.

Financial Arrangements: We enter into discussions about payments only when we are going to contract. This information is confidential.

Copyright: Under the United States copyright law, copyright for any work is secured when the work is created; i.e. an author has copyright protection the moment the work is put on paper and can be visually perceived. When a manuscript is published by Harlequin, every copy bears a copyright notice that entitles the copyright holder to certain additional rights. For more information regarding copyright, write to Copyright Office, Library of Congress, 101 Independence Avenue, Washington, DC 20557-6400.

Manuscripts: Harlequin's requirements on professional presentation:

a) Manuscripts must be typewritten, error-free, double-spaced, and on one side of the paper only. Leave a 1 1/4" margin around the entire page, and be sure to use a good grade of white bond. If you use a computer printer, the print must be of letter-quality.

b) The title page should include the author's real name and address, the title and the approximate number of words. Also indicate pseudonym if applicable.

c) In the upper right-hand corner of each manuscript page, include the author's last name and the page number, e.g. Smith—12, Smith—13, etc.

d) Be sure to make a complete copy for your files.

e) Do not bind or staple your manuscript. Use an envelope or box large enough to contain your manuscript flat.

HARLEQUIN HISTORICALS
300 E. 42nd Street, 6th Floor
New York, NY 10017
(212) 682-6080   FAX: (212) 682-4539

Acquisitions: Tracy Farrell, Senior Editor

Media Type: Paperback, 48 titles per year.

Submissions: Send query letter or complete manuscript with SASE.

Seeking: Historical of 95,000–105,000 words.

Harlequin Historical Guidelines

Set before 1900, Harlequin Historicals are romance of varying lengths that range from Medieval sagas to lighthearted Westerns and everything in between. The heroes and heroines are equally strong-willed and their relationship is the focus of the story. Though historical details give each book a distinct sense of time and place, their purpose is to create an atmosphere rather than provide a history lesson. The level of sensuality in the stories varies according to what is appropriate to the characters and the writing style.

HARLEQUIN INTRIGUE

300 E. 42nd Street, 6th Floor
New York, NY 10017
(212) 682-6080

Acquisitions: Debra Matteucci, Senior Editor and Editorial Coordinator; Denise O'Sullivan, Associate Editor; Julianne Moore, Editor

Media Type: Paperback, 48 titles per year.

Submissions: Please query first. Send the complete manuscript if we request it. Published authors may send synopsis and sample chapters at initial contact. New authors are encouraged. Unagented manuscripts or OK. Absolutely no simultaneous submissions. Agents may call. Usual response time is about 12 weeks.

Seeking: Romantic mystery/suspense of 70,000–75,000 words.

Tips: Both the romantic element and the intrigue must be introduced early and maintained throughout.

Turn-offs/Taboos: Plots dealing with computers, environmental problems, archeology, treasure hunts, or featuring the movie, theater, or sports world.

Editor's Wish List: A manuscript with a perfect mix of romance and suspense. Intrigues are at their best when the romance and intrigue intertwine and play off of each other. Classic romantic conflicts with intrigue and suspense folded in.

Harlequin Intrigue Guidelines

These taut, edge-of-the-seat, contemporary romantic suspense tales of intrigue and desire are so involving you can barely believe they're told in a mere 70,000–75,000 words! Kidnappings, the stalkings of personal ad applicants, or fiancés wrongly accused of murdering their brides-to-be are examples of storylines we love most. Whether a murder mystery, psychological suspense, thriller, espionage tale, or a woman-in-jeopardy, the love story must be inextricably bound to the mystery at the level of the novel's premise. Gripping plots twist, turn, and thicken, ever leading toward a final resolution where all loose ends are neatly tied up, while shared dangers lead right to shared passions. Our hero and heroine's lives are on the line and so are their hearts.

HARLEQUIN LOVE AND LAUGHTER

Harlequin Enterprises, Ltd.
225 Duncan Mill Road
Don Mills, Ontario M3B 3K9
CANADA
(416) 445-5860   FAX: (416) 445-8655

Acquisitions: Malle Vallik, Editor; Leslie Wainger, Senior Editor; Gail Chasen, Editor

Media Type: Paperback, 2 titles per month.

Submissions: Please submit queries, partials, or complete manuscripts with synopses to any of these editors: Love and Laughter Coordinator: Malle Vallik, Editor, Love and Laughter, at the Harlequin Books Canada address listed above, *or* Leslie Wainger, Senior Editor and Editorial Coordinator, or Gail Chasen, Editor, both at Silhouette Books, 300 East 42nd Street, 6th Floor, New York, NY 10017 U.S.A.

Seeking: Romantic comedy of 50,000 words.

Tips: Write the kind of entertaining romantic comedy you would like to read. (Some examples given are from movies: *Moonstruck, Say Anything, Sleepless in Seattle, Roxanne, Only You,* etc.)

Harlequin Love and Laughter Writer's Guidelines

From Gable and Lombard, to Hepburn and Tracy, to Jamie and Paul Buchman in *Mad About You*, we adore romantic comedies and the heroes and heroines in them. In fact, love and laughter are such a natural combination that we've decided to create a new series featuring just that—the lighter side of love.

Your story must be a contemporary romance of 50,000–55,000 words and it must be humorous. Whether your book is a screwball comedy, whether it contains slapstick, whether a cast of secondary characters maintains a running commentary of one-liners, how you tell your love and laughter story is up to you. We, the editors, just like the reader, want to laugh, be entertained, and sigh over the love story.

Other than romance and humor there are no limitations. A high degree of sexual tension should be present in the story, and while love scenes are encouraged, they are not a requirement.

HARLEQUIN MILLS & BOON, LTD.
Harlequin Presents
Eton House, 18–24 Paradise Road
Richmond, Surrey TW9 1SR
UNITED KINGDOM
(081) 948-0444   FAX: (081) 940-5899

Acquisitions: Address submissions to Editorial Department.

Media Type: Paperback, 72 titles per year.

Submissions: Query with a synopsis of 1–2 pages.

Seeking: Contemporary romance of 50,000–55,000 words.

Harlequin Presents Writer's Guidelines

Pick up a Harlequin Presents novel and you enter a world full of spine-tingling passion and provocative, tantalizing romantic excitement! Although grounded in reality, these stories offer compelling modern fantasies to readers all around the world, and there is scope within this line to develop relevant contemporary issues that touch the lives of today's woman. Each novel is written in the third person and features spirited, independent heroines—who aren't afraid to take the initiative!—and breathtakingly attractive, larger-than-life heroes. The conflict between these characters should be lively and evenly matched, but always balanced by a developing romance, which may include explicit lovemaking. Presents novels capture the drama and intensity of a powerful, sensual love affair.

HARLEQUIN MILLS & BOON, LTD.

Harlequin Romance
Eton House, 18–24 Paradise Road
Richmond, Surrey TW9 1SR
UNITED KINGDOM
(081) 948-0444   FAX: (081) 940-5899

Acquisitions: Address submissions to Editorial Department.

Media Type: Paperback, 72 titles per year.

Submissions: Query plus synopsis of 1–2 pages.

Pay Rate: Confidential.

Seeking: Contemporary of 50,000–55,000 words.

Harlequin Romance Guidelines

Written in third person from the heroine's point of view, each book should focus almost exclusively on the developing relationship between the main protaganists. The emphasis should be on warm and tender emotions, with no sexual explicitness; lovemaking should only take place when the emotional commitment between the characters justifies it. These heartwarming stories must be written with freshness and sincerity, featuring spirited, engaging heroines as well as heroes who are charismatic enough to fulfill every woman's dreams! Readers should be thrilled by the tenderness of their developing relationship, and gripped by romantic suspense as the couple strives to overcome the emotional barriers between them and find true happiness in the romance of a lifetime!

HARLEQUIN MILLS & BOON, LTD.
Legacy of Love and Love on Call
Eton House, 18–24 Paradise Road
Richmond, Surrey TW9 1SR
UNITED KINGDOM
(081) 948-0444   FAX: (081) 940-5899

Acquisitions: Tessa Shapcott, Senior Editor; Sheila Hodgson, Senior Editor; Elizabeth Johnson, Senior Editor; Sue Curran, Editor; Sam Bell, Editor; Gillian Green, Editor. Karin Stoecker is the Editorial Director.

Media Type: Paperback, 240+ titles per year.

Submissions: Query first with SASE, or send synopsis and sample chapters, or send the complete manuscript. Return postage should be in international reply coupons (IRCs) for submissions from outside England. New authors are encouraged to send submissions. Although unsolicited and unagented manuscripts are OK, simultaneous submissions are not acceptable. Agents may telephone. Usual response time is 8–12 weeks.

Pay Rate: Average advances and average royalties are confidential. Books are normally published about 24 months after acceptance.

Seeking: Legacy of Love wants historical of 75,000–85,000 words, prefer Regency period, and contemporary of 50,000–55,000 words. Love on Call wants medical romances of 50,000–55,000 words. Our romances include a range of sensuality. See Legacy of Love and Love on Call Guidelines below.

Legacy of Love Guidelines for Authors

We are looking for born storytellers with a love of history, who have an ability to bring a period vividly to life, and create characters who involve and absorb the reader from page one. It goes without saying that the historical detail should be well researched and accurate. You should incorporate enough detail to allow the reader to almost taste and smell the life and times, but do not convey so many facts that the reader feels lectured to and overwhelmed. Don't forget to add "color," examples are: clothing descriptions, necessities of daily life, facial expressions, tones of voice, body language/movement, all of which create a visual picture.

There must be a good central plot, into which the actual historical happenings of people may, or may not, be woven (obviously this decision will depend upon the type and complexity of your main plot). Bear in mind that the general reader is not likely to be familiar with the more esoteric periods, and if you choose to tackle something particularly unusual, its acceptance will depend very much on your ability as a writer. For instance, Oriental settings, ancient Egypt, and the like are difficult to convey successfully.

As well as British history, you could also consider European history.

Look at aspects other than royalty, such as politics, industry, the arts (examples might be the gem trade of Amsterdam, the money markets of Bruges, the arts sponsored by Lorenzo the

Magnificent, Borgia intriguing); all of which could be used as the background of good plots.

It is important that, whatever character type you choose to create, the heroine should be lovable and the hero charismatic. Please note that actual historical characters do not usually feature as either the hero or the heroine of storylines. Should you wish to do this, you should first discuss your ideas with the editor. You should strive to create fully rounded characters within the conventions of your chosen period. Look at all layers and facets of human behavior—mental, physical, emotional—and use tension as well as rapport.

Alongside these aspects you must employ a variety of pace—so that with the highs and lows of emotion, the reader is enthralled, rather than bored by a telegraphed plot and flat, even writing.

The development of the hero and heroine and the growth of their relationship (which must have a happy ending) are vital strands threaded through the plot. Your main characters are the means by which the reader is emotionally caught up into the story and should never be neglected.

There is no bar to the use of sensuality if it seems appropriate to both characters and plot, but we are not in the market for "bodice-rippers." The emotional responses are as important as any physical response, because the emotions generate the overall romantic aura. Certainly you should avoid long absences by the hero and, when he is together with the heroine, they must communicate.

Good use of dialogue can lift a book out of the crowd, but aim for clarity and simplicity. Regency dialogue is a specific skill (beware of overusing slang expressions), but with other periods, it is generally wiser not to overdo period language (Medieval, for example). The effect is often not that sought and can instead create a stiff and stilted feeling, which has the unfortunate effect of holding your characters at a distance from the reader. It is always better to allow your characters to "show" themselves through dialogue, rather than have you explain them through narrative.

Your skill and enthusiasm, warmth, and conviction will imbue a book with that extra special "something" and, if the reader thoroughly enjoys your book, then you will have succeeded.

Love on Call Guidelines for Authors

The theme for this category is present day medicine. Hospital settings are, of course, welcome, but the tree of medicine has many branches—general practice, district nursing, private nursing, physiotherapy, occupational therapy, and specific divisions such as children's, handicapped, casualty—to name but a few. The range of medical themes to be featured and explored within these settings is just as wide.

Of equal importance is the development of the central relationship and the depth of characterization. The practical details of medicine are interesting, but ultimately it is the people who bring a story to life. Subsidiary characters (such as patients) are obviously valuable, but the hero and heroine should carry the story. They are the driving force within your plot, and your success (or lack of it) in developing the chemistry and charisma between them can make or break an otherwise satisfactory story.

More specifically, both hero and heroine will be medical professionals. As such, they will usually work together. If they don't, then opportunities for contact should be wide. Their communication—through action and dialogue—should naturally involve rapport as well as conflict, humor as well as sadness. The world of medicine is rich in human drama—both joys and tragedies—and the emotional ranges should be fully explored. If appropriate to both character and plot, the incorporation of sensuality is welcomed—but not if used gratuitously.

Above all, there should be a happy balance between all strands of the plot, between the love affair and the medical detail, between the characters and their emotions. This way, we can absorb and involve readers into hours of good reading.

MEDICAL DETAIL

Ideally, you will have a thorough knowledge of up-to-date methods and use of drugs. However, convincing use of medical detail in storylines can also come from a lively interest in the subject matter combined with adequate research skills. When creating their medical scenarios, our authors draw upon "secondary" medical experience, gained from talking to family friends and other contacts working in the medical profession, and "desk research," using information from medical journals and textbooks. Below are just a few of the many publications providing information about the medical world.

Journals: *Nursing Times, British Medical Journal, Senior Nurse, Pediatric Nursing, Health Visitor, Heart and Lung, Midwife Health Visitor, Community Nurse, Doctor, GP*, and *Pulse*. Your local reference library will hold current and back issues of some or all of these publications. If not, they should be able to advise you on where they can be found in your area.

Books: *The Oxford Concise Medical Dictionary, Watson's Medical Surgical Nursing and Related Physiology, Family Medical Adviser*, and *Reader's Digest*.

HARLEQUIN REGENCY

225 Duncan Mill Road
Don Mills, Ontario, M3B 3K9
CANADA
(416) 445-5860   FAX: (416) 445-8655

Acquisitions: Maureen Stonehouse, Regency Editor

Media Type: Paperback, four titles per year.

Submissions: Not actively seeking submissions at present.

HARLEQUIN SUPERROMANCE
225 Duncan Mill Road
Don Mills, Ontario, M3B 3K9
CANADA
(416) 445-5860   FAX: (416) 445-8655

Acquisitions: Paula Eykelhof, Senior Editor

Media Type: Paperback.

Submissions: Query first or send cover letter with partial manuscript. Enclose SASE with Canadian postage or international reply coupons. New authors are encouraged. Unagented manuscritps OK. No simultaneous submissions. Agents may call. Usual response time is 6–8 weeks on queries; 4–6 months on manuscripts. See Writer's Guidelines for additional information.

Seeking: Contemporary romance of about 85,000 words.

Harlequin Superromance Writer's Guidelines

These books are Harlequin's biggest romance novels, in scope as well as length. They're complex, compelling stories about complex, compelling people. The key to writing a Superromance novel is characterization: It's essential that your hero and heroine be well-developed, fully explored people whose lives and loves will involve the reader completely. Take advantage of the longer format to create characters whose personalities are formed not only by the events and circumstances of their past, but by their expectations for the future and the network of relationships and responsibilities that surround them. These are characters who define and drive the plot—not vice versa.

We're looking for a wide range of story types and tones (including highly dramatic, humorous, heartwarming, suspenseful, and adventurous stories). Above all, we want exciting, innovative, emotionally genuine, page-turning stories—and we want you to write your story your way.

HARLEQUIN TEMPTATION
225 Duncan Mill Road
Don Mills, Ontario, M3B 3K9
CANADA
(416) 445-5860   FAX: (416) 445-8655

Acquisitions: Birgit Davis-Todd, Senior Editor

Media Type: Paperback, 4 titles per month.

Submissions: Query first with synopsis, first chapter, and SASE (Canadian postage or international reply coupons). New authors are encouraged. Unagented manuscripts OK. No simultaneous submissions. Agents may call. Usual response time is 2–4 weeks on queries; 2–4 months on manuscritps. For Annual Harlequin Temptation contest, query the Temptation Senior Editor and enclose SASE for information.

Seeking: Contemporary romance of 60,000 words.

Tips: Read current Temptation to get a feel for the line.

Editor's Wish List: Strong heroes and heroines and contemporary plots.

Harlequin Temptation Writer's Guidelines

This is Harlequin's boldest, most sensuous series, focusing on men and women living and loving in the 1990s! The stories may be humorous, topical, adventurous, or glitzy, but at heart, they are pure romantic fantasy. Think fast-paced, use the desires and language of women today, add a high level of sexual tension, along with strong conflicts, and then throw in a good dash of "what if . . ." The results should sizzle!

HARPERPAPERBACKS

HarperMonogram
10 E. 53rd Street
New York, NY 10022
(212) 207-7000   FAX: (212) 207-7759

Acquisitions: Jessica Lichtenstein, Senior Editor; Abigail Kamen Holland, Editor; Sharon Morey, Assistant Editor

Media Type: Paperback, 4–6 titles per month.

Submissions: Don't query. Authors may send synopsis and three sample chapters with cover letter and SASE. No unsolicited manuscripts.

Pay Rate: Varies.

Seeking: Contemporary romance, historical and western historical, mainstream, paranormal, time travel. Length is 60,000–95,000 words (see Tip Sheet below).

Tips: Target your submission to the appropriate publisher. Keep your synopsis brief.

Turn-offs/Taboos: A submission lacking a synopsis or containing a synopsis of more than a few double-spaced pages. Anything that isn't fresh and original. Avoid romance clichés in your story and in your writing.

HarperMonogram Tip Sheet

Thank you for your interest in HarperMonogram! Although we do not have any formal guidelines, here is some information that will be helpful to anyone interested in submitting.

HarperMonogram is an exciting new imprint of HarperPaperbacks that was launched in September 1992. In addition to authors with proven track records, we have room for new talent and love to build writers for the future. Many Monogram authors go on to write multiple books for us.

There's no formula for a Monogram romance. We publish historicals and contemporaries, including time travel, historicals with American and European settings, romantic suspense, and much more. Though we're open to practically any kind of romance, we're especially eager for strong historicals these days.

We're also starting to publish Regency romances on a regular basis and welcome submissions in this area. They should follow the traditional Regency format, with an emphasis on strong characterization. Length for Regencies should be 60,000–75,000 words.

If you've read some Monograms, you'll see how original and varied they are. Many of our romances are traditional American or British historicals, including those set in the West, but we also publish more detailed and descriptive historical novels. In the contemporary area, we've had great success with relationship-centered family stories.

One thing we always look for is strong emotional tension between the hero and heroine. The romantic relationship should be the heart of the book, though of course an exciting plot, lively dialogue, and believable characters are also crucial. Humor can work well, too.

Two of HarperMonogram's bestselling authors include Debbie Macomber, author of *Someday Soon*, and Susan Wiggs, author of *Vows Made in Wine*.

HARPERCOLLINS/HARPER PERENNIAL
10 E. 53rd Street
New York, NY 10022
(212) 207-7000

Acquisitions: Tracy Behar, Editorial Manager

Media Type: Paperback, hardcover; 600 per year.

Submissions: Agents must query first. Do not send unsolicited manuscripts. Agents may not call. No electronic submissions. Simultaneous submissions are OK. New authors are encouraged, but only through agents. Usual response time is 6–8 weeks.

Seeking: Women's fiction, ethnic, Gothic, mystery/suspense.

Tips: For best results, submit only through an established, qualified literary agent.

Editor's Wish List: Looking for women's fiction that is literary, not genre-type romances.

HARVEST HOUSE
1075 Arrowsmith
Eugene, OR 97402-9197
(503) 343-0123

Acquisitions: Address correspondence to Manuscript Coordinator.

Media Type: Paperback.

Submissions: Query with SASE, or send synopsis and first three chapters with cover letter and SASE. Unsolicited manuscripts are OK. Response time is 2–8 weeks. If you have not heard anything after 8 weeks, feel free to write and inquire about the status of your submission. While each submission is given individual attention, we are unable to critique manuscripts.

Seeking: Rhapsody line (short category romances) has been discontinued. Looking for historical (Christian), inspirational, sweet. Harvest House book subjects include adult fiction, contemporary issues, Christian living, counseling, cults, family life, juvenile fiction, marriage, women's themes, and more. (No short stories, cookbooks, or poetry.)

Harvest House Author Information Sheet (excerpted)

1) Harvest House Publishers is a strong evangelical Christian publishing company which is progressive and eager to proclaim the gospel, even though sometimes in only parts of the book. Our goal is to publish books that will encourage the faith of our readers and turn their attention to Jesus Christ as the answer to the problems and questions of life. The foundation of our publishing program is to publish books that help the hurts of people and nurture spiritual growth. 2) Harvest House also publishes study books, Bible-related material, topical, contemporary, and fiction works that have a message to promote the gospel. 3) We seek exceptional messages that are original, relevant, well-written, and grounded in the teachings of scripture. We publish books that help men, women, and children grow spiritually strong.

Instructions for Submitting a Manuscript: 1) Type your material, double spaced, on 8 ½" × 11" paper. Use one side of the paper with 1" margins all around. Number pages consecutively, not by chapters. 2) Scripture references in manuscript must state translation or paraphrase from which they were taken. 3) Author is responsible for obtaining permissions for copyrighted material that goes beyond the guidelines of "fair use." 4) Prefer a query letter of one page telling what the manuscript is about, why you wrote it, projected audience, and how the reader will benefit. The table of contents and first two to three chapters can be sent at this stage. Please include an information sheet about yourself—spiritual experience, writing qualifications, education, and previous published works, if any. 5) If we are interested, we will request the remainder of the manuscript. 6) Once a manuscript satisfies our editorial requirements, we assume all costs of production and distribution. Author receives a royalty on each book sold, the rates being comparable with those paid by other publishers in our industry. 7) SASE with every manuscript or query letter. Manuscript will be disposed of unless you include sufficient postage for its return. Do not send the original copy—we cannot assume responsibility for lost/damaged manuscripts.

HEARTSONG PRESENTS
See Barbour and Company, Inc.

KELLY AND KATHRYN PRESENT
(in Taiwan)
Romance Consultants International (RCI)
55 Bergen Street
Brooklyn, NY 11201
(718) 237-1097

Acquisitions: Lynda Ryan, Foreign Rights Director

Media Type: Paperback, 10 titles per month.

Submissions: For original manuscripts, send query letter with synopsis, first three chapters, and "author's kit" (see Tips). Unsolicited manuscripts are OK. Also buying foreign rights to published out-of-print novels.

Pay Rate: Percentage of the advance is paid to authors within one month of the signed contract arriving in Taiwan. Authors are consulted for promotional ideas that will best present their book to the foreign market.

Seeking: Historical (all time periods), inspirational/sweet, mainstream, mystery, paranormal, prairie romance, romantic suspense, time travel. Also seeking entrepreneurial and business nonfiction. Also seeking published authors with rights to out-of-print novels. Regarding word counts, shorter reads are great for foreign market.

Tips: Send an "author's kit" containing your bio, photo, a letter to readers, etc. Make sure photo is glamorous, and letter, too!

Editor's Wish List: Hot contemporary romance that can easily be made into a blockbuster movie!

Note: "Kathryn" of "Kelly and Kathryn Present" is Kathryn Falk, Lady Barrow, the founder and CEO of *Romantic Times* magazine. "Kelly" is Kelly Chu. Her parents founded Sitak Publishing in the early 1970s. Sitak's "Kelly and Kathryn Present" launch title debuted with the Mandarin translation of Judith McNaught's *Until You*. RCI's global marketing strategies promote both books and authors.

KENSINGTON PUBLISHING CORPORATION

Arabesque Books
850 Third Avenue
New York, NY 10022
(212) 407-1559

Acquisitions: Monica Harris, Editor; Paul Dinas, Executive Editor

Media Type: Paperback, hardcover; 3 titles per month.

Submissions: Don't query by letter or phone. Send synopsis and first three chapters. Unsolicited manuscripts are OK, but should be addressed to the specific editor. SASE please.

Pay Rate: Negotiable.

Seeking: Contemporary romance, ethnic, mainstream.

Tips: Read the books in this line.

KENSINGTON PUBLISHING CORPORATION

Denise Little Presents
850 Third Avenue
New York, NY 10022
(212) 407-1559

Acquisitions: Denise Little, Editor

Media Type: Paperback, hardcover: 2 titles per month.

Submissions: Query by letter with SASE or send synopsis and first three chapters. No unsolicited manuscripts.(See Tip Sheet.)

Pay Rate: Variable according to author's experience and track record.

Seeking: Contemporary romance, fantasy, futuristic, historical, mainstream, mystery, paranormal, prairie romance, romantic suspense, time travel, any form of romance. Length of novels is 95,000–120,000 words.

Tips: These books are of exceptionally high quality and must be well-written and emotionally compelling. (See Tip Sheet for additional information.)

Turn-offs/Taboos: Bad writing, inconsistent characterization, poor pacing, illogical plotting, books with whales as main characters.

Editor's Wish List: I want a romance that will knock my socks off!

Note: Denise Little edited *Shades of Rose* by Deb Stover, a romance packed with ghosts, time travel, and humor. *Shades of Rose* is representative of Denise Little's penchant for discovering talented unpublished writers and nurturing them into bestselling authors.

Denise Little Presents Tip Sheet

Beginning in June 1994, we will be publishing two books per month under "Denise Little Presents." The books will average between 100,000 and 120,000 words in length, although Denise will consider something a little shorter or longer if it is brilliant.

Authors should submit to Denise Little at the above address a one-page cover letter describing their project(s), a short synopsis, and either three chapters of the book or a finished manuscript. Please enclose an SASE large enough to hold the project, to be used if the book is not accepted for publication. (If the envelope is not large enough, the project might be modified to fit.)

The requirements for this imprint are:

1) The book must be a romance. 2) The book must have a happy ending. 3) The story must be emotionally gripping throughout, whether the emotion in question is laughter, pathos, or gut-wrenching tension. 4) The writing should be of good quality.

The emphasis in this list is on finding books romance readers will enjoy, not on uniformity of page count and format. So far, Denise Little Presents includes contemporary romance, historical romance, ghost stories, a really bizarre time travel book, and an even odder futuristic. Denise Little Presents is not looking for books set in Aztec or Mayan Mexico, books set in India, poorly written books, books with hackneyed plots, books with flowery or overly ornamented prose, books with graphically described torture scenes, or books with heroes who aren't bipedal and at least marginally humanoid. After that, all bets are off.

This is not your standard tip sheet, but this is not your standard line.

KENSINGTON PUBLISHING CORPORATION
Zebra/Kensington/Pinnacle/Z-Fave
1616 N. Fuller Avenue, Suite 333
Los Angeles, CA 90046
(213) 874-0601

Acquisitions: Beth Lieberman, Consulting Senior Editor of West Coast Development, acquires for all imprints: Zebra, Pinnacle, Kensington, and Z-Fave.

Media Type: Paperback, hardcover.

Submissions: Query letter or send synopsis and entire manuscript. SASE a must.

Seeking: Contemporary romance, historical, mainstream, mystery, paranormal, romantic suspense of about 100,000 words. Also seeking quality nonfiction in the areas of health, self-help, spirituality, humor, and lifestyle.

Editor's Wish List: A great story! Stories with a large scope.

Note: *Shattered Vows* by Pat Warren is an example of this publisher's romantic suspense.

KENSINGTON PUBLISHING CORPORATION
Zebra/Kensington/Pinnacle/Z-Fave
850 Third Avenue
New York, NY 10022
(212) 407-1559

Acquisitions: Ann La Farge, Executive Editor of Zebra Books; Kate Duffy, Senior Editor of Zebra Books; Sarah Gallick, Executive Editor of Kensington hardcover; Tracy Bernstein,

Executive Editor of Kensington trade paperbacks; Paul Dinas, Executive Editor of Pinnacle Books; Elise Donner, Senior Editor of Z-Fave (Young adult novels).

Media Type: Paperback, hardcover; 40 titles per month.

Submissions: Don't query. Send synopsis and first three chapters. Unsolicited manuscripts are OK, but should be addressed to a specific editor.

Seeking: Contemporary romance, ethnic, historical, mainstream, of 100,000–120,000 words.

KRON-KORONA PRESS
601 Gateway Blvd., #800
S. San Francisco, CA 94080
(415) 570-7080

Acquisitions: Anton Lomon, Director U.S. Operations

Submissions: Query first with SASE. May be helpful to have an agent handle foreign rights contracts.

Seeking: Category romances for the Russian book market.

LAREDO PUBLISHING
8907 Wilshire Boulevard
Beverly Hills, CA 90211

Acquisitions: Sam Laredo, Publisher

Media Type: Paperback, hardcover.

Submissions: Query first by letter. No partials.

Pay Rate: Varies.

Seeking: Ethnic romances in Spanish.

MEGA-BOOKS
116 E. 19th Street
New York, NY 10003
(212) 598-0909

Acquisitions: Jenine Leny, Associate Editor

Media Type: Paperbacks, 100+ titles per year.

Pay Rate: This book producer pays a flat fee and no royalties to authors on a work-for-hire basis.

Submissions: Send SASE for current writer's guidelines. No unsolicited manuscripts. Query first with SASE.

Seeking: Young adult series novels; Nancy Drew, Hardy Boys, etc.

MIDNITE INTERLUDE ROMANCE NOVELS
(Starring People of Color)
C Y Publishing Group
P.O. Box 1287
Lanham, MD 20703
(301) 262-5792

Acquisitions: Jacqueline C. Young, Publisher

Media Type: Paperback, 2–3 titles per year.

Submissions: Writers may query first by letter or phone, send synopsis and first three chapters, or send the entire manuscript (preferred). Unsolicited OK. SASE please. Allow up to 3 months for a response. (See Guidelines below for additional information.)

Pay Rate: $200 plus royalties. One half on acceptance, the other upon publication.

Seeking: Ethnic, multicultural, 40,000–60,000 words.

Midnite Interlude Guidelines for Authors (excerpted)

C Y Publishing Group is pleased to consider manuscripts for its publishing program, a line of romance novels starring people of color. One of our goals is to develop talent from within the black community and therefore, we strongly encourage black writers to submit. We plan to publish three to four books per year in the near future, with every hope of expanding.

Romance novels follow basic formulas: Woman meets man. They fall in love. Sparks fly and they become attracted to one another. They separate or have a rift because of some unforeseen event. In between, a story unfolds. They ultimately have a happy ending (marriage, hint of marriage, or some idea that the relationship will work).

Stories should "star" black heroines or heroes and must be completely fictitious. They can be contemporary or historical, passionate, intriguing, sensual, or heart-stirring, with an aura of realism about them. They can take place in any location in the world.

Female Character: As the writer, you have lots of flexibility with this character. After all, she is one of two key players. However, here are a few guidelines we want you to follow:

The story should be told primarily from her viewpoint. She should be at least nineteen, but not over forty. She does not have to be beautiful in the physical sense. For example, she can be slightly overweight or taller than average. However, something about her must intrigue the reader, and the hero.

She does not have to be pristine or virginal. Any sexual encounters should be tastefully done. This area (sex) affords you great flexibility and only you can decide what's best for your story. For example, if being a virgin makes your heroine more believable, then go with it. On the other hand, if it's more realistic for your story to have an experienced heroine, fine, your story will benefit from it.

Male Character: Again you have flexibility and the guidelines for this character are the same (as for the heroine), with one addition: Please don't stereotype this character. He doesn't have to be perfect, just believable.

Additional information: Profanity should be kept to a minimum.

Main characters can certainly have friends, family, children and pets. Characters don't all have to be black, nor do they all have to be central to the story.

Research is important, especially for exotic settings. Write about areas and subjects you know. What you don't know, research.

Don't confuse the reader with details that don't matter to the story.

Originality is wonderful, but not always easy in this kind of writing. To create a story as original as possible, think about what you would like to read and build on that. It is a good idea to read other romances to get a sense of writing styles, plot development, character development, etc. Please don't plagiarize.

Remember, you are writing a romance novel. Let the love shine!

Please be yourself. Don't change the way you write just to make us happy. If you're happy with your manuscript, we'll know it, because it will be reflected on every page.

Manuscript Preparation: Keep a copy for your files. Double-space with 1 1/4" margins on plain white paper, using one side of the page. We also accept manuscripts on 5 1/4" floppy disks, compatible to Word Perfect. If you choose this option, please, no fancy formats. Only the page number is required on each page. With the floppy, please include a synopsis or outline.

Include SASE if you want us to acknowledge receipt of your manuscript. If we accept it, we will inform you within 8–10 weeks and begin a process for publication of your manuscript.

For a sample copy of one of our books, please send $5.79 (postpaid) to: C Y Publishing Group, P.O. Box 1287, Lanham, MD 20703. Thank you for your interest in our program.

MIRA BOOKS
225 Duncan Mill Road
Don Mills, Ontario M3B 3K9
CANADA
(416) 445-5860   FAX: (416) 445-8655

Acquisitions: Dianne Moggy, Senior Editor and Editorial Coordinator

Media Type: In 1996, MIRA will publish approximately 20 paperback originals. We plan to publish 2 paperback originals per month in 1997. Selected titles will be published first in hardcover.

Submissions: Please send a query letter with SASE at initial contact. A query letter will get you the quickest response. (Remember, Canadian postage or IRCs will be required for return postage.)

Pay Rate: Competitive.

Seeking: Women's fiction of 100,000+ words.

Tips: Editor Dianne Moggy emphasized that this is a very difficult market to break into. "We're still concentrating on acquiring authors with proven track records. As the program expands, both established and new-but-talented authors will be added to the list."

Turn-offs/Taboos: Paranormal, time travel.

Editor's Wish List: Really entertaining reads. We are primarily looking for contemporary novels, although we will be doing some historicals, too. MIRA Books is looking for relationship novels, family sagas, romantic suspense—almost anything goes in women's fiction. The romantic element doesn't have to be the central focus of the story, and stories don't necessarily have to have the traditional happily-ever-after ending, with the hero and heroine riding off into the sunset together, but they must have "satisfying" conclusions.

NAL/DUTTON PUBLISHING
Division of Penguin USA (See Dutton)

NEW READERS PRESS
Publishing Division of Laubach Literacy International
P.O. Box 131
Syracuse, NY 13210
(315) 422-9121

Acquisitions: Jennifer Lashley, Office Manager

Submissions: Query first with cover letter, synopsis, and SASE.

Seeking: Short novels for adult readers with limited reading skills. Length is under 10,000 words. Send SASE for free book catalog and author's guidelines.

PALISADES ROMANCES
c/o Questar Publishers, Inc.
P.O. Box 1720
Sisters, OR 97759

Acquisitions: Lisa Bergren, Managing Editor

Media Type: Paperback, 2 per month.

Submissions: Cover letter plus two-page outline and three chapters. (See Guidelines below.)

Pay Rate: Contract basis.

Seeking: Contemporary romance, ethnic, inspirational. We have a special need for African-American, Asian-American, and Hispanic characters. Novel length is 64,000–68,000 words.

Tips: Read at least one of our books and our guidelines before submission. Study the line!

Turn-offs/Taboos: Fantasy, angel themes.

Editor's Wish List: Clean, interesting storyline with strong, admirable heroine.

Writer's Guidelines for Palisades Romances (formerly Harbor Romances) (excerpted)

The word "palisades" means the stakes that form fortress walls. Truly, we want readers to feel safe in our own little "fortress" of fiction; reading a Palisades Romance should be equated with finding refuge. We want to tell an entertaining, uplifting story while ennobling faith and marriage.

Authors published under this imprint should keep these values in mind as they write.

Plot: Storylines may be relatively simple, though there must be enough complexity to maintain interest for the required 64,000 plus words. Subplots that add elements of mystery, suspense, or adventure are fine, as long as the emphasis remains on the central romance. The plot should not be too harsh; readers pick up a romance to be uplifted, not depressed. Keep your reader in mind. She wants to be swept away into an intriguing, delightful story! The story should uplift true love, ennobling marriage—there may be times of trouble—but the relationship always survives. Your heroine may be single or a widow. Tread lightly if she's divorced—her new romance should show that true love is possible and that this is a relationship that will last until death.

Successful storylines are entertaining and portray Christian values.

Style: Generally light and natural; humorous only if it fits naturally into a story. There should be active dialogue, reflecting the way people actually speak, but keep swearing out and provocative language in check.

Sensuality: We want passionate, yet chaste relationships. Even married couples' most intimate scenes are to be left to the readers' imagination. Readers want to understand the incredible draw of our heroes and heroines, but characters must know where to draw the line to maintain their high moral standards. Obviously, stay away from erotica. Think of emotional response over physical response in intimate scenes.

Hero, Heroine, and Setting: We want to see innovative plots, intriguing characters, and interesting settings. Please think beyond teaching professions and do not write about women who can't cook. We like strong characters. The rest is up to you!

Send us a story we cannot refuse. We have a special need for African-American, Asian-American, and Hispanic characters.

Gospel message: Foremost, believable characters! In real life, everyone doesn't come to salvation and people express faith in unique ways. We want characters who echo life: Christian characters who help show the way, but aren't perfect; non-Christians who glimpse the wonders of Christ, but don't always grasp the importance all at once. There can be salvation, but make it work naturally. Beware of platforming or preaching to readers. Clearly depict Biblical principles, values, and morals within the novel.

Submissions Guidelines: Cover letter should include word count, info about yourself (such as publishing credits, why you want to write a Christian romance, how long you've been writing, and your familiarity with romance novels), and why you think your book is right for Palisade Romances. Also send a two-page outline and three chapters of your novel. Include SASE for response.

Please read at least one Palisades novel before submission. Some Palisades titles are: *Refuge, Torchlight and Treasure* by Lisa Tawn Bergren, *Secrets* by Robin Jones Gunn, *Sierra* by Shari MacDonald, and *Westward* by Amanda MacLean.

PARACHUTE PRESS
156 Fifth Avenue, Suite 325
New York, NY 10010
(212) 691-1421

Acquisitions: Melinda Metz, Senior Editor

Media Type: Paperback.

Submissions: Send cover letter with outline/synopsis and sample chapters. Published authors, include writing credits.

Pay Rate: This book packager pays either a flat fee or a royalty, depending on the book and the author's level of experience.

Seeking: Suitable stories for mass-market children's, middle-grade, and young adult fiction, such as the Fear Street and Goosebumps series. Also seeking young adult novels, some with romantic elements, some with mystery, horror, girl's themes. Some series with multiple endings.

Tips: Read current offerings to become familiar with the types of books published by Parachute Press.

Note: Melinda Metz was previously a romance editor at Berkley.

PEACOCK PUBLISHING
P.O. Box 438
Sheffield S1 4YX
England
UNITED KINGDOM
(44 114) 262-0950   FAX: Same

Acquisitions: Shani Lee, Senior Editor of Peacock Amour

Media Type: Paperback, 1 per month.

Submissions: OK to query first by letter, phone or fax. Unsolicited manuscripts also are OK. (Don't forget international reply coupons for response.)

Pay Rate: On acceptance.

Seeking: Ethnic, mainstream of 55,000 words maximum.

Tips: Afrocentric lifestyle must be woven into the fabric of the story.

Turn-offs/Taboos: No strong language or swearing in the dialogue. Intimacy and lovemaking should be tastefully handled.

Editor's Wish List: Simple storylines, but complex enough to sustain interest in the plot. Setting may be anywhere in the world.

Note: A Peacock Amour title, *Significant Other* by Sonia Seerani, has been favorably reviewed in *Affaire de Coeur* and

Black Elegance. It can be ordered directly from this UK publisher for $10.95 (U.S. money order), which includes postage and handling.

PENGUIN-UK
27 Wright's Lane
London, England W85 TZ
UNITED KINGDOM

Acquisitions: Luigi Bonomi, Executive Editor

Media Type: Paperback, hardcover, 5 titles per month. Books may come out in hardcover, softcover, or both, and are backlisted for one to two years.

Submissions: Send a query letter with synopsis and first three chapters. The synopsis should not be longer than 20 pages. It is acceptable to submit to both Penguins, the United Kingdom and the United States, (see Dutton/Signet) at the same time.

Seeking: Manuscripts that will appeal to a world market, especially suspense with romance elements, thrillers, straight mysteries, and large broad-based mainstream novels. Also, a new line, Creed, is in need of novels with paranormal elements.

Tips: Bonomi likes to read Nora Roberts, Patricia Cornwell, Scott Turow, and Sara Paretsky. The types of novels he likes have contemporary settings and are large in scope.

Turn-offs/Taboos: Small-town America, westerns, and historicals.

Editor's Wish List: Bonomi is looking for the next Mary Higgins Clark. He likes to read books about obsession, murder, and dark fantasy.

PENGUIN-USA
See Dutton/Signet

POCKET
Archway Paperbacks/Minstrel Books
1230 Avenue of the Americas
New York, NY 10020
(212) 698-7000

Acquisitions: Patricia MacDonald, Vice President and Editorial Director; Claire Zion, Executive Editor; Ruth Ashby, Senior Editor, Young Adult novels; Carolyn Tolley, Historical Romance Editor

Media Type: Paperback, 300+ per year.

Submissions: Agents and authors may query first to appropriate editor with detailed synopsis and sample chapters. SASE for return of material. (See Guidelines below for additional information.)

Seeking: Claire Zion seeks contemporary romances and mainstream novels. Carolyn Tolley seeks historical romances. Ruth Ashby seeks young adult novels for Archway, especially romantic comedies and suspense thrillers of 35,000 words (160 pages). Patricia MacDonald seeks young adult novels for Archway in the areas of contemporary romance, fantasy, inspirational/sweet, mainstream, mystery, paranormal, romantic suspense, and time travel. For Minstrel Books, which are for younger readers, MacDonald seeks stories with ethnic characters, pioneer America historicals, animal stories, humor, and school and family stories.

Tips: We are a mass-market original paperback house, so stories have to be fast-paced and appeal to a broad audience. Stories that are too specialized should be sent to a hardcover house.

Archway Paperbacks and
Minstrel Books Guidelines (excerpted)

General Information: Our Archway Paperbacks imprint is for young adults, ages 12–16. These books are an average of 160 pages or 35,000 words. Our Minstrel Books imprint is for middle-grade readers, ages 7–11. These books are an average of 96 pages or 6,000–10,000 words.

We publish juvenile fiction with a current setting, school and animal stories, and popular biographies. We do not publish picture books.

Currently, we are very successful with mass-market oriented suspense/thrillers and romantic sagas or comedies for the young adult and scary/funny stories for the middle-grade reader.

You may find it helpful to familiarize yourself with some of the titles we have recently published.

Submission Guidelines: Please send us a proposal first. Include: 1) brief cover letter introducing your work, 2) a very detailed outline of the entire book, 3) (optional) a few sample chapters.

Please enclose SASE as well. If we are interested in seeing more, we will contact you. Submissions will be answered in 3–4 weeks. We look forward to hearing from you.

PUTNAM BERKLEY PUBLISHING GROUP
See Berkley

ST. MARTIN'S PRESS
175 Fifth Avenue
New York, NY 10010
(212) 674-5151   FAX: (212) 677-7456

Acquisitions: Jennifer Weis, Executive Editor; Jennifer Enderlin, Senior Editor

Media Type: Paperback, hardcover; 15–17 per month in mass market, 150 per season in hardcover.

Submissions: For Jennifer Weis: Query first with SASE. OK to send synopsis and first three chapters. Unsolicited manuscripts are OK. For Jennifer Enderlin: Query first with SASE. If you've met J. E. at a writer's conference and she specifically asked to see your work, you may send it.

Pay Rate: Various.

Seeking: For Jennifer Weis: Contemporary romance, historical, mainstream, paranormal, women's suspense. For Jennifer Enderlin: Contemporary romance, historical, mainstream, paranormal, romantic suspense, time travel. Novels are "non-category" length.

Tips: We never have to fill slots on a list, so we're never "desperately seeking" any particular kind of book. We're waiting to fall in love with the right book—Jennifer Enderlin.

Turn-offs/Taboos: Clichés.

Editor's Wish List: Books written from the heart by wonderful storytellers.

SERVANT PUBLICATIONS
Vine Books
P.O. Box 8617, 840 Airport Boulevard
Ann Arbor, MI 48107
(313) 761-8505   FAX: (313) 761-1577

Acquisitions: Ann Spangler, Executive Editor; Beth Feia; Senior Editor

Media Type: Paperback, 40 per year (many are nonfiction titles).

Submissions: Query first with SASE. OK to send synopsis and sample chapters, but not the complete manuscript, unless it has been requested. New authors are only encouraged if they have published in magazines and journals. No unsolicited or una-gented manuscripts. Simultaneous submissions are OK. Agents, please write instead of calling. Usual response time is 60–90 days.

Pay Rate: Books are normally published about 12 months after acceptance. Average advances and royalty rate were not given.

Seeking: Historical of 80,000–120,000 words (prefer 17th–19th century rural America); religious romance of 80,000–120,000 words.

Editor's Wish List: Manuscripts must be from a Christian point of view, displaying Judeo-Christian values, but not preachy. Historical research must be accurate; fast-moving plots work best; strong writing ability a must.

Note: No writer's guidelines were provided.

SEVERN HOUSE PUBLISHERS, INC.

595 Madison Avenue, 15th Floor
New York, NY 10022
(212) 888-4042

Acquisitions: Deborah Smith, Senior Editor

Media Type: Hardcover for libraries, 12 titles per month.

Submissions: We have a strong preference for material to be submitted only by established literary agents. Query first with SASE or send cover letter with synopsis and first three chapters. No unsolicited manuscripts.

Seeking: Contemporary romance, historical (but not Medieval), mainstream, mystery, romantic suspense of 90,000 words.

Note: No writer's guidelines were provided.

SILHOUETTE DESIRE

300 East 42nd Street, 6th Floor
New York, NY 10017
(212) 682-6080

Acquisitions: Lucia Macro, Senior Editor; Isabel Swift, Editorial Director. All Silhouette editors can acquire for all Silhouette lines. Address queries to specific editors.

Media Type: Paperback, 72 per year.

Submissions: *First-time authors are encouraged but must query first*. Send synopsis, sample chapters, or complete manuscript only if requested. Usual response time is 3 months. Agents may call. See Writer's Guidelines (below) for additional information.

Seeking: Contemporary romance, ethnic romance of 55,000–60,000 words.

Tips: Everyone at Silhouette can acquire for all Silhouette lines. Send SASE to request guidelines (and see Guidelines below).

Turn-offs/Taboos: The market doesn't seem to go for stories that have to do with heroes in the arts, sports figures, corporate affairs, or land development "save ye old inn."

Editor's Wish List: I want wonderfully written love stories by authors who study and know the market and can write what the readers want!

General Silhouette Submission Guidelines

Thank you for your interest in Silhouette Books. We do not accept unsolicited complete or partial manuscripts, but ask instead that you submit a query letter. Please indicate what Silhouette series you think your project is appropriate for, if it is completed, what you think makes it special, and list your previous publishing experience, (if any). Also include a synopsis of your story that gives a clear idea of both your plot and characters and is no more than two single-spaced pages. A self-addressed envelope (SASE) will ensure a reply. Should your manuscript be requested, please note the following information:

1. We publish only category romances! Please do not submit any other type of fiction or nonfiction. Your manuscript should take place in the present and be told in the third person, primarily from the heroine's point of view. However, the hero's perspective may be used to enhance tension, plot, or character development.

2. All material should be the author's own original work. Stories that contain scenes or plot lines that bear a striking resemblance to previously published work are in breach of copyright law and are not acceptable.

3. All material must be typewritten, double-spaced, and on 8 1/2" × 11" paper. No disk submissions. Computer-generated material is acceptable, but must be letter quality and pages must be separated. Any material received on computer reams will be returned without evaluation.

4. Do *not* submit your material bound in binders, boxes, or containers of any kind. Secure material by rubber bands. Cover sheets must have your complete name, address, and phone number. Each page should be numbered sequentially thereafter. Please type your name and title in the upper left-hand corner of each page. If we ask to see your manuscript, please include a complete synopsis. Enclose a self-addressed, stamped postcard if you wish acknowledgment of receipt.

5. All material will be evaluated in as timely a fashion as volume allows. Please do not call regarding the status of your manuscript. You will be notified by mail as soon as your work has been reviewed.

6. Do not send any material that is being considered by another publisher. "Multiple submissions" are not acceptable. A literary agent is not required in order to submit.

7. You must enclose a SASE with all material you send in. This will ensure the return of your material. Please send an `

envelope large enough to accommodate your work and adequate postage.

8. This sheet is designed as a guide to aid you in understanding our requirements and standards. However, there is no better way to determine what we are looking for than by reading our books.

(All of Silhouette Writer's Guidelines are copyrighted property of Silhouette Books and are reprinted here with permission. Silhouette Romance, Silhouette Desire, Silhouette Special Edition, and Silhouette Intimate Moments are trademarks and registered trademarks of Silhouette Books.)

Silhouette Desire Writer's Guidelines

Sensual, believable, compelling, these books are written for today's woman. Innocent or experienced, the heroine is someone we identify with; the hero irresistible. The conflict should be an emotional one, springing naturally from the unique characters you've chosen. The focus is on the developing relationship, set in a believable plot. The characters don't have to be married to make love, but lovemaking is never taken lightly. Secondary characters and subplots must blend with the core story. Innovative new directions in storytelling and fresh approaches to classic romantic plots are welcome.

SILHOUETTE INTIMATE MOMENTS
300 E. 42nd Street
New York, NY 10017
(212) 682-6080

Acquisitions: Leslie Wainger, Senior Editor and Editorial Coordinator; Isabel Swift, Editorial Director. All Silhouette editors can acquire for all Silhouette lines. Address queries to specific editors.

Media Type: Paperback, 72 per year.

Submissions: Query first by letter with SASE. No unsolicited manuscripts or partials. Agented or otherwise solicited submissions do not need to query first. See General Silhouette Submission Guidelines on pages 166–169 for more information.

Pay Rate: Average advance is variable. Standard royalty starts at 6%. Books are normally published about 18–24 months after acceptance.

Seeking: Contemporary romance and romantic suspense of 80,000–85,000 words.

Tips: Read within the genre and the specific line to see what works. Remember that these are romances; readers are buying them for the emotions they convey.

Turn-offs/Taboos: Intellectual/non-emotional conflicts; characters who do not arouse reader empathy; books in which the romance is secondary to suspense or some other element.

Editor's Wish List: Books that handle traditionally popular plot lines in a fresh and "big" way; books that compel me to keep turning the pages. Strong characters, a strong story, and lots of compelling emotion.

Silhouette Intimate Moments Writer's Guidelines

Believable characters swept into a world of larger-than-life romance, such is the magic of Silhouette Intimate Moments. These books offer you the freedom to combine the universally appealing elements of a category romance with the flash and excitement of mainstream fiction. Adventure, suspense, melodrama, glamour—let your imagination be your guide as you blend old and new to create a novel of emotional depth and tantalizing complexity, a novel that explores new directions in romantic fiction, a novel that is quintessentially Intimate Moments.

SILHOUETTE ROMANCE
300 E. 42nd Street, 6th Floor
New York, NY 10017
(212) 682-6080   FAX: (212) 682-4539

Acquisitions: Melissa Senate, Senior Editor; Isabel Swift, Editorial Director. All Silhouette editors can acquire for all Silhouette lines. Address queries to specific editors.

Media Type: Paperback, 72 per year.

Submissions: Authors, send query letter first. Agents may call. New authors are encouraged. No unsolicited manuscripts. Unagented manuscripts are OK, but query first. No simultaneous submissions. Usual response time is 6–12 weeks.(See General Silhouette Submission Guidelines on pages 166–169 for more information.)

Pay Rate: Books are normally published about 12–24 months after acceptance. Average advance is variable. Standard royalty starts at 6%.

Seeking: Contemporary romance of 53,000–58,000 words.

Tips: Our romances are conservative. Silhouette Romances are contemporary, warm, and dynamic with a solid base of traditional family values. Stories can be powerfully emotional or humorous and charming, but all must be believable, compelling love stories at heart.

Turn-offs/Taboos: Stories must be fresh, contemporary even when using classic storylines such as marriage-of-convenience. *The hero and heroine cannot consummate their relationship unless they are married.*

Editor's Wish List: Strong, believable characters and conflict. Emotional, believable romance.

Silhouette Romance Writer's Guidelines

Silhouette Romance requires talented authors able to portray modern relationships in the context of romantic love. Although the hero and heroine don't actually make love unless married, sexual tension is a vitally important element. Writers are encouraged to try new twists and creative approaches to this winning formula. Our ultimate goal is to give readers a romance with heightened emotional impact—books that make them laugh or cry, books that touch their hearts.

SILHOUETTE SPECIAL EDITION
300 E. 42nd Street, 6th Floor
New York, NY 10017
(212) 682-6080

Acquisitions: Tara Gavin, Senior Editor; Isabel Swift, Editorial Director. All Silhouette editors can acquire for all Silhouette lines. Address queries to specific editors.

Media Type: Paperback, 72 per year.

Submissions: Authors, send query letter first plus outline of story. Send synopsis and sample chapters only at editor's request after query letter. Agents may call. New authors are encouraged. No unsolicited manuscripts. Unagented manuscripts are OK, but query first. No simultaneous submissions. No electronic submissions. Usual response time is 6–8 weeks.

Pay Rate: Book publishing schedule varies. Average advance is variable. Standard royalty starts at 6%.

Seeking: Contemporary category of 75,000–80,000 words with a strong focus on romance; topics vary.

Tips: A Silhouette Special Edition has a broad range—sensuality depends on the author and what works for the story. Read the line and study the market! Keep in mind who you are writing for and what subjects will be meaningful and entertaining to them.

Turn-offs/Taboos: Too much reliance on contrivance, misunderstanding, or the other woman/other man chestnut.

Editor's Wish List: Our readers look to us to provide stories with a strong focus on the developing romance as well as an awareness of what satisfies the romance reader. The longer length of a Silhouette Special Edition offers authors the opportunity of creating a more in-depth characterization. The broader concept necessary for the length offers the challenge of connecting with the reader in a unique and meaningful way.

Silhouette Special Edition Writer's Guidelines

Sophisticated, substantial, and packed with emotion, Special Edition demands writers eager to probe characters deeply, to explore issues that heighten the drama of living and loving, to create compelling romantic plots. Whether the sensuality is sizzling or subtle, whether the plot is wildly innovative or satisfyingly traditional, the novel's emotional vividness, its depth and dimension, should clearly label it a very special contemporary romance. Subplots are welcome, but must further or parallel the developing romantic relationship in a meaningful way.

SILHOUETTE YOURS TRULY
300 E. 42nd Street, 6th Floor
New York, NY 10017
(212) 682-6080

Acquisitions: Leslie Wainger, Senior Editor and Editorial Coordinator

Media Type: Paperback.

Submissions: Authors, send queries, partials, or complete manuscripts. SASE please. No simultaneous submissions. See General Silhouette Submission Guidelines on pages 166–169 for more information.

Seeking: Contemporary romance of 50,000 words.

Turn-offs/Taboos: Paranormal stories are an absolute no-no.

Silhouette Yours Truly Updated Guidelines

Yours Truly—Silhouette's new line of short, sassy contemporary romance novels about unexpectedly meeting, dating . . . and marrying Mr. Right.

How does the heroine meet Mr. Right? Through a form of written communication, such as a personal ad, an invitation to a wedding, or a misdirected Dear John letter—just to name a few fun and intriguing examples. Hook readers in the snappiest way possible in the first few pages. How does she date him? Considering the compelling romantic conflict standing in their way, they're too busy letting the emotional and romantic tension develop. Plus, she just might date other men—for humorous touches that teach her who she really belongs with . . . the hero. How does she marry him? That depends on the page-turning plot. And in Yours Truly novels, only a satisfying, happy ending is required—marriage isn't.

Touch readers' hearts and tickle their funnybones as your characters explore the trials, tribulations, and triumphs of the hunt for love.

Word Count: 50,000. Tone: Category romance that is very contemporary, fast-paced, fun, flirtatious, entertaining, and up-beat. Level of sensuality: Sexy, but no requirements. Examples of movies that capture the tone and types of stories: *Sleepless in*

Seattle, Four Weddings and a Funeral, Married to the Mob, Crossing Delancy. Absolute No-No: Paranormal elements (Yours Truly novels are an entertaining reflection of real life). Absolute Must: Hero and heroine meet, directly or indirectly, through a form of written communication.

Submission info: Yours Truly is actively seeking submissions from unpublished and published authors. (Silhouette and Harlequin authors: submit to your respective editors.) Send a query or a partial (with a full synopsis) or a complete manuscript with a cover letter and manuscript sized SASE to Leslie Wainger, Senior Editor and Editorial Coordinator or to any member of the editorial staff.

Yours Truly: Love—When You Least Expect It.

STARBURST PUBLISHERS

P.O. Box 4123
Lancaster, PA 17604
(717) 293-0939

Acquisitions: Ellen Hake, Editorial Director

Media Type: Paperback, hardcover; 1–2 titles per month.

Submissions: Submit outline/synopsis, three sample chapters, author's bio and photo, and SASE. No unsolicited manuscripts. (Send SASE for current guidelines.)

Pay Rate: 6%–16% royalty on net price to retailer.

Seeking: All types of inspirational fiction, including adventure, fantasy, historical, mainstream, contemporary, romance, western. "We are looking for wholesome, Christian fiction." Length is 60,000–70,000 words minimum. Also seeking nonfiction in areas of business, children, cooking, health, psychology, recreation, and more.

TOR/FORGE BOOKS

175 Fifth Avenue, 14th Floor
New York, NY 10010
(212) 388-0100

Acquisitions: Melissa Ann Singer, Senior Editor; Claire Eddy, Editor; Natalia Aponte, Associate Editor

Media Type: Mass-market paperback, hardcover. (We buy other rights for licensing.)

Submissions: Prefers phone calls to query letters. (Melissa Ann Singer is at extension 877.) A five minute phone call will help to determine if your work is right for this publisher and to which editor you should submit your manuscript. OK to send synopsis and first three chapters (about 50 pages). Unsolicited manuscripts are OK, but only in proposal form unless author is published novelist. In that case, OK to send complete manuscript. SASE or return postage is a must on all submissions, except agented.

Pay Rate: Industry standard.

Seeking: Ethnic, historical, mystery, paranormal, prairie romance, romantic suspense, time travel. (For in-depth info, please see Chapter 3, "Melissa Ann Singer Gives Writers a Tour, of Tor Books!"

Turn-offs/Taboos: Virtually no turn-offs or taboos, though we sometimes shy away from overly graphic violence, especially rape or violence against children.

Editor's Wish List: Each editor has her own wish list, which is why we recommend calling. Looking at the books we are publishing is a good way of figuring out if your project is right for us.

TOR KIDS
175 Fifth Avenue
New York, NY 10010
(212) 388-0100

Acquisitions: Jonathan Schmidt, Senior Editor/Tor Kids

Media Type: Mass market paperback, hardcover; 3–4 per month.

Submissions: No query letters. No phone queries. Send cover letter with synopsis and first three chapters. Unsolicited manuscripts are OK.

Pay Rate: Depends on each project.

Seeking: Middle-grade through high-school fiction and non-fiction.

Tips: Write, requesting publisher's guidelines for submission to Tor Kids and a copy of the catalog to make sure that your work fits the house.

WARNER BOOKS
1271 Avenue of the Americas
New York, NY 10020
(212) 522-7200   FAX: (212) 522-7990

Acquisitions: Jeanne Tiedge, Senior Editor

Media Type: Paperback, hardcover, audio; 1–2 titles per month.

Submissions: Query first by letter with SASE. No unsolicited manuscripts.

Pay Rate: Advances and royalties vary.

Seeking: Contemporary (long) and historical 110,000–120,000 words.

Note: Warner does not have tip sheets.

DANIEL WEISS ASSOCIATES, INC.
33 W. 17th Street, 11th Floor
New York, NY 10011
(212) 645-3865   FAX: (212) 633-1236

Acquisitions: Elise Howard, Editor-in-Chief; Risa Goldstein, Editor; Gene Hult, Sweet Valley Assistant Editor.

Media Type: Paperback, 1 title per month.

Submissions: $1.93 postage on SASE with your initial query for sample packets—a test for existing series. No phone or FAX queries. OK to send synopsis and sample chapters or unsolicited manuscripts. Unagented manuscripts are OK, as are simultaneous submissions. Agents may call. Usual response time is 6–10 weeks.

Pay Rate: Book producer pays about $3,500 flat fee per book. This varies with experience and ability of the writer.

Seeking: Fantasy (including angels, ghosts, and vampires), juvenile, and mystery, mainstream, and contemporary romance for children, teens, and young adults. See Writer's Guidelines below for more information.

Tips: Read the series before attempting a sample.

Turn-offs/Taboos: Talking down to readers. Heavy moral or religious messages. No graphic sex or violence.

Editor's Wish List: An excellent journeyman writer for young adult, middle-grade, and elementary readers. Light romance, humor, and lighthearted stories.

Writer's Guidelines for Daniel Weiss Associates, Inc.

GENERAL GUIDELINES

We are currently acquiring in a few specific areas. The first of these is the young adult romance category. Guidelines for our new series, Love Stories, are listed. All romance proposals should be addressed to Risa Goldstein, Editor. (Specific guidelines for this series follow.)

Writers for our Sweet Valley series—*Kids, Twins, High,* and *University* are always needed. Please direct inquiries to the attention of Risa Goldstein, Editor, or Gene Hult, Assistant Editor. (Specific guidelines for these series follow.)

We are presently working on various other series for which we need experienced young adult, middle-grade, and elementary writers. If you wish to be considered for these series, please send us your credentials and samples of your writing.

When submitting your proposal, please keep in mind that we cannot acquire individual novels that do not fit in with one of our established series. If you do wish to submit a series proposal, however, we encourage you to do so. Please write a query letter including the subject matter, intended audience, proposed number of books, and proposed book length of your series to Elise Howard, Editor-in-Chief. Also please enclose an SASE with your submission for response and/or return.

SWEET VALLEY SERIES WRITER'S GUIDELINES

Sweet Valley High, with more than 60 million books in print worldwide, is one of the best-selling young adult series ever created.

Sweet Valley Twins, a series for a middle-grade audience, presents the same well-loved characters, four years earlier.

Sweet Valley Kids, a series for elementary readers, explores the lives of the Wakefield twins in second grade.

Sweet Valley University, our newest Sweet Valley series, follows the Wakefields and their friends to college.

All four series are on-going projects, with a new titles appearing each month. As the series' producer, we are in constant need of talented writers who can create humorous dialogue and fast-paced action in the established tone of the series.

Writers are provided with story outlines from which to work. They are responsible, however, for developing the outline into a chapter-by-chapter synopsis for our approval, and creating a subplot that fits in with the main storyline.

Final manuscripts are 185 manuscript pages (45,000 words) for *High,* 135 manuscript pages (33,000 words) for *Twins,* 40–45 manuscript pages (10,000–12,000 words) for *Kids,* and 225 manuscript pages (53,000 words) for *University.*

Writers will find it necessary to read many of the books in the series to familiarize themselves with the characters, setting, and tone.

Writers are given four to six weeks to produce a first draft.

Compensation varies with the experience and ability of the writer.

We require all writers, however experienced, to write a sample of two chapters. Samples will be based on an outline from a book that has already been assigned. Writers interested in receiving sample material, please send an SASE with $1.93 in postage to Gene Hult and specify for which series you would like to write a sample.

LOVE STORIES WRITER'S GUIDELINES

Love Stories are *the* young adult romances of the 90s—individual novels about the wonder and excitement of first love, the ups and downs of what it's like to be part of a couple.

The stories can be told in the first or third person. The role of the boy is essential in these books. He must be a solid, three-dimensional character with dreams and plans of his own. The overall feel of the character is classic and romantic, yet modern, fresh, and forward-looking. The emphasis is solidly on the romance between a boy and a girl—and the conflict that threatens to keep them apart. These stories contain *no sex*, but are full of tender, touching, and even thrilling moments. Heavy on plot and fast-paced, these books must have well-developed, three-dimensional characters.

These books are *not* adolescent problem novels, but instead are an antidote to the weighty sophistication of some of the more recent young adult romances. The characters of *Love Stories* undoubtedly will face the everyday problems of teenagers everywhere, but their tone should remain upbeat. As in all good novels, the drama may be amplified by engaging subplots involving the heroine or secondary characters.

The heroines are between the ages of 14 and 16, and they are having their first real encounters with romance. This means they have moved beyond the first kiss stage and are now involved in actual relationships. Through their eyes, the reader experiences the once-in-a-lifetime thrill and intensity of being part of a couple—the high points and the low. There are no restrictions on settings, but plots must be accessible to the average American teenage girl.

We will consider complete manuscripts accompanied by a detailed plot synopsis, or a detailed plot outline and partial manuscript (two to four chapters). Finished manuscripts should be 45,000 words. All submissions should be typed and double-spaced. Unsolicited submissions must be accompanied by a self-addressed stamped envelope for return to the author. We cannot respond to manuscripts without SASEs.

ZEBRA

(See Kensington Publishing Corporation)

6

Directory of Writer's Networks

International Networks

Australia

ROMANCE WRITERS OF AMERICA
AUSTRALIAN CHAPTER IV-131
22 Glen Eagles Road
Mt. Osmond, Adelaide, South Australia,
AUSTRALIA 5064

Contact Person: Diane Beer, President

Annual Dues: $15, plus membership in RWA National (U.S.A.).

Member Benefits: Members receive newsletter; networking; support; marketing information; vital link between Australian and American writers; opportunity to attend annual August conference (cost varies).

AUSTRALIAN NETWORK OF FUTURISTIC, FANTASY, AND PARANORMAL ROMANCE WRITERS (ANFFPRW)

32 Jetty Street
Grange, South Australia
AUSTRALIA 5022

Contact Person: Gillian Curtin, Network Coordinator

Annual Dues: $30 (Australian).

Member Benefits: Airmail subscription to bimonthly member-written newsletter, *Realms Beyond;* critique partners; writing help; member hotline; mutual support; international members perspective; free author ad in newsletter on space available basis. (Not officially affiliated with RWA.)

ROMANCE WRITERS OF AUSTRALIA (RWAUSTRALIA)

P.O. Box 183
Bexley, New South Wales,
AUSTRALIA 2207

Contact Person: Lynne Wilding, President

Member Benefits: Members receive newsletter; networking; support; marketing information; opportunity to attend annual August conference (cost varies). Not officially affiliated with

Romance Writers of America. Contact president for membership dues and conference information.

Canada

ALBERTA ROMANCE WRITERS ASSOCIATION
223 12th Avenue S.W.
Calgary, Alberta T2R OG9
CANADA
FAX: (403) 283-7325

Contact Persons: Grace Panko, President; Darlene Beaton-Harris, Membership Chair

Annual Dues: $35 (Canadian). New members required to submit 30-page manuscript as sign of serious intent.

Member Benefits: Receive support; monthly newsletter; workshops; meetings; library privileges; networking; hands-on courses; opportunity to attend local quadrennial conference May 1996 (about $160). Annual contests for unpublished writers. Not affiliated with RWA.

FEDERATION OF BRITISH COLUMBIA WRITERS
905 West Pender Street, 4th Floor
Vancouver, B.C. V6C 1L6
CANADA

Contact Person: Corey Van't Haaff, Manager

Annual Dues: $50 (Canadian).

Member Benefits: Receive quarterly newsletter; grievance assistance; phone accessible. BC's largest writing group has two annual literary competitions. (Informally affiliated with RWA.)

MARSHLANDS ROMANCE WRITERS—RWA #127
RR #2
Sackville, New Brunswick E0A 3CO
CANADA

Contact Person: Tory LeBlanc, President

Annual Dues: $20 (Canadian).

Member Benefits: Monthly meetings; monthly newsletter; critiques; discussion; updates on publishing industry; advice to realize potential; local writing contests for unpublished in area. SASE for rules.

RWA ONTARIO
P.O. Box 69035, St. Clair Center P.O.
12 St. Clair Avenue, East
Toronto, Ontario M4T 3A1
CANADA
(416) 236-6934 (voice mail)

Annual Dues: $35 (Canadian).

Member Benefits: Lectures by published authors/editors; workshops; tape library; reference library; market news; annual contest.

SASKATCHEWAN WRITER'S GUILD
Box 3986
Regina, Saskatchewan S4P 3R9
CANADA

Contact: Send SASE to address above for information.

United Kingdom

ROMANTIC NOVELISTS' ASSOCIATION
5 St. Agnes Gate
Wendover, Buckinghamshire HP226DP
ENGLAND
(01296) 623260   FAX: (01296) 623601

Contact Person: Hilary Johnson, Membership Secretary

Annual Dues: £20 sterling, full membership for published romance novelists; £50 sterling for new writers.

Member Benefits: Group membership of the New Cavendish in London; provides link between professional romantic novelists and publishing business; new writer's award; offers help and advice to aspiring romantic novelists. Each September, new writers submit a manuscsript for assessment; manuscripts with potential are submitted by RNA to publishers.

U.S.A National and Regional Associations and Conferences

AFFAIRE DE COEUR CONVENTION

Call *Affaire de Coeur* at (510) 569-5675 or check the magazine for the latest conference information.

ASSOCIATION OF AUTHOR'S REPRESENTATIVES (AAR)

10 Astor Place, 3rd Floor
New York, NY 10003
(212) 353-3709

An association of literary agents. For $5 and SASE with two first class stamps, AAR will send a brochure with list of members.

THE AUTHORS GUILD

330 W. 42nd Street
New York, NY 10036-6902
(212) 563-5904   FAX: (212) 564-5364

Contact Person: Mr. Paul Aiken, Assistant Director

Annual Dues: First year is $90. Thereafter, dues based on income earned from writing. Must be published: one book within past three years or three magazine articles within past 18 months.

Member Benefits: Free agency and publishing contract reviews by Guild legal staff; legal and tax information; symposia; seminars keep members current on publishing developments; more than 6,700 authors in many genres; conferences.

FICTION WRITER'S CONNECTION
P.O. Box 4065
Deerfield Beach, FL 33442-4065
(305) 426-4705

Contact Person: Blythe Camenson, Director

Annual Dues: $59 ($54 for students/seniors).

Member Benefits: Writers receive free critiquing; newsletter featuring interviews with agents/editors; toll-free hotline; publishing tips; seminars; annual contest open to all (SASE for rules). (Not affiliated with RWA.)

FUTURISTIC, FANTASY, AND PARANORMAL CHAPTER—RWA (FF&P)
6047 E. Elmwood Avenue
Philadelphia, PA 19142

Contact Person: Judy Di Canio, President

Annual Dues: $10, plus membership in RWA.

Membership Benefits: Brings writers a treasure trove of information! FF&P helps writers find others who are familiar with both science fiction/fantasy and romance elements in books. This subgenre chapter provides member roster, bimonthly newsletter

Out of This World, critique partners if desired, lots of info relating to this subgenre, with focus on marketing and answers to research questions. Annual contest open to all unpublished RWA members or published members who have not sold book in three years. (SASE for rules/entry form.)

NATIONAL WRITER'S ASSOCIATION
1450 S. Havana, Suite 424
Aurora, CO 80012
(303) 751-7844
e-mail: NWA.STAFF@GENIE.COM

Contact Person: Sandy Whelchel, Executive Director

Annual Dues: $50 Regular members, $60 Professional members (members must be published for professional membership).

Member Benefits: Aspiring or published, all are welcome. Free marketing service; contract evaluation; research reports; advice; advocacy action; bimonthly magazine; *Professional Freelance Writers Directory;* annual conference/contest opportunities. SASE for contest rules or conference brochure. (Not affiliated with RWA.)

ROMANCE READERS ASSOCIATION
P.O. Box 24584
San Jose, CA 95154
FAX: (408) 978-9363

Contact Persons: Terri Farrell, President; Debbie Meckler, Vice President

Annual Dues: $25

Member Benefits: Members receive *Romantics at Heart* newsletter; contest opportunities; book signing news. (Not affiliated with RWA.)

ROMANCE WRITERS OF AMERICA (RWA NATIONAL)
13700 Veterans Memorial, Suite 315
Houston, TX 77014
(713) 440-6885   FAX (713) 440-7510

Contact Person: Allison Kelley, Executive Manager

Annual Dues: $60

Member Benefits: Members receive bimonthly magazine with focus on technique and book markets; opportunities to enter contests and attend annual national conference (about $300); 100+ affiliated chapters provide support and personal interaction for romance writers in many geographical areas.

ROMANCE WRITERS OF AMERICA (NATIONAL ON-LINE CHAPTER)
P.O. Box 3835
Granada Hills, CA 91394-0835
(800) 848-8990 (CompuServe's customer service line)

Contact: Karen Pershing, President

Annual Dues: $15, plus membership in RWA and CompuServe.

Member Benefits: Brings writers together from the United States and other countries. This communication-by-modem chapter is located in CompuServe's Literary Forum. Offers on-line critique; discussions; on-line newsletter; tip sheets; workshops; research; contest and conference news as close as your modem. Hourly on-line charges may apply.

ROMANTIC SUSPENSE NETWORK
517 S. 51st Avenue
Omaha, NE 68106-1362
(402) 558-1869

Contact Person: Cathy Nelson

Annual Dues: $15 ($20 overseas).

Member Benefits: Brings readers a newsletter about this subgenre of romance; interactive newsletter with readers, publishers, and writers; members informed of changes in publishing industry. (Not affiliated with RWA.)

ROMANTIC TIMES CONVENTION
October, 1996, Baton Rouge, LA

Call *Romantic Times* (718) 237-1097 or check magazine for info. Offers intriguing workshops; research bookstore; romance book fair; awards ceremony; opportunities to interact with authors, editors, agents, booksellers, and readers.

ROSE PETALS AND PEARLS

115 Eastmont Drive
Jackson, TN 38301
(901) 422-6223

Contact Person: Diane Kirk, Founder

Annual Dues: $20.

Member Benefits: Quarterly newsletter dedicated to the preservation of romance genre; Reader's Room opened for Women's Crisis Center; bookfair with proceeds to charity; helps women's literacy programs; annual romance readers' cruise conference (speakers' travel costs covered). (Not affiliated with RWA.)

SCIENCE FICTION AND FANTASY WRITERS OF AMERICA

5 Winding Brook Drive
Guilderland, NY 12084

Contact Person: Peter Dennis Pautz, Executive Secretary

Annual Dues: Dues vary for different types of memberships.

Member Benefits: Send SASE for details of types of membership, requirements, dues, and list of member publications.

SCI-FI ROMANCE!

P.O. Box 496
Endicott, NY 13761-0496

Contact Person: SASE to Jennifer Dunne at above address or e-mail for newsletter to yeep@aol.com

Annual Dues: None.

Member Benefits: By SASE or e-mail, readers can receive newsletter and learn about the science fiction romance subgenre through book reviews, articles about the publishing industry written by agents and editors. Research and writing questions are explored, and more. (Not affiliated with RWA.)

SISTERS IN CRIME
P.O. Box 442124
Lawrence, KS 66044
(913) 842-1325

Contact Person: M. Beth Wasson, Executive Secretary

Annual Dues: $25, U.S.; $30, other countries.

Member Benefits: Purpose of SIC is to combat discrimination against women in mystery field, educate publishers and general public about inequalities in treatment of female authors, and raise level of awareness of contributions by women mystery writers. First annual conference in Houston, TX ($185); newsletter; speakers bureau; GEnie electronic forum; Women of Color Outreach; Young Adult, Juvenile, and Children's writer's outreach; clipping service.

WESTERN WRITERS OF AMERICA, INC. (WWA)
P.O. Box 1104, 500 Second Street
Magdalena, NM 87825

Contact Person: S. Gail Miller, Editor of *Roundup* magazine and Publicity Coordinator

Annual Dues: Professional requirements for full membership ($60).

Member Benefits: Since 1952, 600+ members have fostered literature of the American West. Annual Spur Awards for published works in a dozen categories. Bimonthly professional writer's magazine. Conference is held every June. 1996 conference is in Albuquerque; 1997 is in Cheyenne, Wyoming. Not affiliated with RWA, though many writers are members of both.

WOMEN'S NATIONAL BOOK ASSOCIATION (WNBA)
160 Fifth Avenue
New York, NY 10010
(212) 675-7805

Contact Person: Sandra Paul

Annual Dues: Varies.

Member Benefits: Educational opportunities; networking; literacy volunteer opportunities; brings together women and men who work with and value words; provides opportunities for exchange of info, ideas, contacts, and support. Eleven U.S. chapters. (Not affiliated with RWA.)

WRITERS GUILD OF AMERICA—EAST (WGAe)
555 W. 57th Street, Suite 1230
New York, NY 10019
(212) 757-4360 (registration info)
or (212) 767-7800

Works Registration: For $20, WGAe registers nonmembers' written works for film, TV, radio, novels, short stories, etc. Also available to nonmembers are *WGA Directory* ($17.50) and *The WGA Journal* ($40/yr for 11 issues). (Professional credits required for membership.)

WRITERS GUILD OF AMERICA—WEST (WGAw)

8955 Beverly Boulevard
West Hollywood, CA 90048
(310) 205-2500 (registration information)

Works Registration: (See Writers Guild of America—East.)

Local (U.S.) Networks by State

Alabama

GULF COAST RWA

6504 Creekwood Court
Mobile, AL 36695

Contact Person: Judith Bland, President

Annual Dues: $16, plus membership in RWA National.

Member Benefits: Members receive *Silken Sands* newsletter to assist in active pursuit of romance writing; group attracts writers from all along Gulf Coast (Mississippi, Alabama, Florida); opportunity to attend annual May conference at Gulf Shores (about $125); annual writing contests for unpublished and published authors (SASE for rules).

HEART OF DIXIE
P.O. Box 2099
Gadsden, AL 35903

Contact Person: Linda Winstead Jones, President

Annual Dues: $20, plus membership in RWA National.

Member Benefits: Members receive monthly newsletter; monthly meetings with variety of programs for beginners and seasoned writers; special price for May workshop in Huntsville. Members are from North Alabama, Tennessee, Georgia, and Florida. About one third of members are published. Many programs presented by Heart of Dixie's published authors.

Arizona

ARIZONA AUTHORS ASSOCIATION
3509 E. Shea Boulevard, Suite 117
Phoenix, AZ 85028
(602) 867-9001

Contact Person: Eva Lee Martin, President

Annual Dues: $40.

Member Benefits: Discounts on seminars and books; networking with other writers; bimonthly newsletter; market news; conference news; information about other writers groups; contests (SASE for rules).

DESERT ROSE CHAPTER—PHOENIX RWA #60
2553 S. Playa Avenue
Mesa, AZ 85202-6926

Contact Person: Dawn Creighton, President

Annual Dues: $18, plus membership in RWA National.

Member Benefits: Monthly meetings; networking; critique groups; mentor program; member discount on annual September Desert Dreams Conference (about $120); occasional hands-on workshops; interaction with published authors who share expertise.

NORTHERN ARIZONA RWA
484 Wakas Trail
Flagstaff, AZ 86001
(520) 525-2403

Contact Person: Anita Gunnufson

Annual Dues: $12, plus membership in RWA National.

Member Benefits: Unites romance writers through newsletter and bimonthly meetings. First conference is planned for June 1996. Only romance writers' group in Northern Arizona. Meetings rotate between several cities in the area.

TUCSON RWA #58
681 N. Hearthside Lane
Tucson, AZ 85748
(520) 751-9141

Contact Person: Evelyn Marie Snover

Annual Dues: $15.

Member Benefits: Monthly meetings with networking; talking to fellow authors anytime; manuscript critiques.

VALLEY OF THE SUN RWA— WEST SIDE CHAPTER
4164 W. Crocus Drive
Phoenix, AZ 85023
(602) 843-9594

Contact Person: Theresa Meyers, President

Annual Dues: $15, plus membership in RWA National.

Member Benefits: Brings writers together with high quality networking; monthly newsletter and meetings; reference tapes and library; outstanding programs; retreats; booksignings; local publicity assistance for published authors; annual Hot Prospects Contest for unpublished authors (SASE for rules).

WRITERS OF THE PURPLE PAGE— YUMA, AZ, RWA CHAPTER

P.O. Box 228
Winterhaven, CA 92283
(619) 572-0876

Contact Person: Pinkie Paranya, President

Annual Dues: $15, plus membership in RWA National.

Member Benefits: Members reap benefits of newsletter and meetings twice per month (second meeting is critique group). This small group enables chapter to do things that larger groups cannot, for instance, meet at someone's home for discussion. Annual contest in the works.

California

INLAND VALLEY RWA #26

2828 W. Via Verde Drive
Rialto, CA 92377
(909) 823-1477

Contact Person: Janelle Denison, President

Annual Dues: $20, plus membership in RWA National.

Member Benefits: Brings writers a monthly newsletter; critique group twice per month; support for published and unpublished authors; annual writing contest for unpublished writers (SASE for "Put Your Best Hook Forward" contest rules).

MONTEREY BAY CHAPTER RWA

P.O. Box 806
Capitola, CA 95010
or
137 Rustic Lane
Santa Cruz, CA 95060
(408) 427-2275 (evenings and weekends)

Contact Person: Suzannne Barrett, Vice President/Program Chair

Annual Dues: $20, plus membership in RWA National.

Member Benefits: Timely, informative programs; high quality networking; all-day workshops twice per year; critique groups; extensive tape and reference library; newsletter; excellent national contest for all RWA unpublished members. The Silver Heart Contest consists of synopsis and first chapter, up to forty pages (SASE to Capitola address for contest rules/entry form); contest entries receive critiques; newcomers welcome.

ORANGE COUNTY CHAPTER RWA

P.O. Box 395
Yorba Linda, CA 92686-0395

Contact Person: Margaret Esther, Membership Director

Annual Dues: $35 for new members (renewals $30), plus membership in RWA National.

Member Benefits: Joins writers together in the largest chapter of RWA (400+ members); monthly meetings feature speakers who are agents, editors, or best-selling romance authors; special workshops for published and unpublished; monthly newsletter; mentor program; speaker tapes available; libraries; annual Orange Rose contest is open to all RWA members (SASE for rules).

SAN DIEGO CHAPTER RWA
P.O. Box 22805
San Diego, CA 92192

Contact Persons: Marilyn Forstot, President; Diana Saenger, President

Annual Dues: $25, plus membership in RWA National.

Member Benefits: Monthly *Romantically Speaking* newsletter; monthly workshops and meetings ($5 meeting fee); and special events, including editor dinners; annual writing contest (SASE for rules). First annual conference scheduled for 4/96 in Old Town.

SAN DIEGO STATE UNIVERSITY CONFERENCE
College of Extended Studies Extension Program
5250 Campanile Drive
San Diego, CA 92182-1920
(619) 594-5152   FAX: (619) 594-7080

Contact: Writer's Conference Registration

Annual conference; usually held in January. Three-day event (about $225) features read-critique sessions in all genres; editors/agents interaction with writers; speakers; specialty workshops; research emporium. From romance writing to agent shopping, screenwriting, children's markets, and nonfiction workshops, this conference sells out quickly.

WOMEN'S FICTION WRITERS— SACRAMENTO RWA
P.O. Box 215884
Sacramento, CA 95821

Annual Dues: $25, plus membership in RWA National.

Member Benefits: Gives writers professional access to 100+ members, of which 30 are published; monthly meetings include editors, writers, and agents as guest speakers; newsletter; California Gold Synopsis Contest (open to unpublished writers and to authors not published in five years; SASE for rules).

WRITERS OF KERN
P.O. Box 6694
Bakersfield, CA 93386-6694
(805) 871-5834

Contact Person: Debbie Bailey, President

Annual Dues: $18.

Member Benefits: Monthly meetings (except the third Saturday of September, which is annual conference), with speakers/authors on topics pertaining to writing; weekly and biweekly critique groups for several fiction genres including romance, nonfiction, and screenwriting; monthly newsletter with marketing tips, conference and contest news; access to club library; writing contest held May–June (SASE for rules). Affiliated with Bakersfield College Foundation.

THE WRITING CENTER
416 Third Avenue
San Diego, CA 92101
(619) 230-0670

Contact Person: Judy Reeves, Director

Annual Dues: $25

Member Benefits: Grants members access to gathering place for writers; discounted classes (some free); brown-bag-lunch writers and journal groups; workshops and readings in all genres; newsletter; annual writing contest in short fiction, nonfiction (SASE for rules/entry form); retreats; journals. Some classes offer childcare for small fee.

Colorado

COLORADO ROMANCE WRITERS
P.O. Box 448
Eastlake, CO 80614
(303) 440-9296

Contact Person: Kathy Williams, President

Annual Dues: $20, plus membership in RWA National (interest in seriously pursuing a career in romance writing is required).

Member Benefits: Offers monthly meetings; interesting programs; monthly newsletter; critique groups; published writers' support group; annual booksellers-distributors tea; promotional materials sent to booksellers; biannual conference in Denver (about $85); contests for published and unpublished writers (SASE for rules).

PIKES PEAK ROMANCE WRITERS (PPRW)
P.O. Box 16976
Colorado Springs, CO 80935

Contact Person: Pam McCutcheon, President

Annual Dues: $21, plus membership in RWA National.

Member Benefits: A quality monthly newsletter; meetings; programs; critique groups; lending library; workshops; networking; annual retreat; annual bookseller tea; Writer of the Year Contest for published members of PPRW; Top of the Peak Contest open to all unpublished writers of romance (prize is registration fee for RWA's national conference). Supports Annual Pikes Peak Writers Conference and hosts awards dinner. (Affiliated with RWA.)

PIKES PEAK WRITERS CONFERENCE
P.O. Box 1579, 5550 N. Union Boulevard
Colorado Springs, CO 80901

Contact Person: Jimmie H. Butler, Director

Annual conference sponsored by Friends of the Pikes Peak Library District in April, features editors/agents and workshops/lectures in all genres including romance, sci-fi, young adult, TV scripts, magazine writing. Write for brochure.

Florida

FIRST COAST ROMANCE WRITERS—RWA #108
21 Dondanville Road, #40
St. Augustine, FL 32084
(904) 471-4834

Contact Person: Marge Smith

Annual Dues: $15, plus membership in RWA National.

Member Benefits: Reaps writers a harvest of monthly newsletters; monthly meetings with speakers and workshops; up-to-date market news; promotes excellence in romantic fiction; helps writers become published and establish careers; provides support, encouragement, and inspiration through recognition for achievements and attainments of personal goals; annual one day workshop in Jacksonville; annual "Spice, Sizzle and Steam" contest, open to all fiction writers (SASE for rules/entry form).

SOUTHWEST FLORIDA ROMANCE WRITERS, INC. (SWFRW)
16150 Bay Pointe Boulevard, N.E., B-307
North Fort Meyers, FL 33917

Contact Person: Joyce Henderson, President

Annual Dues: $25, plus membership in RWA National.

Member Benefits: Lets writers in on RWA news, publishing news, and updates; networking; writing workshops; critiquing; guest speakers; annual conference in October (approximately $65–$75); annual writing contest for all pre-published RWA members, excluding SWFRW members. Members must write women's or young adult fiction.

Georgia

GEORGIA ROMANCE WRITERS (GRW)
P.O. Box 142
Acworth, GA 30101
(404) 974-6678

Contact Persons: Marian Oaks, Membership Chair; Ellen Taber, President

Annual Dues: $20, plus membership in RWA National.

Member Benefits: Grants writers entrance into one of the largest and most active chapters of RWA. GRW addresses the needs of published and unpublished writers in all genres with support, networking, peer critiques, expertise sharing, hands-on workshop, *The Galley* monthly newsletter, firsthand knowledge about publishing industry—editors, agents, markets, and how-to writing-skills help. Opportunity to attend Annual Moonlight and Magnolias Conference, held every September; Annual Maggie Awards for RWA members (SASE for contest rules and/or conference brochure).

Hawaii

ALOHA CHAPTER—HAWAII RWA #72
P.O. Box 240013
Honolulu, HI 96824-0013

Contact Person: Lynde Lakes, President

Annual Dues: $15, plus membership in RWA National.

Member Benefits: Opens door to writers' fellowship; encouragement; tapes; videos; programs; newsletters; market news; fun! We need you and we want you to succeed! Some of the top romance writers belong to Aloha and they want you to join them! Sometimes holds annual conference. Annual writing contest (SASE for info.).

Illinois

COUP D'ESSAI
411 East Roosevelt Road
Wheaton, IL 60187
(708) 668-3316

Contact Person: Susan Donohue, President

Annual Dues: $20.

Member Benefits: Opens up opportunities for all serious writers of romantic fiction. This experimental group evolved from romance writing classes offered by the College of DuPage. Weekly meetings; critique groups; guest speakers; weekend writer's retreats; annual awards dinner; newsletter. Coup d'Essai has applied for chapter status with RWA National. Thursday meetings are on DuPage campus; Saturday breakfast groups at members' homes.

Note: *Romance Writer's Pink Pages* is on the reference booklist for romance writing students at the College of DuPage.

LOVE DESIGNERS WRITERS CLUB, INC.

1507 Burnham Avenue
Calumet City, IL 60409
(708) 862-9797

Contact Person: Virginia Deweese

Annual Dues: $20, plus membership in RWA National.

Member Benefits: Benefits writers with support group; encouragement; knowledge exchange; *Rendezvous* magazine; opportunity to attend annual October Autumn Authors Affair Conference (about $50) in Lisle (SASE for conference brochure). (Affiliated with RWA.)

LOVE ON THE RIVER—RWA #109

17580 Rt. 5 West
East Dubuque, IL 61025

Contact Person: Karen Litscher, Secretary

Annual Dues: $20, plus membership in RWA National.

Member Benefits: Brings writers up-to-date market news; networking with fellow writers; supportive critiques; RWA information; variety of writers in different genres; annual writing contest (SASE for rules/entry form).

PRAIRIE HEARTS—RWA #43
607 W. Park
Thomasboro, IL 61878
(217) 643-2592 (evenings/weekends)

Contact Person: HiDee Ekstrom, President

Annual Dues: $12, plus membership in RWA National.

Member Benefits: Entitles writers to monthly group meetings; critiquing opportunities; contact with published authors; support and encouragement; annual contests for unpublished writers; annual conference; small group (10–15 members) works together for the good of all members; welcomes new members; SASE for contest/conference info.

WINDY CITY RWA
P.O. Box 3523
Lisle, IL 60532
(708) 495-4731

Contact Person: Stacy Verden, President

Annual Dues: $20, plus membership in RWA National.

Member Benefits: Newsletters, plus monthly meetings, which feature a presentation by published author or professional, or alternately, a critique session/business meeting. Close group has respect for each other's work; new members always welcome; professional and social interaction; retreats.

Iowa

HEART OF IOWA
1885 E. Berry Road
Cedar Rapids, IA 52403
(319) 365-2474

Contact Person: Roxanne Rustand, President

Annual Dues: $24, plus membership in RWA National.

Member Benefits: Entitles writers to monthly meetings that include a variety of speakers and stimulating discussion; contest and workshop info; networking with aspiring and published writers; members encouraged to contribute articles to newsletter, which is distributed to RWA chapters nationwide.

IOWA ROMANCE NOVELISTS
P.O. Box 145
Minburn, IA 50167
(515) 677-2200

Contact Person: Roxanne Rene-Erb, President

Annual Dues: $20, plus membership in RWA National.

Member Benefits: Offers members opportunities for awards for published and unpublished writers for reaching personal goals; free writing worksheets; two different types of meetings each month (critique and regular); newsletter; annual workshop; June Awards Luncheon in Des Moines; annual "Query Me Away" contest open to any RWA member (SASE for rules/entry form).

Kansas

WICHITA AREA ROMANCE AUTHORS
1120 Schweiter Drive
Wichita, KS 67211
(316) 265-2458

Contact Person: Starla Criser, President

Annual Dues: $20, plus membership in RWA National.

Member Benefits: Offers writers a bimonthly newsletter; market news updates; awards for achievements in writing field; critiquing and brainstorming sessions; educational programs; Tattered Rose Contest and Hook Contest are for chapter members only.

Louisiana

COEUR DE LOUISIANE, INC.
P.O. Box 109
Marksville, LA 71351-0109

Contact Person: Donna Caubarreaux, Treasurer

Annual Dues: $15.

Member Benefits: Promotes excellence in book-length commercial fiction; helps writers become published and establish careers; provides continuing support through monthly newsletter, monthly meetings with speakers; critique partners/groups; discount on conference held April/May in Alexandria (about $100); two contests (synopsis and query letters). SASE for contest or conference information. (Not affiliated with RWA.)

Maryland

MARYLAND ROMANCE WRITERS
P.O. Box 435
Hunt Valley, MD 21030-0435
(410) 744-4843 or (410) 461-4662

Contact Persons: Sheila Caruso and Maria Gorman, Co-Presidents

Annual Dues: $24, plus membership in RWA National.

Member Benefits: Monthly meetings, featuring guest speakers; monthly newsletter; critique groups; reference library; tapes on writing and publishing; writing workshops; networking. (Affiliated with RWA.)

NATIONAL CAPITAL NOVELISTS
3435 Brookhaven Road
Pasadena, MD 21122-6434

Contact Person: Rhonda Harding Pollero, President

Annual Dues: $30, plus membership in RWA National.

Member Benefits: This RWA chapter affiliate works to meet the needs of published and unpublished writers; thirteen members of group are published; newsletter with monthly contest for unpublished chapter members only; monthly meetings; all-day workshops; small, intimate group; critique groups; "Adopt an Author" program; booksignings.

Massachusetts

CAPE COD WRITERS' CONFERENCE

c/o Cape Cod Conservatory of Music and Arts
2235 Route 132
West Barnstable, MA 02668
(508) 375-0516

Contact Person: Marion Vuilleumier, Executive Director

Cape Cod Writer's Center, with support from the NEA, Massachusetts Cultural Council, and others, has sponsored more than three decades of multi-genre writers' conferences (about $410). Scholarships and college credit available. Individual manuscript evaluations by agent/editor arranged in advance.

NEW ENGLAND CHAPTER, INC.
98 Dartmouth Avenue
Dedham, MA 02026
(617) 320-9078

Contact Person: Betsy Eliot, President.

Annual Dues: $20, plus membership in RWA National.

Member Benefits: Benefits members from all over New England with networking; improving writing skills through critique service; monthly meetings/workshops; *N.E.W.S.* (*New England Writers Newsletter*); Annual "Let Imagination Take Flight" Conference (about $110); discount entry fee to local First Kiss unpublished writers contest. For contest rules, send SASE to: Blanche Marriott, 27 Woodland Street, Lincoln, RI 02865. For conference brochure, SASE to Betsy Eliot.

Michigan

MID-MICHIGAN RWA #2
29224 East Lafayette
Sturgis, MI 49091-9544

Contact Person: Joyce Coker, Chapter President

Annual Dues: $20, plus membership in RWA National.

Member Benefits: Networking; critiquing; one-on-one writer support to help reach goals of publication; support after publication; access to chapter library; annual May retreat ($12 per day); very friendly RWA chapter!

Minnesota

THE LOFT: A PLACE FOR WRITING AND LITERATURE
Pratt Community Center
66 Malcolm Avenue Southeast
Minneapolis, MN 55414
(612) 379-8999

Annual Dues: $40 for individuals ($20 low-income/student).

Member Benefits: Provides writers with free admission to readings; monthly writers' magazine; discounts on classes; free entry to Loft contests. Six award programs motivate Minnesota writers, who annually compete for $7,500 Loft-McKnight grants awarded for promising fiction, etc. Awards of Distinction winners receive grants up to $10,500. National Poetry and Fiction Prize Contest (open to all) offers $1,000, plus publication in *Michigan Quarterly Review*.

MIDWEST FICTION WRITERS
P.O. Box 47888
Minneapolis, MN 55447

Contact Person: Candace Schuler, President

Annual Dues: $25, plus membership in RWA National.

Member Benefits: Attend monthly meetings and programs; receive monthly newsletter; attend pre-meeting workshops about writing basics presented by published authors (4–8 times per year for small fee); enjoy networking with 80 members, of which more than 20 are published in book-length romantic fiction; opportunity to attend biannual conference (cost varies); annual writing contests are instrumental in helping many writers become published authors (SASE for rules/entry form).

Missouri

MID-AMERICA ROMANCE AUTHORS
P.O. Box 32186
Kansas City, MO 64171

Annual Dues: $25, plus membership in RWA National.

Member Benefits: Brings members a monthly newsletter; monthly meetings and workshops; critique groups/service; quarterly reader and bookseller newsletter; subscriptions to review publications; reduced fee for annual February conference ($85–$99); national writing contest for unpublished writers is open to all ($20 entry fee; SASE for rules/entry form).

OZARKS ROMANCE AUTHORS
P.O. Box 4812
Springfield, MO 65808
(417) 886-2289

Contact Person: Weta Nichols, Vice President

Annual Dues: $15, plus membership in RWA National.

Member Benefits: Entitles writers or aspiring writers to great speakers at monthly meetings; critique group; seminars; mentor program. Friendly members are helpful with writing problems. Opportunity to attend annual September writers' conference in Springfield; annual first chapter and synopsis contest open to all writers (SASE for rules/entry form). (Affiliated with RWA.)

THE WRITERS PLACE
3607 Pennsylvania
Kansas City, MO 64111
(816) 363-8010

Contact Person: Judy Ray, Executive Director

Annual Dues: $25.

Member Benefits: The Writers Place is a nonprofit community center. Access to library and place for public readings and meetings. Membership also includes monthly literary calendar for Kansas City area; newsletter; discounts on events and workshops; annual September conference (cost varies). (Not affiliated with RWA.)

Montana

HEART OF MONTANA RWA CHAPTER
1809 Mountain View Drive
Great Falls, MT 59405

Contact Person: Rita Karnopp, President

Annual Dues: $15, plus membership in RWA National.

Member Benefits: Bimonthly newsletter; bimonthly meetings with guest speakers; critique sessions. If you have an interest in the West, this is the place to be. Nothing beats "Big Sky" country.

Nebraska

CAMEO WRITERS
1864 Eldorado Drive
Omaha, NE 68154
(402) 493-0322

Contact Person: Pauline Hetrick, President

Annual Dues: $15, plus membership in RWA National.

Member Benefits: Membership with focus on education, motivation, and mutual support; insightful assessment of the art and craft of writing; coming together with other writers for learning, artistic growth, and instruction with goal of publication.

ROMANCE AUTHORS OF THE HEARTLAND
801 Moore Drive
Bellevue, NE 68005
(402) 734-5804

Contact Person: Ginny McBlain, President

Annual Dues: $20, plus membership in RWA National.

Member Benefits: Entitles new member to packet of how-to articles, guidelines, and market information; bimonthly newsletter; critique groups; critiques by mail for out-of-town members; monthly pre-meeting workshop; monthly programs on good writing techniques; field trips; members share expenses when traveling to conferences; local conference plans; Hot Stuff Contest for unpublished writers includes line-edited critique. For rules/entry form, send SASE to Mo Webster, 802 Galway Circle, Papillion, NE 64086.

Nevada

CACTUS ROSE RWA
4615 Faircenter Parkway, #285
Las Vegas, NV 89102
(702) 254-3173

Contact Person: Mary Ellen Bly, Treasurer

Annual Dues: $15, plus membership in RWA National.

Member Benefits: Critique groups to help improve writing; speakers and programs on writing; opportunity to enter "Dazzling Hook" Contest (SASE for rules). Because chapter is in Las Vegas, well-known authors frequently visit and offer to speak.

New Jersey

NEW JERSEY ROMANCE WRITERS
P.O. Box 513
Plainsboro, NJ 08536
(609) 275-8323

Contact Person: Shirley Hailstock, President

Annual Dues: $45, plus membership in RWA National.

Member Benefits: Interesting monthly workshops; monthly newsletter; access to chapter library; critique program; annual fall New Jersey conference (about $120); free author advertising in newsletter; featured author program; first chapter contest for all RWA members (SASE for rules); "Put Your Heart in a Book" Contest; quarterly bookseller guide; resource booklet.

New York

LAKE COUNTRY ROMANCE WRITERS
c/o Patricia Ryan
P.O. Box 26207
Rochester, NY 14626

Contact Person: Patricia Ryan, President

Annual Dues: $15, plus membership in RWA National.

Member Benefits: Provides education, networking, support, and friendship for romance writers with serious interest in careers. Thirty members (five published) welcome newcomers and offer meetings; critiques; published author program; workshops; newsletter; contest. For annual Great Confrontations Contest rules, send SASE to Nancy Vandivert, 1215 Lake Point Drive, Webster, NY 14580-9585.

NEW YORK CITY CHAPTER, INC.—RWA

P.O. Box 3722, Grand Central Station
New York, NY 10163
(212) 781-0067, Ext. 3 (RWA/NYC Hotline)

Contact Person: Rita Madole, President

Annual Dues: $20 (all members must also be members of RWA National and be interested in being a published writer—no associate status).

Member Benefits: Monthly meetings; monthly network dinners; "From Dream to Reality" workshop; wine and cheese reception for editors and distributors; RITA/Golden Heart contest lottery in which several members win their entry fees to a national writer's contest; chapter retreat and outings; free publicity in newsletter and P.O. box rental for published authors; more. (SASE for Love and Laughter contest/critique for unpublished writers.)

SARATOGA CHAPTER OF RWA

12 Cortland Drive
Ballston Lake, NY 12019
(518) 399-4523

Contact Person: Lisette Belisle, President

Annual Dues: $25, plus membership in RWA National.

Member Benefits: Offers meetings twice per month; newsletter; critique; workshops. We welcome published and unpublished writers and encourage progress at an individual pace.

SOUTHERN TIER AUTHORS OF ROMANCE—STAR RWA
HC 75, Box 993A
Greene, NY 13788

Contact Person: Michele J. Masarech, President

Annual Dues: $12, plus membership in RWA National.

Member Benefits: Offers writers a chance to network with an eclectic, talented group of writers who write mainly romance, but nonfiction, children's, young adult, horror, sci-fi, paranormal, fantasy, and mystery. Large tape library and critiquing offered. Meetings in Binghamton area.

WESTERN NEW YORK ROMANCE WRITERS INC.
135 Colony Street
Depew, NY 14043
(716) 685-1425

Contact Person: Vera M. Hodge, Membership Coordinator

Annual Dues: $25, general membership; $15 long-distance membership. Members must be actively pursuing or engaged in publishing romance fiction, and must be members of RWA National.

Member Benefits: Monthly meetings and workshops by professionals (agents, authors, editors); access to tape library/reference materials; critique groups; bimonthly newsletter; annual conference in Buffalo (about $45). Being a smaller group offers members a chance to really know one another and be supportive, and makes the chapter a great place to network.

WRITERS & BOOKS
740 University Avenue
Rochester, NY 14607
(716) 473-2590

Contact Person: Joseph Flaherty, Executive Director

Annual Dues: $30.

Member Benefits: Membership into second-largest community-based literary arts organization in the United States. Offers discounts on workshops (one-day and ongoing) taught by published authors; inexpensive writers' retreat house in Finger Lakes hills; readings; social events; support of community services. (Not affiliated with RWA.)

North Carolina

BLUE RIDGE ROMANCE WRITERS
P.O. Box 188
Black Mountain, NC 28711
(704) 669-8421

Contact Person: Yvonne Lehman, President

Annual Dues: None, so far. We take donations as necessary. Members must belong to RWA National.

Member Benefits: Fellowship; encouragement; inspiration; information; critiques; support. About a dozen members have various expertise, from one author who has published 30+ books, to unpublished authors getting up the courage to submit manuscripts to publishers. We enjoy, and benefit from, a varying range of members' accomplishments.

CAROLINA ROMANCE WRITERS
416 Lamar Avenue
Charlotte, NC 28204
(704) 332-8214

Contact Person: Peg Robarchek, Chapter Advisor

Annual Dues: $20, plus membership in RWA National.

Member Benefits: Leads to opportunities for writers as twenty active members offer access to expertise of published authors; monthly newsletter; access to library of educational books and tapes; up-to-date market information; monthly educational programs; critique groups; plotting groups; annual spring conference in Charlotte (cost varies). Since chapter is small, establishing supportive relationships is easy.

LOWER CAPE FEAR CHAPTER RWA
P.O. Box 1153
Long Beach, NC 28465

Contact Person: Whitney Walters, Newsletter Editor

Annual Dues: Must belong to RWA National.

Member Benefits: Great newsletter; support, information, and resources for writers and unpublished authors; informs and educates writers; offers quality information for writers in all genres, so that they can produce marketable work and further their writing careers; brings writers together with editors and agents for the mutual benefit of all.

NORTH CAROLINA WRITERS NETWORK
P.O. Box 954
Carrboro, NC 27510

Annual Dues: $35 regular; $15 fulltime students under 25, senior citizens, or writers with disability. Members are at all stages of writing development.

Member Benefits: Nonprofit literary organization dedicated to helping writers of all levels, wherever they are located. Sponsors workshops and readings. Offers bimonthly newsletter (24–28 pages); reduced fees on many competitions, workshops, and conferences; critique service; opportunity to network with other writers, agents, and editors; two annual conferences (June's cost is free–$25; November's cost is about $100); many writing contests in all genres with cash prizes. (Send SASE to request contest rules/entry forms or conference information.)

Other: Not affiliated with RWA, but is glad to list RWA's local events in their newsletter and annual resource guide.

Ohio

WOMEN FICTION WRITERS ASSOCIATION
609 S. Washington Street
Millersburg, OH 44654
(216) 674-9413

Contact Person: Lorraine A. Moore, President

Annual Dues: $12 plus membership in RWA National.

Member Benefits: This chapter offers monthly meetings, support, critiques, and networking within a small group; members encouraged to reach for their goals. Great Beginnings Contest (first ten pages) is open to all unpublished RWA members (SASE for rules/entry form).

Oregon

CASCADE CHAPTER RWA #59
P.O. Box 30135
Portland, OR 97230
(503) 284-2021

Contact Person: Janet L. Brayson, Treasurer

Annual Dues: $12, plus membership in RWA National.

Member Benefits: Grants access to extensive tape library on writing topics; basic writing series of workshops (10 weeks); quarterly one-day workshops; monthly meetings; 80 friendly members who are willing to help with writing questions.

HEART OF OREGON RWA

1210 Woodside Drive
Eugene, OR 97401
(503) 345-0540 (after 10:00 A.M.)

Contact Person: Suzan Greenlee, Treasurer

Annual Dues: $12, plus membership in RWA National.

Member Benefits: Offers much to writers of all levels of expertise through monthly program and newsletter, workshops, annual first chapter competition for all unpublished RWA members (with full critiques by judges), annual May writing conference (about $140). For conference or contest info, send SASE to Ann Simas, 1140 Waverly Street, Eugene, OR 97401-5235.

MID-WILLAMETTE VALLEY RWA

490 Lochmoor Place
Eugene, OR 97405
(503) 687-8879

Contact Person: Sharon A. Morris, President

Annual Dues: $15 plus membership in RWA National.

Member Benefits: Access to wonderful speakers at our meetings. Every three months, we bring our manuscripts for a group critique—putting into practice what we have learned.

ROMANCE WRITERS OF AMERICA OUTREACH
1140 Waverly Street
Eugene, OR 97401-5235
(503) 485-0583

Contact Person: Ann Simas, RWA Outreach Chairperson

Annual Dues: $20, plus membership in RWA National.

Member Benefits: Outreach offers critiquing contest; Networking-by-Mail Program matches critique partners by mail; resource directory; 20-page bimonthly newsletter; chapter atmosphere via mail for those who don't live near a chapter, or who are looking for more; contest is for Outreach members only.

Pennsylvania

VALLEY FORGE ROMANCE WRITERS
6047 Elmwood Avenue
Philadelphia, PA 19142
(215) 729-6746

Contact Person: Judy Di Canio, President

Annual Dues: $20, plus membership in RWA National.

Member Benefits: Offers writers entrance to informative meetings at Wayne library, presented by a variety of speakers; networking with writers interested in the same goals; monthly newsletter *Romantic Penns;* annual contest (send SASE for rules); support; information.

Tennessee

EAST TENNESSEE ROMANCE WRITERS (ETRW)
60 Lake Shore Lane
Chattanooga, TN 37415

Contact Person: Pat Dieter, President

Annual Dues: $15, plus membership in RWA National.

Member Benefits: Meetings with networking one-on-one with peers and professionals; workshops for beginners; monthly newsletter with publishing industry news; published authors help and advice group; annual conference (cost and location varies).

RIVER CITY ROMANCE WRITERS
RWA #23 (RCRW)
1056 Perkins Terrace
Memphis, TN 38117
(901) 682-7531

Contact Person: Martha Shields, President

Annual Dues: $15, plus membership in RWA National.

Member Benefits: A seriously professional chapter dedicated to helping members become published by offering critique group registry; workshops; chapter library; published author's network; annual writing contest (first chapter) open to any writer; annual March "Duel on the Delta" Conference (about $75). For contest rules, send SASE to Amelia Bomar, 867 Green Acres, Hernandeo, MS 38632.

Texas

AUSTIN WRITERS' LEAGUE
1501 W. 5th Street, Suite E-2
Austin, TX 78703
(512) 499-8914   FAX: (512) 499-0441

Contact Person: Angela Smith, Executive Director

Annual Dues: $40 regular; $35 senior citizen or student.
Members should have an interest in writing.

Member Benefits: Largest regional writing group in Texas with
more than 1,600 members; checkout privileges for 1,000+ titles
on writing and publishing in library/resource center; free workshops; agent-author conference every summer (about $175);
monthly newsletter; monthly meetings/programs; 12+ study
groups in many genres; tour promotions for Texas writers/litera-
ture; resume posting in job bank; Violet Crown Book Awards for
published members. (Not affiliated with RWA.)

NORTHWEST HOUSTON RWA
7086 Edgewater Drive
Willis, TX 77378
(409) 856-8564

Contact Person: Laura Powell, President

Annual Dues: $15, plus membership in RWA National.

Member Benefits: Monthly newsletter; monthly meetings with
informative speakers; yearly one-day workshop and manuscript

critiquing; annual MICA Awards Contest in many categories of romance (SASE for rules/entry form).

ROMANCE WRITERS OF AMERICA— EAST TEXAS CHAPTER #37

P.O. Box 56
Tyler, TX 75710
(503) 531-0104

Contact Person: Vince Brach, President

Annual Dues: $15, plus membership in RWA National.

Member Benefits: Monthly meetings with speakers; participate in critique sessions; conference and contest opportunities (send SASE to request info); fellowship; networking; chapter newsletter. RWA-ETC attracts both published and unpublished authors due to emphasis on excellence and professionalism.

WEST HOUSTON RWA #28

1302 Crystal Hills
Houston, TX 77077-2215
(713) 496-5263

Contact Person: Anne Dykowski, President

Annual Dues: $15, plus membership in RWA National.

Member Benefits: Access to membership that includes 38 active published authors; group is very focused on publication of their romance novels; networking with others familiar with the publishing world; newsletter; tape library; local March conference (about $125); Emily Contest (first chapter) is open to RWA members (SASE for contest rules/entry form).

Virginia

CHESAPEAKE ROMANCE WRITERS (CRW)
P.O. Box 5345
Hampton, VA 23667

Contact Person: W. Michelle Fronheiser, President

Annual Dues: $15.

Member Benefits: Provides a monthly newsletter, market news, audiotape library, monthly meetings with programs geared to help writers at all levels of their careers, and networking with other authors. CRW offers programs to veteran authors as well as the novice. At meetings we have tip sheets, a book exchange, market news sharing, support and motivation. Sponsors annual bookseller's luncheon, First Peake Contest and Last Line Contest (SASE for rules/entry forms), and October conference with editor/speaker from major publishing house (cost is about $50).

VIRGINIA ROMANCE WRITERS

P.O. Box 35
Midlothian, VA 23112
(804) 748-0343

Contact Person: Vickie Lojek, President

Annual Dues: $25, plus membership in RWA National. Members should be actively pursuing a writing career and support romantic fiction.

Member Benefits: Positive energy develops around this active chapter of RWA. Members working together show focus, ability, and leadership. 45% of members are published. Offers monthly newsletter, monthly meetings with great programs, workshops, tapes and books in lending library, critique groups, support of fellow writers, market news, biannual conference in Williamsburg (about $100), Fool for Love Writing Contest for unpublished writers (SASE for contest rules/entry form).

Washington

NORTHWEST WASHINGTON CHAPTER RWA #121

P.O. Box 3496
Arlington, WA 98223

Annual Dues: $12, plus membership in RWA National.

Member Benefits: Monthly meetings with excellent speakers, support of the other members in a close-knit atmosphere, annual "Happily Ever After" Writing Contest (SASE for rules/entry form).

Washington, D.C.

WASHINGTON ROMANCE WRITERS

P.O. Box 21311, Kalorama Station
Washington, D.C. 20009

Contact Person: Mary Kilchenstein, President

Annual Dues: $30, plus membership in RWA National.

Member Benefits: Monthly meetings; critique groups coordination; mentor program; mini-workshops; publishing industry news; day-long conferences; weekend retreat; extensive research library; monthly newsletter; quarterly booksellers newsletter; booksellers' luncheon; annual spring conference in Harper's Ferry, West Virginia (about $280–$300 inclusive of meals and hotel).

Wisconsin

WISCONSIN ROMANCE WRITERS OF AMERICA (WISRWA)

6940 S. Timber Ridge Lane, #10308
Oak Creek, WI 53154

Contact Person: Leslie J. Parker, President

Annual Dues: $30, plus membership in RWA National.

Member Benefits: Great support groups; monthly meetings; critique groups; publishing news; marketing assistance for romance and related genres; networking; bimonthly newsletter; Milwaukee area spring conference (about $80); fall workshop; contest for unpublished writers with deadline of March 1st. (Send SASE for conference or contest information.)

Note: If writer's networks did not mail their updated information in time to meet publication deadlines of this edition, their listing was deleted.

7

Fourteen Little Secrets to Help You Get Published

*D*id you know some romance writer's markets are so secret, they aren't even in this book? That's because editors don't talk about them, and don't solicit for them openly. In fact, the only way you may hear about this secret market is through other writers who may tell you of an opportunity, in the magazine *The Gila Queen's Guide to Markets,* or on an electronic bulletin board.

Secret #1: This secret market is romance anthologies, many published by commercial romance publishers on a seasonal basis, some published by magazines doing a "best of" collection, and some published by small presses that do anthology collections of novellas on a regular basis.

How many times have you been in a bookstore and seen thematic anthologies of short romances by three to five authors, published as a collection of romantic Christmas stories, summer or bride themes, Halloween or Valentine's Day stories? Some publishers also use anthologies to introduce and test the market for a new line, which is what Silhouette Shadows did, before they changed to full length novels in that line.

You may recognize one or two author's names in each anthology, but some will be newcomers or perhaps only have one or two books out.

Short stories and novellas can help writers break into the market. True, some anthologies are by "invitation only," to authors who already write for that house. But it never hurts to send a query letter to either an editor at one of the commercial publishers or to the shorter fiction markets listed in the next section, some of whom regularly do novellas.

Being an author in an anthology won't make you a lot of money. Remember, the royalties are divided between participating authors, although the lead author, whose story is first in the anthology, sometimes receives a bigger percentage. The purpose is to break in, get your name out there, and build up your credibility with readers. A true feather in your cap would be to have a story in an anthology with an author whom readers already know well. Her name draws her readers and will also help them discover you!

Secret #2: Talent isn't enough to succeed. A romance writer has to have perseverance, as well as a big supply of postage stamps and envelopes. Sharon Wagner, a prolific novelist with over 60 published novels, including *Dark Cloister*, always keeps *at least seven* different projects circulating to editors. She started her successful career by writing fiction for magazines and smaller markets, and worked her way up through the different book markets, writing for almost every house, from Avon to Zebra.

The "rule of seven" is a part of her success. This is a secret that will keep you at the keyboard instead of waiting for the mail and fretting about a single project. When an editor calls you and says she wants to buy your book, you'll be able to say "which one?"

Secret #3: Did you know that some rejection letters are really "maybes"? If an editor gives you a detailed critique, immediately write a thank-you letter and ask, if you corrected all the flaws, would she take another look? This technique, originally perfected by used-car salesmen, works for romance writers, too. Sometimes, "no" really means "maybe," except in the bedroom. Remember that.

Secret #4: You may be able to penetrate the romance market by writing romance audioscripts for small companies, writing short stories for magazines, even for the confession markets, where many professional authors make their start.

Secret #5: Enter contests sponsored by magazines and writer's associations. It's often worth the entry fee to get objective feedback on your manuscript. I was a judge for a national contest where the manuscript I loved didn't win the contest. I made comments about the fabulous manuscript, which were forwarded through the contest committee to the author. Judge and unpublished writer then exchanged a couple of letters, encouraging on one side, hopeful on the other. The writer who was a finalist in that contest is now the bestselling romance author of *Shadow Star*, Lori Handeland.

Secret #6: Utilize your connections from within your local writers' association to jumpstart your career. Accessibility to editors can be as simple as volunteering to call them to do an interview or request market news for your association's newsletter. The next thing you know, you may be sending your manuscript or pitching a query to that editor!

Secret #7: Don't break the basic rules. The romance genre has its own unwritten rules, unique characteristics, and plot devices. Readers have certain expectations of a romance novel and you, as the "creative director," need to tailor your manuscript to meet those expectations, while still being original and creative enough to make the story fresh and new.

Submissions have their own rules, too. Editors like to see clean manuscripts, properly formatted, with no typos or staples. And don't forget SASE!

Secret #8: Concentrate on one goal at a time, so that every manuscript is the best work you've ever written. And when you've finished it, send it out and start something else. Immediately!

Secret #9: Female Empowerment. You have a much better chance of selling any material if the heroine isn't co-dependent on the hero. She should have her own dreams and goals that readers can identify with, her own life besides the hero. She is with him because she chooses to be.

Secret #10: Why Editors Love Query Letters. Not only do they go quickly, but the editor can tell if the author is able to express the theme, characters, and plot of the manuscript in a concise, entertaining way, and one that will fit their current needs.

Secret #11: Editor and agent appointments at conferences. It's not enough to have writing talent. Learn how to verbally pitch the gist of your book to agents or editors in two minutes or less. Practice on your critique group or writer friends until you are smooth and sure of yourself.

Your personal connection with an editor or agent at a conference makes a stronger impression than a query letter. Meet people at conferences. Give out your business card and ask questions. Conferences are for networking with people in the business. Get your money's worth.

Remember, you are competing with other authors for the editor's or agent's attention. It doesn't hurt to request seating next to them at luncheons or offer them a ride to the airport after the conference. If you get an appropriate opportunity, ask if they are interested in hearing a quick pitch.

Secret #12: Write down your goals for the next year, as well as the steps you will need to take to attain those goals. Keep to your writing schedule. After all, what is more important, your romance writing career or the dust bunnies in the corners?

Secret #13: Isolated from other writers? Get a modem and get connected! GEnie electronic network and CompuServe both have great electronic bulletin boards. On GEnie you can even talk with editors and get to know their likes and dislikes. Shy? Well, you can lurk, can't you?

Secret #14: Write to authors whose books you've read and enjoyed. They often will send you an informational or promotional newsletter or personal reply to answer your brief questions about the business. An SASE is always polite if you expect a response.

Romance writing is a business where successful authors help their unpublished competitors to succeed. Please remember *that* when you are rich and famous.

Directory of Non-Book Markets

*T*his section includes markets for shorter romantic fiction, such as novellas, novelettes, short stories, confessions for magazines, anthology markets, and audio scripts.

AFFAIRE DE COEUR
3976 Oak Hill Drive
Oakland, CA 94605-4931
(510) 569-5675

Acquisitions: Louise Snead, Publisher

Submissions: Don't query. Send the complete manuscript. Unsolicited manuscripts OK, but simultaneous submissions are not. Don't forget SASE. Average response time is up to 6 months.

Pay Rate: Payment upon publication for first North American serial rights.

Seeking: Contemporary romance, historical, inspirational fiction, or ethnic fiction. Also need romance novel industry news, how-to writer's articles. Word counts are 1,000–2,000.

Tips: We are looking for articles about writing and authors, publishing, and author's bios. Reviews galleys and published novels.

AMELIA, SPSM&H, AND CICADA
329 "E" Street
Bakersfield, CA 93304
(805) 323-4064

Acquisitions: Frederick A. Raborg, Jr., Editor

Submissions: Queries are not necessary. Send the complete manuscript. Unsolicited manuscripts and simultaneous submissions OK. Average response time is 2 weeks to 3 months. For contest rules, send request with SASE.

Pay Rate: Payment upon acceptance; $10 to $35 (see individual magazines under Seeking below). Publishing schedule is about 12 months after acceptance.

Seeking: For *Amelia,* need contemporary romance, mainstream, ethnic, romantic suspense, mystery, western, science fiction. Especially wants excellent romantic science fiction or western with well-constructed characters. Word counts are up to 4,500. Pays $35 for fiction over 2,000 words; $10 per thousand under 2,000 words.

For *Cicada,* We use fiction with an emphasis on the Oriental, especially Japanese, though we have used stories set in China and other Asian locales. All types are welcome to 2,000 words maximum. Payment $10 on publication, plus one copy. (Also uses poetry with Oriental emphasis.)

For *SPSM&H* (stands for Shakespeare, Petrarch, Sidney, Milton, and Hopkins), we use stories with romantic or Gothic themes, to 2,000 words maximum. Especially welcomed are tales that somehow incorporate the sonnet. Payment $10 on publication, plus one copy. (Also uses sonnets and sonnet sequences, experimental or traditional.)

CONTEST DEADLINES AND GUIDELINES

Here are just a few of the contests that we offer. (Send SASE for complete writer's guidelines and details for more than 60 of our annual writing contests.)

Anna B. Jantzen Romantic Poetry Award: Deadline is January 2. $100 prize for best romantic poem, of any type, up to 100 lines. Entry fee: $4.

Amelia Erotic Poetry Award: Deadline is May 1. $100 for best erotic poem, any form to 50 lines. Entry fee: $4 each poem.

Amelia Erotic Fiction Award: Deadline is July 1. $100 is offered for best short story, any type, to 3,000 words, with an erotic theme. Entry fee: $5.

Amelia Romantic Fiction Award: Deadline is October 1. $100 for best romantic fiction up to 2,000 words. Entry fee: $5.

BLACK SECRETS/JIVE/INTIMACY

Sterling/Macfadden, Inc.
233 Park Avenue South, 5th Floor
New York, NY 10003
(212) 780-3500

Acquisitions: M. Mahon, Editor

Submissions: Don't query. Send the complete manuscript. Unsolicited submissions are OK. Usual response time is 2 months.

Pay Rate: $75 per standard confession story; $100–$125 for special features and service articles; $50 for reprints. Payment is after publication. Buys first North American serial rights/all rights.

Seeking: Confessions, romantic suspense, ethnic, and poetry.

Tips: Send interesting love stories. Endings should be happy or sad.

Turn-offs/Taboos: No stories about rape, incest, murder; no depressing stories. Please don't submit stories with more than two love scenes.

Editor's Wish List: I would like to see stronger heroines.

Writer's Guidelines

For *Jive, Intimacy,* and *Black Secrets* magazines, we strive for the stories to lean toward romantic lines. This does not mean that the stories should not have true-to-life experience plots. We simply want to project romance, love, and togetherness, rather than to overwhelm our readers with violence or anything too depressing.

Make the stories believable. We do not want to deviate from reality. All endings cannot be happy ones, but we want to try, whenever possible, to cast an optimistic outlook.

Hopefully, you can follow these guidelines and will soon be sending in your manuscripts. There is no limit to how many you can submit at one time. It is good to submit material as frequently as you can, so that outlines for upcoming months can be made. However, if you send us an excessive amount of manuscripts to evaluate, you must be patient, for it will take a longer period of time to get back to you. Here are the guidelines:

1. Stories must be written from a young, black, female perspective with romance in mind. (This is not to discourage male writers.)
2. Stories must be true-to-life confessions with interesting plots.

3. Stories need to exude an aura of romance.
4. Stories should have at least two descriptive love scenes. Each should be one page in length.
5. Stories must be written in the first-person voice of the heroine.
6. Stories should be written in the past tense, but keep action current.
7. Stories must be typed and double-spaced, with each page numbered and identified either with your name or the title of the work.
8. Each manuscript should follow a professional manuscript format—including your name, address, and a daytime phone number.
9. Stories should be 18–20 pages.

Allow at least 2 months for confirmation of acceptance or rejection.

GUIDELINES FOR WRITING LOVE SCENES

All stories must have two love scenes. They should be romantic in nature and they should allude to the couple making love. Do not use graphic description. Describe the feelings and thoughts of the heroine at that moment.

In the case of writing love scenes for us, less is best! Use tags to describe an act of love. Consult *The Romance Writer's Phrase Book* by Jean Kent and Candace Shelton. This is an excellent workbook for obtaining romantic tags and getting an idea of how to keep them more romantic than sexual. Love scenes should be light, romantic, and should have an air of magic/fantasy about them.

We'd also like to see a bit more of the psychological aspect of the couple's romantic encounters, e.g., how the woman feels after it is over, how it will affect their relationship, how the man is affected, and so on.

In our quest to give our publications a more romantic look, we must enlist the help of our writers. We look forward to working with you.

BYLINE
P.O. Box 130596
Edmond, OK 73013
(405) 348-5591

Acquisitions: Kathryn Fanning, Managing Editor, reads fiction and nonfiction. Betty Shipley is Poetry Editor.

Submissions: Don't query. Send complete manuscripts. Include phone number. SASE a must or no response. Double-space manuscripts, no right justification, no variety of fonts.

Pay Rate: Payment upon acceptance. $100 for fiction; $50 for advice features; fillers $15–$35; poetry $5–$10. Buys first North American serial rights. Also sponsors four contests per month (small entry fees). SASE for contest details.

Seeking: All types of fiction, including romantic suspense, confessions, contemporary romance, ethnic, fantasy, futuristic, historical, inspirational, mainstream, mystery, paranormal, poetry, western, thriller. 2,000–4,000 words, please. Also need advice features of 1,500–1,800 words. Stories will not be read if longer than specified.

Tips: We like all types of fiction, but prefer no writing theme since our articles and poetry must have a writing theme for variety's sake.

Turn-offs/Taboos: No obscene language, graphic sex, abuse, AIDS, alcoholism, class reunions.

Editor's Wish List: We love sensory detail, figures of speech, conflict and a change in the central character at the end of the story. Send for guidelines before submitting (SASE). We buy from new and veteran writers alike.

DEAD OF NIGHT
916 Shaker Road, Suite 228
Longmeadow, MA 01106-2416

Acquisitions: Lin Stein, Editor

Submissions: Closed to submissions until 1/1/96. After then, don't query but send complete manuscripts with SASE.

Pay Rate: For fiction, 4–7¢ per word (up to $150) for first North American serial rights, plus a one-time reprint right, in case we decide to do a "best of" issue in the future. Payments mailed on quarterly basis.

Seeking: Horror, fantasy, mystery and sci-fi in a different vein. Besides general fiction, specializes in vampire-related fiction (may be allegorical and fangless), including romantic suspense, fantasy, and thriller. SASE for detailed guidelines. Sample copy for $4.

Turn-offs/Taboos: Abundance of elves, unicorns, dragons.

GLIMMER TRAIN PRESS
812 S.W. Washington Street, #1205
Portland, OR 97205

Acquisitions: Linda Davies, Co-President

Submissions: For regular submissions, send complete manuscript during the months of January, April, July, and October. Simultaneous submissions are OK. Include SASE for response.

To enter the $1,200 plus publication Short Story Contest for New Writers during February/March or August/September, writers who haven't had their fiction appear in a national publication with circulation over 5,000, can send $11 entry fee and one or two stories in same envelope. Staple the contest entries, type name, address, and phone on first page of each story only, no SASE. Winners will be telephoned. All entrants receive a copy of the issue containing the winning entry.

Pay Rate: $500 upon acceptance, for first publication rights and nonexclusive anthology rights.

Seeking: Mainstream fiction of 1,200–7,500 words.

Turn-offs/Taboos: Don't send stories with heavy dialect, story fragments, poetry, children's stories, or nonfiction.

I'LL TAKE ROMANCE!

P.O. Box 22-0380
Brooklyn, NY 11222-0380
FAX: (718) 349-3946

Acquisitions: Charlene Keel, Editor-in-Chief

Submissions: Send complete manuscript with SASE and cover letter with phone number.

Seeking: Blue Ribbon Fiction (a regular feature) features short romantic stories that inspire and touch the heart. Good place for beginners to break into the market.

LH PRODUCTIONS

P.O. Box 3205
Guttenburg, NJ 07093
(201) 662-1064

Acquisitions: Linda Hurwitz, Executive Director

Submissions: Send complete short story with SASE and cover letter. New authors, unsolicited manuscripts, and writers without agents are encouraged.

Pay Rate: Advances and royalty figures are confidential.

Seeking: Contemporary romance, mainstream, romantic suspense, and thrillers of approximately 8,000–10,000 words.

Tips: We are looking for sensual or sexy romances that offer the listener a brief romantic escape on 30-minute audiotape.

Turn-offs/Taboos: Graphic violence, rape, incest.

Editor's Wish List: Well-written sensually charged short stories that can be read by a man to a female listener.

LH Productions Writer's Guidelines

LH Productions is a young audio publishing company actively seeking short stories. Stories should be approximately 8,000–10,000 words (about 30 minutes). Two 30-minute stories comprise a one-hour audio cassette. Offerings include work from both published and unpublished authors and represent original stories as well as those previously printed.

We are interested in contemporary romances. They can range from thrillers to stories dealing with everyday issues and situations in a manner that is exciting and erotically and emotionally satisfying. When the story ends, the reader should feel positive.

LH Productions wishes to offer the listener a brief romantic escape. The listener is a sophisticated woman of the 90s. She may be a traveling businesswoman or a busy homemaker. Often, she may not be a romance reader. In any case, she is a woman with little free time. She wants to relax and enjoy a short fantasy interlude.

To add to the sensual or sexy mood, stories will be read by a man only. A challenge to our authors, where possible, is to write a story that can be read by the man as the woman would like to hear it. In any event we want authors to use their imaginations and expand the boundaries of contemporary romance.

We are looking for well-written short stories that take risks and stretch traditional guidelines. They should be sensually and erotically charged. Good examples found in full-length published stories are Suzanne Forster's *Come Midnight,* Joan Hohl's *Compromises,* and Catherine Coulter's *Impulse.*

LYNX EYE

ScribbleFest Literary Group
1880 Hill Drive
Los Angeles, CA 90041
(213) 550-8522

Acquisitions: Pam McCully, Co-Editor

Submissions: Don't query. Send complete manuscripts with SASE. Simultaneous submissions OK with notification.

Pay Rate: $10 per piece, plus five copies of *Lynx Eye.*

Seeking: All well-written work, including contemporary romance, ethnic, fantasy, futuristic, historical, inspirational, mainstream, mystery, paranormal, poetry, romantic suspense, thriller, and western fiction. Also seeking essay/social commentary. Word counts are 5,000 maximum.

Lynx Eye Writer's Guidelines

Thank you for your interest in *Lynx Eye* and ScribbleFest Literary Group. ScribbleFest is a new organization dedicated to the development and promotion of the literary arts, whether new or established, by providing a showcase for your work.

Each issue of *Lynx Eye* includes short fiction, essays, poetry, and artwork. Prose should be 500–5,000 words. Poetry should be 30 lines or less. Our format is 5.5" × 8.5" so artwork should not exceed 4" × 6". If you have an excellent piece of work, send it. Also, each issue contains the special feature "Presenting": in which an unpublished writer or artist makes their print debut.

Never-before-published works only. We acquire first North American serial rights to your work. All other rights remain with you. We pay $10 per piece upon acceptance. You also receive five copies of the issues in which your work appears.

Manuscripts must be typed. Dot matrix or photocopies OK, but must be legible. Artwork must be camera ready. Include your phone number. SASE for reply from us. If you need confirmation that we have received your submission, also include a self-addressed stamped postcard. We are committed to the written word and anxiously await reading yours.

MODERN ROMANCES
233 Park Avenue, South
New York, NY 10003
(212) 979-4800   FAX: (212) 979-7342

Acquisitions: Eileen Fitzmaurice, Editor

Submissions: Never query first. Send the complete manuscript with SASE. Unsolicited manuscripts are OK, but simultaneous submissions are not acceptable. Response time is about 9 months.

Pay Rate: Payment for stories is upon publication at the rate of 5¢ per word; $2 per line for poetry. We buy all rights.

Seeking: Confessions, contemporary romance, inspirational, mainstream, poetry, romantic suspense. All stories are to be written in first-person viewpoint. We also buy nonfiction.

Tips: Of course, read the magazine! Know your market and write accordingly.

Turn-offs/Taboos: Graphic language, sexist topics, overdone themes.

Editor's Wish List: Short well-written stories. Our narrators/readers are strong-minded individuals with traditional beliefs. Traditional people in nontraditional situations.

Modern Romances Guidelines

Thank you for your interest in *Modern Romances* magazine. We would like to see your work. However, we do not issue "official" guidelines. As an alternative, we suggest that you read several issues of the magazine for an idea of the style of stories we print.

Manuscripts should be typed, double-spaced, and between 2,500 and 12,000 words. Only those stories offering us all rights and written in the first person will be considered.

Subject matter can be anything from light romance to current social concerns that would be of interest to our readers. Each manuscript we receive will be considered and a reply will be sent to you between 3 to 9 months after we receive your work. We do not acknowledge receipt of manuscripts. Please enclose a SASE for your manuscript's return.

We also accept light romantic poetry, such as love poems or poems with a holiday/seasonal theme. Maximum length, 24 lines. Payment of poems is based on merit.

We look forward to reading your story. Best of luck!

MURDEROUS INTENT
Madison Publishing Company
P.O. Box 5947
Vancouver, WA 98668-5947

Acquisitions: Margo Power, Editor/Publisher

Submissions: Please send a cover letter and brief publishing bio with your manuscript. Send hard copy (paper) now and be prepared to supply a computer disk with your story saved in ASCII text on acceptance. Don't forget SASE if return is desired. We will assist you in preparing the disk if needed. Please observe all manuscript conventions, using double-spaced text, one side of the page only on white bond paper with 1" margins all around, and dark readable type (on hard copy) in 12 pt. Courier font. Never send the only copy of your manuscript.

Pay Rate: Fiction or nonfiction, payment for first North American serial rights is $10, plus two free contributor's copies per story or article, on acceptance. Occasionally pays more for nonfiction. Author will be expected to sign a contract stating that the work is original and that she/he is the author. Reprints are acceptable if author states such at time of submission and author owns reprint rights. Send clips of previous publications, including publication date and name of magazine. Fillers pay $2.

Seeking: Mystery, romantic suspense (with emphasis on suspense). Word counts are 2,000–4,000 words, occasionally to 6,000 words. Also, annual mystery contest with cash prize and publication for winners.

Tips: Write good stories from the heart and send them in.

Turn-offs/Taboos: Husband kills wife/wife kills husband—we get way too many. True crime, excessive violence, foul language, explicit sex.

Editor's Wish List: Humorous mysteries—more mystery/ suspense in 2,000–4,000 word length. We love stories with a good sense of character, location, and ethnicity.

Murderous Intent Writer's Guidelines

Muderous Intent, a magazine of mystery and suspense, is a quarterly magazine targeting the readers and writers of mystery/ suspense who not only want to be entertained, but challenged.

Fiction: Send us only your best short stories, no longer than 6,000 words (we prefer 2,000–4,000). Short shorts considered and we are actively seeking 250–500 word flash mysteries that have a beginning, middle and twist ending. We will also consider cross-genre mysteries (i.e. horror, sci-fi, romance) if the strongest emphasis is on the mystery/suspense. Give at least a hint of the mystery on the first page and keep suspense high. Plot and character are of equal importance.

Nonfiction: We are looking for articles (no longer than 4,000 words) applicable to writing or reading mysteries. For example, articles covering forensics, police procedures, district attorneys and how their offices operate, weaponry, crime scenes, medical examiners, private investigators, criminal defense lawyers, DNA testing, and so on. We are open to anything pertaining to the mystery field but the articles must be authentic and you must include sources. Rarely, we may consider a true crime article. Fillers are mystery related cartoons, poetry, etc.

Subscriptions are $15 per year for four intriguing, unputdownable issues. For a sample copy of *Muderous Intent,* send five first-class stamps and $3.95.

MYSTERY TIME—HUTTON PUBLICATIONS
P.O. Box 2907
Decatur, IL 62524

Acquisitions: Linda Hutton, Editor

Submissions: Don't query. Send complete manuscript with SASE. All envelopes must be typed.

Pay Rate: $5 upon acceptance for first rights.

Seeking: Mystery, romantic suspense, thrillers, and poetry under 1,500 words.

Rotten Romance Contest—Annual deadline February 14th post-
mark. Cash prize for the best or worst opening sentence
(original) of a romance novel you *never* wrote, no length
limit. Submit typed with SASE. No entry fee; one entry per
person. Type all envelopes.

Mystery Mayhem Contest—Annual deadline Agatha Christie's
birthday, September 15th. Cash prize for best or worst
opening sentence of the mystery novel you *never* wrote, no
length limit. Submit typed, with SASE. No entry fee; one
entry per person. Winner will be published in *Mystery
Time.* Type all envelopes.

Tips: We favor women protagonists, especially older women.
Avoid excessive gore and violence. A touch of humor is always
welcome.

Turn-offs/Taboos: Cover letter touting author's previous publications.

Editor's Wish List: Beautifully typed manuscripts with no
coffee-cup stains on any page.

NEW ENGLAND WRITERS' NETWORK
P.O. Box 483, 175 Fifth Avenue, #2001
Hudson, MA 01749-0483

Acquisitions: Liz Aleshire, Fiction Editor; Judy Baker, Poetry
Editor; Glenda Baker, Editor-in-Chief and Nonfiction Editor

Submissions: Fiction and essay submissions are only accepted
between June 1–August 31st. Submissions at other times will be
returned. Poetry may be sent anytime. Don't query. Send entire
manuscript in proper format with SASE.

Pay Rate: $10 for short stories; poetry and essays paid in copies.
Buys one-time North American serial rights at the time of acceptance, which revert to the author upon publication.

Seeking: Encouraging submissions of novel excerpts (under 2,000 words), as well as any type of short fiction (under 2,000 words), personal essays up to 1,000 words, and poetry up to 32 lines. We briefly critique all manuscripts sent to us, so enclose SASE with adequate postage to do so.

Turn-offs/Taboos: If submitting a novel excerpt, do not send entire novel; we'll just return it unread. The editors will not pick the excerpt for you. It's up to the author to determine which 2,000 words can semi-stand alone. (Send along a 50-word or less synopsis with the novel excerpt.) No suicide or depressing stories or poems. No pornography. Writers must adhere to length guidelines. No previously published material.

Editor's Wish List: Our mission is to educate, encourage, and inspire—especially novice writers. We are looking for quality writing in any genre.

NEW MYSTERY
175 Fifth Avenue
New York, NY 10010

Acquisitions: Linda Wong, Editor

Submissions: Unsolicited manuscripts are OK. Send short story with cover letter and SASE ($1.24 postage on 9" x 12" envelope).

Pay Rate: $25–$1,000.

Seeking: Mystery, romantic suspense, thrillers, and book reviews of 3,000–5,000 words.

Tips: Read the magazine; $27.77 a year for 4 issues.

Editor's Wish List: Sympathetic character in terrible trouble.

PEOPLENET

P.O. Box 897
Levittown, NY 11756-0911

Acquisitions: Robert Mauro, Editor/Publisher

Submissions: Unsolicited manuscripts OK. SASE please.

Pay Rate: 1¢ per word.

Seeking: Disabled and romance fiction of about 500 words or
less. Each story must have a man or woman with a disability as
the primary character. No sob stories or "super crip" stories, just
stories about love, trust, and acceptance. Also accepts nonfiction
articles about disabled adults who find, keep, and enjoy a loving
relationship.

Tips: Name and address in upper-left corner of the first page of
your story. Number all pages and double-space.

A PLACE TO ENTER

1328 Broadway, Suite 1054
New York, NY 10001

Acquisitions: Odessa Drayton, Executive Editor

Submissions: Don't query. Send complete manuscript with
cover letter and SASE. Unsolicited OK. Double-spaced a must.
Include preliminary page stating author's name, approximate
word count, address, and phone number. Reports in 10–12
weeks. No simultaneous submissions.

Pay Rate: $50 a story, upon publication, plus one copy of magazine. Buys first North American serial rights. Byline and short bio given.

Seeking: Contemporary fiction, contemporary romance, and ethnic romance by emerging writers of African descent. We prefer 6,000 words but will accept up to 10,000 maximum.

Tips: We get two categories of submissions: ready and not yet ready. The difference between the two is the time invested in editing, stripping, and tightening the manuscript. Invest the time and increase your chances of being published dramatically. We acquire 16–25 manuscripts per year. Sample copies are $8.50.

Editor's Wish List: We publish only short fiction. *A Place to Enter* is a quarterly journal featuring short fiction by writers of African descent. We do accept novel excerpts that conform to our length and other requirements.

PLOT MAGAZINE
P.O. Box 1351
Sugar Land, TX 77487-1351

Acquisitions: Christina Russell, Managing Editor

Submissions: Unsolicited material is OK, with SASE. Simultaneous submissions OK with notification. Reports within 90 days.

Pay Rate: $10, plus contributor's copy. Buys first North American serial rights, which revert to author upon publication.

Seeking: Short stories in the genres of suspense, fantasy, science fiction, and horror.

Tips: We exist to encourage new and emerging genre writers.

PRISONERS OF THE NIGHT

MKASHEF Enterprises
P.O. Box 688
Yucca Valley, CA 92286-0688

Acquisitions: Alayne Gelfland, Editor-in-Chief

Submissions: Query first by letter or send unsolicited manuscripts. Manuscripts are only read September 15th through March 31st, and the sooner you submit after September 15th, the better your chances of consideration; waiting until February or March will pretty much cancel your chances for consideration. During the non-reading period, no submissions will be responded to, though guidelines are always available. Always include appropriate sized SASE. A computer disk plus hard copy is OK in WordPerfect 4.2 or 5.1 or ASCII files. Hard copies must be sent even if you include a disk copy. No simultaneous submissions. Proper manuscript form includes double-spaced pages, numbered consecutively, and your name and address on the first page of the manuscript. (See Writer's Digest's *Novel and Short Story Market,* for an example.)

Pay Rate: 1¢ per word for fiction; $5 per poem; $10 for art.

Seeking: All stories based on vampire-related themes, especially fantasy, futuristic, historical, mystery, paranormal, romantic suspense, and thrillers.

Tips: Study my guidelines carefully and/or read the magazine. Be original! POTN stresses the romanticism of vampires, rather than the horror aspects. Past, present, and future settings, as well as sci-fi elements, are all welcome. 1,500–5,000 words is the preferred length, but longer stories (not over 10,000 words) will also be considered.

Turn-offs/Taboos: Stereotypes, AIDS, ghosts, werewolves, hitchhikers, stranded motorists saved by vampires from nearby convenient castles, bars, singles clubs, prostitution or sleazy sex, "counts," and "countesses." No media related characters from Star Trek, Lestat, etc.

Editor's Wish List: Unique, inventive, provocative, original visions of the vampire. Strong plot, emotional substance, richness of atmosphere both physical and metaphysical, depth of character, and enticing sensuousness. Sensuous can refer to the way light plays across a satin bed cover, wind blowing through hair, a scent on the wind, the feel of a hand against a cheek.

PUBLISHERS SYNDICATION INTERNATIONAL
1377 K Street, N.W., Suite 856
Washington, D.C. 20005

Acquisitions: A. P. Samuels, Editor; Mary Staub, Sleuth Editor (See Writer's Guidelines)

Media Type: Paperback, Hardcover, *The Post*, Novelettes.

Submissions: Send complete manuscripts, including word count and SASE. Unsolicited and unagented manuscripts are OK. New authors are encouraged. No simultaneous submissions. No phone calls from agents. Specify computer type, disk size and density, and word processing program used, in case a disk copy of the story is requested. Usual response time is 4–6 weeks, sometimes longer. SASE is required for return.

Pay Rate: Upon acceptance; 1–4¢ a word, plus royalty. Byline is given. (Sleuth novelettes pay 3/4–3¢ a word.)

Seeking: Romantic adventures of 9,250 words (approximately), buys 12/yr.; mystery/suspense of 9,250 words (approximately), buys 12/yr.; romance of 30,000 words (approximately), buys 12/yr.; miscellaneous subjects of 30,000 words (approximately), buys 12/yr.; mystery of 30,000 words (approximately), buys 12/yr.;

and "Sleuth" novelettes of 10,000 words. (See Writer's Guidelines for additional information.)

Tips: Romances should not contain explicit sex, as they are for a general audience. Mysteries should be similar to Sherlock Holmes. No blood and guts violence.

"Sleuth" novelettes are solved by the reader, who has a choice of multiple suspects. Solution and justification for solution should be typed on a separate page. Include pencil sketches of floor plans or street maps that will involve the reader.

Publishers Syndication International Writer's Guidelines

Pays on acceptance plus royalty. Byline given. Reports in average of 4–6 weeks, sometimes longer. SASE required for return. Will buy first time manuscripts if good enough. Photocopies OK. No simultaneous submissions, please. Prefer letter quality printing.

THE POST

Mystery/suspense of 9,250 words; romantic adventure of 9,250 words. No explicit sex, gore, sadism, or horror. Manuscripts must be for a general audience. Just good plain storytelling with a unique plot. Constant booze, chain smoking, or swearing are not necessary to a well-written, action-filled story.

Some stories of 4,500 words are considered if they are exceptional.

Post pays 1–4¢ per word on acceptance, plus royalty.

NOVELETTES

Romance of 30,000 words (no explicit sex); mystery of 30,000 words; miscellaneous subjects of 30,000 words.

Novelettes pay 3/4–3¢ per word on acceptance. Show word count on submissions. (The type of mystery we are looking for is devoid of references that might offend. Sherlock Holmes would be a good example of the type of mysteries we require.)

SLEUTH

Sleuth requires mysteries that involve the reader. A story may contain one or two pencil diagrams: a street map with placement of figures pertinent to the story, floor plans, seating arrangements, etc. The reader must solve the mystery. Your solution to the mystery and reasoning should be on a separate page. Remember you need multiple obvious suspects.

Submit the entire manuscript. Reports in 4–8 weeks. Byline is given. SASE please. Pays on acceptance. Length is 10,000 words and pay is ³⁄₄–3¢ per word. No simultaneous submissions please. Show word count. No blood and gore. Looking for good mysteries that convert the reader into a detective.

PULPHOUSE: A FICTION MAGAZINE
Box 1227
Eugene, OR 97440

Acquisitions: Dean Wesley Smith, Editor

Submissions: Unsolicited manuscripts are OK. Send entire manuscript with SASE, or they are tossed. Response time is 1 month.

Pay Rate: 4–7¢ per word.

Seeking: Romantic suspense, romance, fantasy, futuristic, mainstream, mystery, paranormal, thriller, western fiction of 50–7,000 words. We publish short stories, novelettes, and novellas in our magazine.

We also use controversial, innovative, futuristic slanted nonfiction up to 5,000 words. We consider general topics, interviews, breaking news, and any ideas that will interest both a sci-fi and mass-market audience. For articles, query first. Payment varies for nonfiction.

Tips: We like science fiction, fantasy, and horror and fiction that combines those genres. We like mysteries, suspense, romance, western, and mainstream fiction, too. We like well-written stories, clean easy-to-read manuscripts, and SASEs of appropriate sizes. A high-quality photocopy is fine. So is letter-quality dot matrix.

Include a cover letter. We're friendly editors, honest, and we like to know whose work we're considering. A two paragraph letter is nice, but don't tell us about the story. Let the story tell us about the story.

Turn-offs/Taboos: Slow openings.

Editor's Wish List: Stories with an edge. The magazine will tell you more about us. Pick up a copy at a newsstand or subscribe, $15 a year/4 issues; $19 a year, Canadian and overseas subscriptions. In the fall of 1995, we will launch two new magazines, *Abrupt Edge, a Magazine of Horror and Dark Fantasy,* and *Mean Streets, The Magazine of Mystery and Suspense.* We want to hear from talented writers in those genres as well.

RADIANCE, THE MAGAZINE FOR LARGE WOMEN

Box 30246
Oakland, California 94604
(510) 482-0680

Acquisitions: Alice Ansfield, Editor/Publisher; Catherine Taylor, Senior Editor; Carol Squires, Assistant Editor

Submissions: Authors may query first by letter or FAX, or send complete manuscript. Unagented and unsolicited are OK. Average response time is 3 months.

Pay Rate: Upon publication, writer receives contributor copy plus $15–$50 for fiction, image articles, poetry; book reviews $35–$75; features/profiles $50–$100. Payment can increase once we develop a good working relationship with a writer and can count on your professionalism, service, quality, and reliability.

Seeking: Contemporary romance, inspirational, mainstream, and poetry. Fiction is 1,500–3,000 words and themes focus on body image, health, well-being, food and eating, work, politics, fashion, cultural attitudes, self-esteem, and acceptance.

Other topics are nonfiction profiles (interviews or first-person accounts relating to life as a large woman). We like strong, intimate, in-depth profiles about a person's life and philosophy.

Tips: Read our magazine before submitting anything. See what our focus is, our tone, our philosophy. See how your writing and ideas can enhance our magazine's mission and purpose.

Turn-offs/Taboos: Nothing too preachy, sentimental, unsubtle, religious (dogmatic).

Editor's Wish List: Inspiring stories about women all sizes of large, finding themselves, fulfilling their dreams, their love, their lives. Empowerment themes. Confronting obstacles.

Radiance Writer's Guidelines

Radiance is a quarterly magazine now celebrating its tenth year in print with more than 50,000 readers worldwide. Its target audience is the one woman in four who wears a size 16 or over—an estimated 30 million women in America alone. *Radiance* brings a fresh, vital new voice to women all sizes of large with our positive images, profiles of dynamic large women from all walks of life, and our compelling articles on health, media, fashion, and politics. We urge women to feel good about themselves now—whatever their body size. *Radiance* is one of the leading resources in the "size acceptance movement," linking large women to the network of products, services, and information just for them.

DEPARTMENTS

Up Front and Personal: Interviews or first-person accounts relating to life as a large woman from all walks of life. We like strong, intimate, in-depth profiles about a person's life and philosophy.

Health and Well-Being: Articles on health, fitness, emotional well-being related to women in general and large women in particular. Also profiles of healthcare professionals sensitive to the needs of large women. Articles on food and cooking.

Perspectives: Cultural, historical, and social views of body size and female beauty.

Expressions: Interviews with artists who are either large themselves or whose work features large-sized women.

Getaways: Travel articles on vacation spots, getaways of all types anywhere in the world. Prefer if article somehow includes ideas or special tips for women of size.

On the Move: Articles about plus-sized women who are involved in some sort of sport or physical activity.

Images: Interviews with designers or manufacturers of plus-sized clothing or accessories. Prefer if the store/designer caters to women all sizes of large, i.e., includes "supersize" women over size 26. Can also be articles on color, style, wardrobe planning, and accessories.

Inner Journeys: Articles on personal growth and inner-directed approaches to feeling better about oneself. Can be profiles of people doing this work or general information.

Book Reviews: Books relating to women, body image, health, eating, politics, psychology, media, fashion, cultural attitudes, and so on.

Short Stories and Poetry: Related to body size, self-acceptance. Especially want fiction or poetry that is more than the "woman hates self until meets man to love her" type of writing.

DEADLINES FOR SUBMISSION
Winter, June 15; Spring, September 15; Summer, December 15;
Fall. March 15.

TO WRITERS
Query us far in advance of the deadline if you want assurance
that your articles will be considered for a particular issue. Our
usual response is about 3 months. Include your name, address,
and phone number on the title page and type your name and
phone number on subsequent pages. Keep a copy of anything
you submit to us. Remember to indicate availability of photos,
artwork, illustrations (or ideas for them), in your query or with
your article. High-quality photos or art can greatly enhance an
article's desirability. If you do send photos, please make sure they
are marked with a caption and the photographer's name, phone,
and address.

    At this time, payment is made on publication. We intend to
pay upon acceptance in the near future. And as we grow, we will
continue to increase payment to writers, photographers, illustrators, etc. We appreciate and value your work.

RAVEN'S TALE
Graphic Knight Publications
57910 Apple Lane
New Hudson, MI 48165

Acquisitions: (Mr.) Gerry Zelenak, Managing Editor

Submissions: Don't query. Send unsolicited manuscript with
cover letter and SASE. Manuscripts are to be double-spaced and
follow general guidelines found in *The Writer's Market*. We also
accept electronic submissions on IBM compatible 3 1/2" disks.

Pay Rate: $10 per story; $5 for poetry. Buys first North
American serial rights. We also buy one-time reprint rights to

material that has been published elsewhere. All rights revert to author upon publication.

Seeking: Although our main audience is horror and fantasy fans, we are interested in romance stories within those genres, especially fantasy, futuristic, mystery, romantic suspense, thriller, and horror fiction of 5,000 words or less. Also buys artwork (pen and ink) and poetry.

Turn-offs/Taboos: No love poetry or sugarcoated poems. No pornography.

Editor's Wish List: A sword and sorcerer story with a strong female lead. A story that will scare our readers to death while falling in love with the hero/heroine.

RED HERRING MYSTERY MAGAZINE
P.O. Box 8278
Prairie Village, KS 66208
(913) 642-1503

Acquisitions: Donna Trombla, Editor

Submissions: Query first. Submit complete short story manuscript with cover letter containing author bio and SASE. One story per submission. Advise editor if story is simultaneous submission. Submit seasonal stories 6 months in advance. If your story is accepted, we will request a copy on Macintosh or IBM 3 1/2" disk in Word Perfect, Word, QuarkExpress, or PageMaker.

Pay Rate: $5, plus contributor copy, paid upon publication. Stories are published 3–12 months after acceptance. Reprint rights revert to author 3 months after publication.

Seeking: *Red Herring* publishes mystery and romantic suspense (maximum 6,000 words). We are also seeking contemporary romance, ethnic, fantasy, historical, mainstream, mystery, romantic suspense, and literary essays of up to 3,500 words for our literary magazine, *Potpourri,* a not-for-profit publication that pays in author copies. (Same address as *Red Herring,* but *Potpourri's* editor is Polly Swafford.)

Tips: Editors seek well-developed, thought-provoking mystery fiction with well-crafted character development. Send only your best work.

Turn-offs/Taboos: No gratuitous sex. No violence. No true crime.

Editor's Wish List: Entertaining, well-written stories with a variety of new and different plots.

RED SAGE PUBLISHING, INC.
P.O. Box 4311
Seminole, FL 34645
(813) 391-3847

Acquisitions: Alexandria Kendall, Senior Editor

Submissions: We are accepting novella submissions from 15,000-25,000 words for an anthology. Query first with a one-page synopsis (clear emotional and physical conflict defined) and the first 10 pages of the story. Please include writing credentials, but we do welcome unpublished authors. SASE for response and return of your submission.

Pay Rate: $50 advance plus a percentage on novellas editions.

Seeking: Contemporary romance, ethnic, fantasy, futuristic, historical, mainstream, mystery, paranormal, romantic suspense, thriller, and western fiction.

Tips: Character-driven, highly sensual to erotic novels.

Turn-offs/Taboos: We can't publish over 25,000 words in length. Don't send full-length novels.

Editor's Wish List: Excellent writing! Great characterization and creative and fun sensuality—this doesn't mean sensuality can't be intense.

Red Sage Writer's Guidelines

Sensuous, bold, spicy, untamed, hot, and sometimes politically incorrect, *Secrets* stories concentrate on the sophisticated highly intense, adult relationship. These character-driven stories always concentrate on the love and sexual relationship between the hero and heroine.

Hero: He may be the fearsome warrior, the rogue, the conqueror, or the imposing captain of industry. He's always intelligent, good-looking, usually rich, may be humorous, larger-than-life, strong-willed, domineering in a sexy way, and very much the ultra alpha male. He is the kind of man who epitomizes every woman's fantasies and is a devastatingly wonderful lover.

Heroine: She may be the Indian captive, lady of the manor, CEO of a corporation, or a traveler to distant stars. She is, above all, intelligent. She has strength, femininity, and independence. She may be humorous. She is a woman the reader likes and identifies with.

Relationship: We are searching for romance authors who dare to go where today's romance authors are forbidden to go. Highly intense love relationships involve an equally intense sexual relationship, that is sometimes politically incorrect. We are looking for a high level of sexual tension throughout the story to maintain the necessary edge and arousing feel. These love scenes should be sophisticated, erotic, and emotional.

Plot: The more difficult or intriguing the conflict, the more interesting the story. Tension and conflict can make love scenes excruciatingly effective. Always a happy ending.

Setting: Historical, contemporary, mainstream, science fiction, mystery, adventure, fantasy—let your imagination be your guide.

ROSEBUD

P.O. Box 459
Cambridge, WI 53523
(608) 423-9609   FAX: (608) 423-4394

Acquisitions: Rod Clark, Editor

Submissions: Submissions may be unpublished or previously
published, provided the author retains the rights to resell.
Submissions must be double-spaced with author's name at the
top of each page. Please allow 10–12 weeks for response. Upon
acceptance, author will be asked to send a disk if available.

Pay Rate: $45 plus two extra copies.

Seeking: This quarterly seeks contemporary romance and
ethnic romance, as well as general short stories, articles of
1,200–1,800 words, and poems that fit loosely into one of the following categories:

City and Shadow (urban settings)
Songs of Suburbia (suburban themes)
These Green Hills (nature and nostalgia)
En Route (any type of travel)
Mothers, Daughters, Wives (relationships)
Ulysses' Bow (manhood)
Paper, Scissors, Rock (childhood, middle age, old age)
The Jeweled Prize (concerning love)
Lost and Found (loss and discovery)
Voices in Other Rooms (historic or of other cultures)
Overtime (involving work)
Anything Goes (humor) 300–600 words
I Hear Music (music)
Season to Taste (food)
Word Jazz (wordplay) 300–600 words
Apples to Oranges (miscellany, excerpts, profiles) of 300–600 words

Tips: We are looking for new voices and are willing to take extra effort with new writers to make sure that the published result surely shines.

Editor's Wish List: Something has to happen in the pieces we choose, but what happens inside characters is much more interesting to us than plot manipulation. We like good storytelling, real emotion, and authentic voice. Sample copies are $5.50.

SHORT STUFF FOR GROWNUPS
P.O. Box 7057
Loveland, CO 80537

Acquisitions: Donna Bowman, Editor/Publisher

Submissions: Unsolicited manuscripts are OK. Send complete manuscript with cover letter that includes author bio. We usually have a contest for the February issue (SASE for rules).

Pay Rate: $10–$50 for stories up to 1,800 words; $1–$5 for less than 500 words.

Seeking: Contemporary romance, historical, mainstream, mystery, romantic suspense, and thriller of up to 1,800 words.

Tips: We are seasonal and like stories to reflect this. Three-month lead time for holiday material (any holiday). Sample copies are $1.50.

Turn-offs/Taboos: No graphic sex, profanity, obscene language.

Editor's Wish List: Stories with good dialogue and definite endings. Hate those cliffhangers or "lady or the tiger" endings.

SHOW AND TELL
93 Medford Street
Malden, MA 02148
(617) 321-3649

Acquisitions: Donna Clark, Editor/Publisher

Submissions: Send complete manuscript with cover letter and SASE. Unsolicited OK.

Pay Rate: $5 token payment.

Seeking: Romance can be contemporary, sweet, historical, and interracial. Show how love transcends all. In westerns, we want historically themed action adventures, tall tales, and heroic tales before 1900. Posses and gunfights welcome! Science fiction, earth-futuristic, or other worlds plots welcome. Spaceships, aliens, and technology heartily received. Seeking also juvenile, time travel, fantasy, historical, mainstream, romantic suspense, thrillers (especially whodunnits, mystery, and scavenger hunts). All fiction should be 500–5,000 words. We also need nonfiction interviews and profiles.

Tips: A good story that balances showing and telling will likely be accepted.

Turn-offs/Taboos: Excessive expletives, horror, occult, political, social, and racial soap-boxing. No gay/lesbian fiction, abortion, extramarital affairs, or AIDS.

Editor's Wish List: More science fiction, juvenile, and humorous submissions! *Show and Tell* subscriptions are $20 per year for 12 issues.

SOUND PUBLICATIONS
10 E. 22nd Street, Suite 108
Lombard, IL 60148
(708) 916-7071 (but please, no phone calls)

Acquisitions: Address submissions to Fiction Editor

Submissions: We prefer to see a synopsis with sample chapters, cover letter with publishing credentials, and other relevant information. Always include SASE for response and return of material. Unsolicited submissions are OK, as are unagented manuscripts and simultaneous submissions. Double-space submissions with letter quality (or near) print. Our usual response time is 1–2 months.

Pay Rate: No advance; royalties negotiable.

Seeking: Contemporary romance, mainstream, mystery, paranormal, romantic suspense, and thrillers. Word count is anywhere between 30,000–80,000, but we're flexible. We're open to any level of sensuality, but we don't want to see anything violent or that which borders on pornography.

Tips: We publish original fiction in the format of old-time radio theater, with different actors taking on the character roles.

Editor's Wish List: Fast-paced and lots of dialogue.

'TEEN MAGAZINE
Petersen Publishing Company
6420 Wilshire Boulevard
Los Angeles, CA 90048-5515

Acquisitions: Roxanne Camron, Editor

Submissions: OK to either query first by letter or send unsolicited manuscripts.

Pay Rate: About $200 for fiction manuscripts, but varies.

Seeking: Confession, contemporary romance, inspirational, mainstream, and romantic suspense fiction of 2,500–4,000 words.

Tips: Subject matter and vocabulary should be appropriate for an average 16-year-old reader. Fiction should have teenage girl as the central character.

'Teen Guidelines for Writers

At the present time we are buying fiction and nonfiction on a limited basis only. We are looking for realistic, upbeat stories concerned with current teen interests and teen problems handled sensitively.

If you are interested in submitting nonfiction, please send query letters only in a quick summary or outline form along with an SASE. Don't send completed nonfiction manuscripts. Also send a resume and copies only of any recently published work that gives evidence of your writing style. Please keep in mind that rarely are the ideas themselves original. Rather, we are looking for an angle or approach to teen subjects that is fresh and innovative.

If we are interested, we will contact you to discuss rates, length, and other pertinent information. Please be advised that we do not pay kill fees and that the agreed-upon purchase is for all rights.

Payment is $200 upon acceptance for all rights. You will hear from us within 10 weeks if your material is accompanied by SASE. Material will not be returned without sufficient postage. Thanks for thinking of 'Teen. We wish you the best of luck.

TRUE CONFESSIONS

233 Park Avenue South
New York, NY 10003
(212) 979-4800   FAX: (212) 979-7342

Acquisitions: Jean Sharbel, Editor

Submissions: Queries are not necessary. Please do not send synopsis and partials. Send the complete manuscript. Unagented and unsolicited are OK. Usual response time is up to 6 months. No simultaneous submissions.

Pay Rate: 5¢ a word. Pays on last day of publication date. Publishes about 1–6 months after acceptance.

Seeking: Confessional, contemporary romances, and mainstream with romance elements of 1,500–8,000 words. Inspirational story length depends on whether it's a story or an article. (All stories are based on true incidents. No fiction.)

True Confessions Writer's Guidelines

All the stories in *True Confessions* are true.

If you would like to send us your story on speculation, we would be happy to read it. Write it in the first person, as you would tell it to a friend, and type it on one side of each sheet of paper, leaving double spaces between the lines. If you do not have a typewriter, please print neatly on one side of each sheet of lined paper.

If we publish your story, we will buy all world rights and pay you at our regular rate—5¢ cents a word. Payment is made during the last week of the month of issue. For example, checks for stories printed in our June issue are mailed out during the last week of June.

Please include SASE with your story so that we may return it to you if it does not meet our needs. If we decide not to publish your story, you should expect to hear from us only if you have enclosed a return envelope and sufficient postage. It is advisable for you to keep a copy of your story in case anything should happen to the original.

Because of the vast number of stories we receive, it usually takes at least 6 months for us to give you a report about your story.

Please enclose SASE with any correspondence to *True Confessions*. Otherwise, we cannot guarantee a reply.

TRUE EXPERIENCE
233 Park Avenue South
New York, NY 10003
(212) 979-4903

Acquisitions: Fiction Editor: Jean Press Silberg (212) 979-4896 (direct line); Associate Editor: Cynthia Di Martino

Submissions: All stories are written in first person, past tense. Submit the complete typed, double-spaced manuscript with SASE. Unsolicited and unagented manuscripts are OK. Average response time is 1–2 months.

Pay Rate: 3¢ a word, upon publication. Publishes about 3 months after acceptance. No byline, buys all rights.

Seeking: Confessional of 7,000–20,000 words.

Tips: Cynthia Di Martino reports, "We're looking for true-to-life stories about current topics women are interested in, although we're glad to accept a good love story."

TRUE LOVE

233 Park Avenue South
New York, NY 10003
(212) 979-4895   FAX: 979-7342

Acquisitions Editor: Kristina M. Kracht

Submissions: Don't query; send the complete manuscript. Unsolicited manuscripts are OK, but no simultaneous submissions are accepted. The usual response time is 6–9 months. Please be patient with us! We get to stories as soon as we can. We love timely stories and lots of modern romance. No historicals.

Pay Rate: We buy all rights. Payment is upon publication, at the rate of 3¢ per word.

Seeking: Confessional, contemporary romance, inspirational, mainstream, ethnic, and mystery or romantic suspense of 1,000–10,000 words.

True Love Writer's Guidelines

True Love is a women's magazine written for women, by women, but we also welcome male writers. Each month we print between 10 and 12 stories, several poems, and features such as "How I Know I'm in Love" and "The Life I Live." The best way to learn our editorial style is to read the magazine itself and study the range of possibilities.

We look for modern, well-written stories that involve real people and real emotions. Our subject matter ranges from light romance to inspirational to current social concerns. Some aspect of love and romance will usually figure in, but it need not be the primary focus of the story. Characters will often face a conflict or solve a problem in their lives that can inspire *True Love* readers.

Due to the amount of stories we receive, it may take up to 9 months for us to respond. But don't let that discourage you—

we are always on the lookout for a good story! Don't forget to include your phone number in case we have any questions.

All stories should be typed, double-spaced. Stories can range from 2,000–10,000 words. No byline is offered. A large envelope with sufficient postage must be included for the manuscripts to be returned.

TRUE ROMANCE
233 Park Avenue South
New York, NY 10003
(212) 979-4898   FAX: (212) 979-7342

Acquisitions: Pat Byrdsong, Editor

Submissions: Don't query first; send the complete manuscript. Unsolicited manuscripts are OK, but simultaneous submissions are not. Usual response time is 3–6 months.

Pay Rate: We buy all rights. Payment is on publication at the rate of 3¢ per word.

Seeking: All stories are confessions of 2,000-10,000 words.

Tips: An excellent market for beginning writers. I read all manuscripts and often work with writers. I suggest that writers read three or four issues before sending. Do not talk down to our readers. Contemporary problems should be handled with insight and a fresh angle. We always need good romantic stories. Stories featuring ethnic characters are accepted, but stay away from stereotypical plots and characteristics. Our greatest needs are for stories from 2,000–4,000 words.

True Romance Writer's Guidelines (excerpted)

True Romance features first-person narratives written for average, high-school educated women who are juggling family and work responsibility, but family comes first. After a long day she wants to read a compelling, realistic story about people she can identify with. Our readers do not want to read stories about men and women who lead glamorous lives. Stories must be set in towns, cities, and neighborhoods where hardworking Americans live.

Emotionally charged stories with a strong emphasis on characterization and well-defined plots are preferred. Stories should be intriguing, suspenseful, humorous, romantic, or tragic. The plots and characters should reflect the average American's values and desires.

"I want stories that cover the wide spectrum of America. A good story will have a well-defined plot and characters. I want to feel as though I intimately know the narrator and his/her motivation. If your story is dramatically gripping or humorous, you have an excellent chance of making a sale. Realism is the key to a sale at *True Romance*," says Pat Byrdsong, editor.

Do not send query letter; send completed manuscripts. Seasonal materials should be sent 6 months in advance and marked "seasonal material" on the outside of the envelope. No multiple submissions or photocopies of stories. We buy all rights. Manuscripts should be typed double-spaced. Letter-quality printed word processed manuscripts are also acceptable. Dot matrix is OK if letter quality. Send SASE for response and return of your manuscript.

WHAT'S LOVE?
93 Medford Street
Malden, MA 02148
(617) 321-3649

Acquisitions: Donna Clark, Editor/Publisher

Submissions: Send unsolicited manuscripts and SASE. Use proper manuscript format. Response time is 4–6 weeks.

Pay Rate: $10 for stories by subscribing authors plus 1/4 subscription. For novelettes, pay is $50.

Seeking: Stories written from the heart. Contemporary, ethnic, fantasy, futuristic, historical, sweet teen, inspirational, mainstream, mystery, romantic suspense, thriller, western, time travel, and ancient world romances from 1,200–5,000 words. Also seeking romance novelettes of 8,000–15,000 words.

Tips: I want writers who can write with tension and a true romance style. Portray people and circumstances with a bite of realism while you give readers a fantasy ride. All stories must end happily. $22 for 12 issues by subscription.

Turn-offs/Taboos: No explicit sex, pornography, gay couples, or illegal practices.

Editor's Wish List: I am especially interested in time travel and ancient world romance.

Note: Donna Clark is also the author of *Stars,* a bestselling book published by Dare to Dream Publishing.

WOMAN'S WEEKLY
Kings' Reach Tower
Stamford Street
London SE1 9LS
ENGLAND
(071) 261-5000   FAX: (071) 261-6322

Acquisitions: Gaynor Davies, Fiction Editor

Submissions: Don't query by letter or FAX. Send unsolicited manuscripts with large SASE (British postage or IRCs) for response and return of manuscript, if necessary. Eight weeks response time. No individual criticisms of stories.

Pay Rate: By negotiation.

Seeking: Contemporary romance, historical romance, and romantic suspense. Short stories can be any length from 1,000 words to 3,500. We occasionally print stories up to 5,000 words long, but they must have sufficiently strong plots and backgrounds to sustain the reader's interest. We are particularly looking for the one-page twist-in-the-tale type of about 1,000 words. The twist shouldn't be shocking or macabre, but neither should it be contrived.

We also seek serials, which should have all the compelling qualities of short stories—strong characters and background—and must also have riveting cliffhangers to keep the reader going back to the newsagent week after week. There should be a central hook to hang the action on: an emotional or practical dilemma that the heroine has to face. A strong sub-plot and well-researched background are essential. Historicals are just as welcome as contemporary serials. Serials can be between 2 and 8 parts. The opening installment is 7,000 words, and each subsequent installment is 4,200 words. You may submit the whole of your manuscript or just the first part with a brief synopsis. A synopsis alone cannot be considered.

Tips: Unfortunately we cannot offer criticism, but if your short story or serial shows promise, we will contact you and suggest alterations.

Turn-offs/Taboos: Although we are more flexible these days, there are still several don'ts to bear in mind: while we welcome stories that reflect real life, they shouldn't contain explicit sex or violence. The main characters, while living firmly in the 1990s, should be basically decent, caring people.

We have experimented with ghost stories over the past year or two, but these haven't proved all that popular with our readers and we only rarely print them. Similarly, we have yet to read a science fiction story we feel our readers would be able to swallow.

Depressing stories are out. All short stories submitted should have a warm quality. Ideally, they should have happy endings so that the readers feel uplifted and full of hope. If a totally happy ending wouldn't be realistic given the theme of your story, then it must have at least an element of optimism. Until recently, we printed a lot of stories about such themes as bereavement, retirement, loneliness in old age, and so on. We will be looking for younger, more lighthearted fiction in the future.

No handwritten work, typescripts only, double-spaced on one side of the paper with wide margins.

Woman's Weekly Writer's Guidelines

Woman's Weekly has always been well-known for it's short stories and serials, and fiction remains one of the most popular aspects of the magazine. Our readers talk about relaxing with our short stories and serials, switching off or taking a break from the daily routine. However, we are no longer looking for predictable boy-meets-girl romances or nostalgic looks at the past. Romance and nostalgia can be important parts of a story, but there should be other elements, too.

We want our stories to portray up-to-date characters in believable, modern situations. We like stories about children, teenagers, family problems, funny stories, and even stories with a crime or thriller element, so long as they are not violent, threatening, or too incredible. In other words, fiction that grips the readers rather then sending them to sleep!

One of the main reasons we reject stories is that we can tell from the word go what their outcome will be. Unless there's an element of tension or uncertainty, readers won't bother to finish a story. And unless they can believe in the characters, they won't get involved in the first place. The best way to achieve this involvement is to be subtle in your writing. Show, don't tell, is the useful maxim to bear in mind. And don't give away too much. Tempt your reader on with more and more clues about a situation or character as the plot unfolds.

Note: This is the most popular women's magazine in the United Kingdom with sales of 800,000 weekly!

WOMAN'S WORLD
270 Sylvan Avenue
Englewood Cliffs, NJ 07632

Acquisitions: Brooke Comer, Fiction Editor

Submissions: Don't query. Send the complete manuscript. Unagented and unsolicited stories are OK. Average response time is 6–8 weeks.

Pay Rate: Buys first North American serial rights. Payment is on acceptance. $500 for mystery to $1,000 for contemporary romance.

Seeking: Contemporary romance of 1,900 words; mystery of 1,200 words.

Tips: Read what we buy! Simple plot with poignant twist. Heroine must emerge wiser and happier at the end.

Turn-offs/Taboos: I hate unprofessional formats! (Single spaced, underlined). I hate it when writers don't follow our obvious formula. No alcohol. No obscenities. No graphic sex.

Editor's Wish List: Let dialogue and succinct details tell what people feel and think. Long descriptive passages are boring, unless you're Faulkner (you're not). Send SASE for our new guidelines.

WRITER'S BLOCK MAGAZINE
Box 32, 9944 33 Avenue
Edmonton, Alberta T6N 1E8
CANADA

Acquisitions: Shaun Donnelly, Publisher/Editor

Submissions: Don't query. Send completed manuscript with SASE. Unsolicited OK.

Pay Rate: 5¢ per word for fiction; poems $25 and up.

Seeking: Contemporary romance, fantasy, futuristic, historical, inspirational, mainstream, mystery, poetry, romantic suspense, thriller, western. Also seeking nonfiction romance writing tips, humor, etc., 5,000 words maximum. Twice annually, we sponsor writing contests (March 1/September 1). Send SASE for rules/entry form. (U.S. residents mailing to Canada, please remember to use IRCs for return postage, or Canadian postage if you have it.)

Tips: Because we pay well, we've become a hard market to crack. Send only your best.

Turn-offs/Taboos: Cannot accept overtly sexual material or profanity.

Editor's Wish List: Clever well-written stories with good character development and imaginative plots.

Writer's Block Guidelines

Our magazine spotlights exceptional stories in the following genres: horror, mystery, science fiction/fantasy, romance, and western. We also accept poetry and, increasingly, humor. Quarterly issues appear in March, June, September, and December.

Our guidelines are simple enough. We like to see well-written pieces that conform to one or more of the above mentioned genres. Submissions should be typed, double-spaced, and reasonably well-proofed. We accept dot matrix printouts, and if the work is available on disk we'd like to know. Tell us what program you use, but don't send the disk until we ask for it. Like most magazines, we lean toward shorter stories and ask that authors try not to exceed 5,000 words. We try to respond in 4–6 weeks and always respond personally—no form letters! Please include SASE and a short bio with your submission.

Simultaneous submissions are accepted—multiple submissions are not.

Contest: In addition to ordinary submissions, we also sponsor the *Writer's Block* Contest. Guidelines are the same as above except that stories/poems must be accompanied by a $5 entry fee and multiple submissions are allowed (to a maximum of three stories or five poems, please!). Prizes include an assortment of hardcover books in your genre, publication, and cash (over and above ordinary payment). Contest deadlines are March 1 and September 1.

9

Booking
Hollywood

omance Novelist's Screenplay in CBS's Top Ten Television Programs of the Year!

This is not a fantasy. It really happened to romance author Maggie Davis (a.k.a. Maggie Daniels and Katherine Deauxville), who co-scripted the adaptation of her contemporary romance novel, *A Christmas Story*. Starring Olivia Newton-John and Gregory Harrison, *A Christmas Story* aired in December 1994 to rave reviews and a viewing audience of millions! Negotiations are in the works for more of Davis's romance novels to be adapted for television.

Webster's Dictionary defines booking as an engagement, and Maggie Davis has definitely "booked" Hollywood!

Not to be outdone by Davis, Harlequin engaged TV viewers in its own version of how a Sunday afternoon should be spent, and it was not watching the Super Bowl! Instead viewers tuned-in to romantic made-for-TV movies transformed from Harlequin romance novels.

For theatergoers and video renters, the love-and-laughter choices range from romantic comedies like *Forget Paris, French Kiss, Only You,* and *Speechless,* to romantic dramas like *First Knight, Wuthering Heights,* and *Forrest Gump,* as well as romantic romps like *Don Juan De Marco,* and even animated Disney romances such as *Pocahontas!*

Because of its versatility and popularity, the genre of romance is gathering more fans than ever before for the silver-screen industry as well as cable and network television.

Film and TV producers are realizing that women are the primary moviegoers and that they will pay $5–$7 a seat to see happily-ever-after screen romances. Viewers want to feel good when the movie is over, and many producers are looking specifically for romantic comedies, currently the hottest trend. They seek to acquire rights to novels for screen adaptations as well as original screenplays.

Some writers think of screenplays as the golden door to fame and fortune. The one screenplay in about 40 thousand that actually gets produced by a WGA signatory film company can net the author about five times (or more) the amount of the average romance novel advance. A brilliant screenplay or novel, the right agent with sharp skills in negotiating specific rights, and a producer with deep pockets are just some of the variables necessary to make it.

The odds are against success. Yet it can happen, and the rewards are great enough to make writers ask "when," instead of "if."

An agent has become a must for booking Hollywood. The business has gotten too complicated and too cutthroat for writers to work their own way through the labyrinth of the Hollywood biz, but don't let that discourage you from pursuing your goals.

Protecting Your Work

Here are a few things you can do to protect your work and your interests:

Register Your Screenplay: In the film business, plagiarism is not rampant, but it does happen. For a mere $20 fee, the WGA will register for you any written materials for film, TV, radio, or theater. WGA will also register manuscripts for novels, short stories, lyrics, and poetry. The protection of WGA registration lasts for five years and can be renewed. Call one of the registration information numbers listed below (Mini-Guide to Hollywood) for instructions.

Get an Agent to Read and Represent Your Screenplay: Besides writing a novel or screenplay that appeals to the mass market, obtaining an agent is one of the most difficult, but most important, aspects of booking Hollywood.

There are agents listed in this book who handle screenplays; WGA also has a list. Here are a few ways to get an agent to read your screenplay. (After that, your story will tell the agent whether or not he or she should represent the property):

1. A client of that same agency writes you a letter of recommendation and referral. You include it with your query letter.

2. You don't have a referral, but you can write a bang-up query letter, one that will make an agent phone you ASAP.

3. You can pitch your idea well in a phone call or in person, if necessary. What this boils down to is convincing an agent in three minutes or less that your screenplay or novel is unique, has mass-market appeal, is an easy sell, and will net the producer millions of dollars if produced.

4. You have a completed screenplay of the proper length and in the proper screenplay format. You meet an agent at a conference and wow him or her with a one- or two-page sample of your written dialogue skills.

5. Perhaps you own the film rights to a previously published novel (even out-of-print novels) and want to sell adaptation rights. Then you contact an agent who is scouting for a producer, and your novel fits their desired subject matter (i.e., contemporary romantic comedy/strong female lead, etc.).

Perhaps you can think of other ways to get an agent read-and-represent to happen. Truthfully, if you do not get an agent, you will have a very hard time breaking into this lucrative and ultra-competitive market.

What kind of screenplays have the best chance of being acquired? Linda Stuart says, "As a story analyst at Paramount, I knew that the studio was primarily interested in commercial screenplays with mass-audience appeal. So I steered clear of small, arty scripts that were too limited in scope, even though the writing may have been strong." (Quoted from *Getting Your Script Through the Hollywood Maze,* 1993.)

Although nearly everyone wants to write romantic screenplays for Paramount, Turner, CastleRock, or Warner, these are tough markets to crack, even with a fabulous screenplay and an agent who can pitch winningly.

The previous edition of this book listed the direct contact addresses of film producers. But recently the market has tightened up so much that the majority of producers are currently accepting agented screenplays only. Your best bet for success is to submit your novel or screenplay to the agents listed in this book.

A Trick of the Trade: Line up your ducks! Authors who have their agents negotiate movie and TV rights at the same time they sell their novel to a publisher are playing it smart, and seeing their novel as a multiple opportunity instead of a one-dimensional product. Just think of the possibilities: novel, feature film, network or cable TV movie, video sales and rentals, perhaps even spin-off products like T-shirts and posters. Don't laugh, but when Winston Groom wrote the line, "Life is like a box of chocolates," do you suppose he ever imagined that someday he would be able to walk into a Wal-Mart and actually *buy* a box of Forrest Gump Chocolates? And let us not forget the *Bubba Gump Shrimp Company Cookbook!*

Strategies for Booking Hollywood

1. The big picture: Get used to thinking of a novel as commercially valuable and as a potential multi-media opportunity. Use your foresight and envision your novels as movies, VHS rentals, audiotapes, even T-shirts!

2. Production costs: A film with historical settings can cost 10 times more to produce than contemporary settings. Because of these production costs, a contemporary novel will have a better chance of making it as a screen adaptation.

3. Writing style: A novel with a high percentage of dialogue (versus narrative) makes it a better candidate for adaptation to the screen (and to audiotapes).

4. Dialogue tip: Limit small talk that does not advance the plot or reveal character.

5. Rule of thumb: One page of dialogue equals about one minute of actual film time. Too short is almost always better than too long.

6. Contracts: Some book publishers have boiler-plate contracts that do not spell out specific rights. Ask your agent to negotiate for acquisition of these rights individually. Even if your novel is never made into a movie, you've covered your assets in advance.

7. How-to: Get your hands on a real script, so that you can understand how to mix sparkling dialogue with plot action. Public libraries have a small selection of popular screenplays on their shelves. There are also several companies that sell copies of scripts for less than $15 (The Write Stuff Catalog: 1-800-989-8833). Anything by Nora Ephron (*When Harry Met Sally*) is highly recommended as a learning tool.

8. Contacts: Join the GEnie electronic network. Experienced and novice writers in the writer's forum exchange gossip, market information, contest news, even good, bad, and ugly experiences with selling to Hollywood. There are also downloadable scripts in the library of the "writers" bulletin board. Check the network for other electronic bulletin boards, aspiring screenwriters groups (see The Writing Center in San Diego), and classes and conferences, where you can meet and mingle with the best of the professionals and wanna-be screenwriters. (Screenwriters such as J. Michael Straczynski often run panel workshops at various writer's conferences.)

Mini-Guide to Hollywood

Here are some related resources to get you started on your way to Oscardom:

WGAw
8955 Beverly Boulevard
West Hollywood, CA 90048
(310) 205-2500 (registration information) or (310) 205-2540

WGAe
555 W. 57th Street, Suite 123
New York, NY 10019
(212) 757-4360 (registration information) or (212) 767-7800

Publications of WGAw include:
WGA Directory. $17.50. Contains names, credits of people in the film industry, and their contact phone numbers.
  The Journal. $40 per year for 11 issues. Single/back copies $5.

List of WGA agents: Send SASE and check for $2. Informative pamphlets are $3.50 each. Specify "Creative Rights," "Plagiarism," or "Working With Writers."

  Other helpful publications include:

Daily Variety
P.O. Box 7550
Torrance, CA 90504
(800) 552-3632

$169 yr. (plus sales tax for CA residents)/240 issues.

This trade magazine carries all the daily news about the film industry.

Hollywood Scriptwriter
1626 N. Wilcox, #385
Hollywood, CA 90028
$44 yr./12 issues

This monthly newsletter contains advice and interviews with successful scriptwriters, plus market listings and yearly survey of agents.

Screenwrite Now!
P.O. Box 7, Long Green Pike
Baldwin, MD 21013
(410) 592-3466

$48 yr./6 issues

Highly recommended bimonthly magazine of professional advice on writing better screenplays.

Variety
5700 Wilshire Boulevard, Suite 120
Los Angeles, CA 90036
800-323-4345

$167 yr./52 issues.

Contains weekly box office reports, film production listings, reviews and industry news.

Helpful Books

The Complete Book of Scriptwriting by J. Michael Straczynski
The Elements of Screenwriting by Irwin R. Blacker
Feature Filmmaking at Used Car Prices by Rick Schmidt
Getting Your Script Through the Hollywood Maze by Linda Stuart
How to Make It in Hollywood by Linda Buzzell
How to Write for Television by Madeline DiMaggio
Madison Avenue Handbook by Peter Glenn Publications (800) 223-1254
The New Screenwriter Looks at the New Screenwriter by William Froug
Successful Scriptwriting by Jurgen Wolff and Kerry Cox

The above-mentioned books are enlightening and should serve to keep you from developing tunnel vision about your writing career. Think of your romance novel or screenplay as an octopus with each of the tentacles leading to a different marketing opportunity for the same product.

Keep an open mind toward perfecting your writing craft and keep working toward your own vision of "booking Hollywood."

See you at the movies!

Directory of Writer's Publications

AFFAIRE DE COEUR
3976 Oak Hill Drive
Oakland, CA 94605-4931
(510) 569-5675

$35 yr./12 issues (U.S.), $65 (Canada)

Well-written articles about writing romance, author profiles,
romantic travel pieces, in-depth book reviews, and short fiction
target romance readers and romance writers.

BOOKLOVERS MAGAZINE
P.O. Box 93485
Milwaukee, WI 53203-0485
(414) 541-7510

$10 yr./4 issues

Author features, book reviews of new and older books in print,
librarian's column, bookstore and book group profiles, short
stories, and poetry provide eclectic reading for writers of all genres. (E-mail rjammer@omnifest.uwm.edu)

BOOKLOVERS, ROMANCE READER SERVICE
P.O. Box 100987
Denver, CO 80250
(303) 935-2672   Visa/MC Order line: (800) 370-1463

$16 yr. bulk rate, $32 first class or foreign

Mail-order catalog that reads like a magazine, with each issue
featuring author profiles, romance novel reviews, and romance
previews.

BYLINE MAGAZINE
P.O. Box 130596
Edmond, OK 73013
(405) 348-5591

$20 yr./11 issues

How-to write and how-to sell features, thoughtful first-person essays, editor interviews, conference listings, many writing contests (small entry fees, cash prizes), short fiction, and poetry appeal to beginning-to-intermediate writers in many genres.

CANADIAN WRITER'S JOURNAL
Box 6618, Depot 1
Victoria, B.C. V8P 5N7
CANADA

$15 yr./4 issues

Informative, well-written how-to articles, writer's resources, markets, poetry, fiction, annual fiction contest, and book reviews target writers of all levels of expertise.

CREATIVITY CONNECTION
610 Langdon Street, #224
Madison, WI 53705-1195
(608) 262-4911

$18 yr./4 issues

Book/magazine reviews, writer/small press profiles, workshop listings, motivational articles, and markets, inspire and instruct writers in all genres in interactive newsletter. Affiliated with University of Wisconsin Outreach.

FICTION WRITER'S GUIDELINE
P.O. Box 4065
Deerfield Beach, FL 33442
(305) 426-4705

$39 yr./6 issues

Free to members of Fiction Writer's Connection, *Fiction Writer's Guideline* reports publishing scams/stormy weather, plus technique articles, editor/agent interviews, writer's book reviews, and new market listings for a well-rounded publication targeted at intermediate to advanced writers who are serious about success.

THE GILA QUEEN'S GUIDE TO MARKETS
P.O. Box 97
Newton, NJ 07860

$30 yr./12 issues (U.S.), $34 (Canada), $48 (overseas)

Best periodical for prolific writers with up-to-date market listings in all genres, plus thought-provoking writers' articles with emphasis on publication. (Checks payable to Kathryn Ptacek.) E-mail address: k.ptacek@genie.com

GOTHIC JOURNAL
Publisher: Kristi Lyn Glass
19210 Forest Road North
Forest Lake, MN 55025

$24 yr./6 issues

Bimonthly book reviews, industry profiles, author bios, genre articles, upcoming titles, and market news targets writers/readers of romantic suspense/mystery, Gothic, and supernatural romance novels.

HISTORICAL GAZETTE
P.O. Box 1901
Manhattan, KS 66502-0022
(913) 776-7731

$15 yr./6 issues

Historical romance writers will enjoy interviews of historical authors, information on upcoming releases, and short articles on historical people, places, and events.

HOUSEWIFE-WRITER'S FORUM
P.O Box 780 Dept RWPP
Lyman, WY 82937
(307) 782-7003

$18 yr./6 issues ($4 sample copy)

Book reviews, articles on writing fiction and nonfiction, market listings, short fiction, success stories target the beginning writer who is a stay-at-home mom.

I'LL TAKE ROMANCE!
P.O. Box 22-0380
Brooklyn, NY 11222-0380
FAX: (718) 349-3946

$15 yr./4 issues (charter subscription rate)

New romantic lifestyle magazine includes book/audio reviews, publishing news, writers' question/answer page, bookstore news, romantic travel, decorating ideas, recipes, and short fiction of interest to romance writers as well as a broader audience.

MANDERLEY
P.O. Box 679
Boonville, CA 95415
(707) 895-3822   Order line (800) 722-0726.

Free upon request!

In-print book catalog specializes in 700+ romantic books and classic videos of interest to well-educated women who read widely. Original reviews, not "canned" from marketing promotions. Includes nonfiction romance writing titles. (Authors, send galleys ASAP.)

THE MEDIÆVAL CHRONICLE
P.O. Box 1663 (Dept. RWPP)
Carlsbad, CA 92018-1663
$12 yr./6 issues (U.S.), $15 Canada

Medieval romance writers, you need this newsletter! Contains articles about Dark Ages, Middle Ages, and Tudor period, as well as information on upcoming Medieval romances. Meet new authors and discover hard-to-find research sources.

MYSTERY READERS JOURNAL
P.O. Box 8116
Berkeley, CA 94707
(510) 339-2800   FAX: (510) 339-8309

$24 yr./4 issues

Professional journal with thematic book reviews (Senior Sleuths, History Mysteries, etc.) author profiles, and insider articles written by bestselling authors that reveal the "story behind the story" of their novels, conference and mystery weekends listings, and industry news by Janet Rudolph, owner of "Murder on the Menu," a company that performs live murder-mystery events on ships, in theatres, and on boardwalks!

PANDORA'S BOX
Romance Writers of America
13700 Veterans Memorial Drive, Suite 315
Houston, TX 77014
(713) 440-6885

$20 yr./6 issues

For professionals, 32-page magazine (available to RWA members only) is dedicated to uncensored truth about romance publishing. Written by authors who tell all through rabble-rousing letters, perks 'n problems articles, secret industry news, best-seller lists, and other items so candid that no other magazine dares to print them! With news of romance novels lauded by the Smithsonian, an agent indictment log, a mid-list meltdown, and a writing-is-not-for-sissies attitude, *Pandora's Box* is a must have!

PAPERBACK PREVIEWS MAGAZINE
P.O. Box 6781
Albuquerque, NM 87197
(800) 872-4461

$20 yr./12 issues

Monthly newsletter/book catalog lists new releases with mini-synopses. Several reviews. Not a book club, no purchase required.

PUBLISHER'S WEEKLY
P.O. Box 1979
Marion, OH 43302
(800) 842-1669

Subscription price varies. Request professional discount.

Contains bestseller lists; book/audio reviews and previews; publishers' news, including new editors, acquisitions, sell-outs, and takeovers; and booksellers' convention news.

RAWHIDE & LACE
P.O. Box 11593
Bainbridge Island, WA 98110

$16 yr./4 issues, $17 to Canada (in U.S. funds)

For western romance writers and aficionados of the American frontier, *Rawhide & Lace* serves up a chuckwagon full of fascinating historical articles, book reviews, author interviews, Old West recipes, facts about adobe, Native American tribes and customs, cattlemen and outlaws, Spanish influence on western expansion, *Little House on the Prairie,* and more. *R&L* will either save a trip to the library or whet the appetite for more research!

THE READER'S VOICE
2646 Wyoming Avenue, South West
Wyoming, MI 49509-2370

$15.50 yr./6 issues (send for foreign rates)

Contains insightful articles and survey results on romance-genre topics (such as, "should heroes cry?"), author profiles, romance writers' conferences, writer's and readers' personal essays, humorous anecdotes, and editorials.

THE REGENCY PLUME NEWSLETTER
Marilyn Clay, Publisher/Editor
711 D. Street Northwest
Ardmore, OK 73401

$12 yr./6 issues

Regency writers subscribe to this newsletter devoted to accurate depiction of Regency period. Enrich your knowledge of Regency history, clothes, food, maps, customs, courtship, and cosmetics with information from expert in field. Facts substantiated with entertaining excerpts from diaries and letters of the time. Three annual writing contests ($25 entry); winners are judged by Regency romance editor. Highly recommended.

RENDEZVOUS
1507 Burnham Avenue
Calumet City, IL 60409
(708) 291-8337

$45 yr./12 issues ($24 for 6 issues or $4 single copy)

Love Designers Writer's Club publication includes candid new book reviews of romance, fantasy, Gothic, mystery, and women's fiction, plus market news column. Staff written (no freelance articles), and no advertising. Recommended reading.

ROMANCE WRITERS' REPORT (RWR)
Romance Writers of America
13700 Veterans Memorial Drive, Suite 315
Houston, TX 77014
(713) 440-6885

Bimonthly free with RWA membership

Professional journal contains romance writing articles, book market listings, writing contests, industry news, book release titles list, news of RWA events, board decisions, and more.

ROMANTIC TIMES
55 Bergen Street
Brooklyn, NY 11201
(718) 237-1097

$42 yr./12 issues (fourth class), $60 first class, $66 Canadian
(Newsstand price $4 U.S., $5 Canada)

Redesigned/revamped to meet romance writers' needs, as well as
reader fans, publishing industry pages feature editor and agent
profiles, letters, publishers' news, foreign markets, convention
info, trends, historical research and how-to writing articles, author profiles, audio romance news, film picks, bookstore news,
lifestyles of the rich and romantic, and more than 100 book reviews per month. Upbeat tone with a sassy sprinkling of male
cover models makes *Romantic Times* entertaining and informative for aspiring as well as veteran romance writers.

SCI-FI ROMANCE!
P.O. Box 496
Endicott, NY 13761-0496

(Free with SASEs or e-mail request to Jennifer Dunne at
yeep@aol.com)

Tightly targeted toward writers of sci-fi romance, *Sci-Fi
Romance* defines this growing subgenre well, zooms in on markets with helpful articles and publisher's needs listings, book reviews, and intelligent transmissions from readers/writers who
know that many women readers appreciate science in their romantic fiction!

THE WRITER
120 Boylston Street
Boston, MA 02116
(617) 423-3157

$28 yr./12 issues

Articles on writing techniques by professionals, plus market listings in various genres and conference and contest listings. May issue annually publishes listings of romance fiction magazine markets.

WRITER'S BLOCK MAGAZINE
Box 32, 9944 33rd Avenue
Edmonton, Alberta T6N 1E8
CANADA

$15 yr./4 issues U.S., $12 Canada

Interesting and well-written magazine mixes exceptional short stories of romance, western, sci-fi, and so on, with writer's articles on character development, plot, and publication information. Writing contests twice per year.

WRITER'S DIGEST
1507 Dana Avenue
Cincinnati, OH 45207
(800)333-0133

$27 yr./12 issues, $37 by surface mail to Canada

Blueprint and step-by-step how-to articles on writing techniques for all genres; publishing issues; market, contest, conference, and agent listings; editor and author interviews; writing lifestyle essays; and writers' resources make *Writer's Digest* a general purpose magazine for aspiring to advanced writers of fiction, nonfiction, and poetry.

WRITER'S EXCHANGE
Box 394
Society Hill, SC 29593

$10 yr./4 issues

Articles on genres and writing techniques, tips and thoughts on writing, marketing ideas, markets, promotion ideas, plus writer's personal experiences, contest news, and industry updates for beginning to intermediate writers in all genres.

WRITERS GAZETTE
899 Williamson Trail
Eclectic, AL 36024

$15 yr./3 issues

Newsletter contains book reviews; market listings; contest and conference news; writing related articles on techniques, computers, bookkeeping, audioscript writing; first sale essays, photojournalism, plus short fiction, and poetry. Helpful to beginning to intermediate writers in all genres.

WRITER'S WORKSHOP REVIEW
511 West 24th Street
Vancouver, WA 98660

$20 yr./12 issues

Writing-related nonfiction, including market listings, electronic networks for writers, software reviews, writing book reviews, plus short stories in genres of romance, sci-fi, suspense, humor, and fantasy, appeal to a wide writing audience, from beginners to professionals.

APPENDIX

Electronic Networks for Writers

You debate and schmooze; you get conference, contest, and market news; you category cruise and find friends to chase away those writing blues. There are plenty of writer-friendly networks whose members will welcome your input and be glad to share what they know. With a computer, a modem, communications software, and a phone line, you can gain access to gigabytes of information at reasonable on-line hourly rates (if a local number is available). Happy cyber-surfing!

America Online, (800) 827-6364. Real-time chats and conferences, e-mail, writers' message boards, etc.

CompuServe, (800) 848-8990. Many services offered to romance writers and romance readers. See listing in Chapter 6 under Romance Writers of America National On-Line Chapter.

GEnie Electronic Network, (800) 638-9636. Many interests including RomEx (Romance Writers Exchange), Writers, and Sci-Fi/Fantasy message boards; real-time roundtable discussions; libraries; shareware. Everyone welcome. 9600 baud available. Rates as low as $3 hour!

Internet. Using your internet connection and a search function like the Web Crawler with the key words "romance" and "writer" will turn up some interesting information, including the Romance Writer's Home Page. Since information on the Internet changes quickly, addresses are not listed here.

Prodigy, (800) 776-3449. Books and Arts/Writers message boards, e-mail, conferences, etc.

RWL. This free romance writers' and readers' electronic mailing list is a place to post and read messages about the genre. To subscribe, send this message:

subRW-L<your first name><your last name>

to this e-mail address:

listserv2cornell.edu

Index